Psychology's Ghosts

Psychology's Ghosts

The Crisis in the Profession and the Way Back

Jerome Kagan

Yale UNIVERSITY PRESS

New Haven & London

Published with assistance from the Mary Cady Tew
Memorial Fund.

Yale University Press books may be purchased in quantity for
educational, business, or promotional use. For information,
please e-mail sales.press@yale.edu (US office) or
sales@yaleup.co.uk (UK office).

Set in Janson type by Newgen North America.
Printed in the United States of America.

Library of Congress Cataloging-in-Publication Data
Kagan, Jerome.
Psychology's ghosts : the crisis in the profession and the way back /
Jerome Kagan.
p. cm.
Includes bibliographical references and index.
ISBN 978–0-300–17868-5 (clothbound : alk. paper)
1. Psychoanalysis. 2. Mental illness. 3. Psychology,
Pathological. I. Title.
BF173.K28 2012
150.1—dc23
2011032204

A catalogue record for this book is available from the
British Library.

This paper meets the requirements of ANSI/NISO Z39.48–1992
(Permanence of Paper).

10 9 8 7 6 5 4 3 2 1

Contents

Preface

This book had an odd gestation because its conception was unintended. I had been brooding on the abstract nature of many psychological concepts that were indifferent to both the settings in which observations were gathered and the types of participants providing the information. Although a few published reports pointed to the profound influences of the context, most of the empirical studies in our premier journals were ignoring this message. As I began to write a draft of a paper on this theme, I read a book by Derek Bok summarizing the research on subjective well-being. The scientists who gathered verbal reports of lifetime happiness seemed to be assuming that the meanings of equivalent levels of lifetime happiness offered by residents of Saudi Arabia, Bangladesh, Venezuela, Nicaragua, Ghana, Norway, and the United States were essentially similar. This premise violated my understanding of the different life circumstances and ethical values in these societies, another example of ignoring the local context.

Soon thereafter, I read several books on the diagnostic practices and therapeutic regimens of psychiatrists and clinical psychologists concerned with mental illness. Here, too, most of the experts were suppressing the effects of the person's social class and culture and assuming that a report of depression by an Ojibwa in Manitoba had the same origins as a similar report by a lawyer in Los Angeles. As I read more extensively in the vast literature on mental disorders, it became clear that a summary and critique of this body of knowledge would be useful and, in addition, would support the idea that each person's life setting influenced the probability of adaptation.

By now two years had passed, and the outline of the present manuscript assumed a form with an initial semblance of coherence. The primary themes would be the significance of the context in which individuals from different social classes and cultures try to cope with each day's responsibilities through their private interpretations of experiences in their distinctive contexts. The critical tone of this discussion made me uncomfortable, and I understood that a critique without some constructive suggestions would not be persuasive enough to promote reforms. The obligation to propose some new practices motivated the final chapter.

This book represents my understanding of the current state of psychological research. Most psychologists studying humans want to measure their representations of experience, thoughts, plans, motives, feelings, emotions, values, and behaviors and the patterns of brain activity that precede or accompany these phenomena. This domain, like ancient Gaul, is divided into three parts. The territory in the south is peopled with scientists trying to discover the events in brain and body that are believed to be the foundations of psychological processes that emerge from a cascade of events that necessarily incorporate events in the environment. At the northern end are sociologists, economists, political scientists, and cultural anthropologists studying the phenomena produced by groups of individuals. The valley between contains psychologists who measure the properties of single agents nurturing the hope of providing bridges between their neighbors and themselves. In this brief book, I focus primarily on the ideology and practices of this third group, many of whom strive to hold the territories together against forces in each pushing for autonomy.

Every intellectual discipline has a unique history marked by intervals of confidence and theoretical coherence alternating with periods of doubt and conceptual confusion. The young field of psychology has passed through several phases since its birth in German universities in the late nineteenth century. This new member of the academy was sired by the union of philosophers and sensory physiologists who believed that human perception, thought, emotion, and morality would be illuminated by studying the relations between objective indices of biological processes and the murkier mental processes that distinguished humans from other animals.

It is not surprising that the first cohort of psychologists chose physics (the acknowledged queen of the natural sciences) as a better model for their concepts and metrics than biology. Had they chosen the latter, they would have been more concerned with the processes that transform knowledge and action, as well as more sensitive to patterns of evidence, and would have recognized that the specific setting in which measurements were recorded often limited the generality of the abstract concepts they favored. Unfortunately, these first investigators were hampered by a lack of methods to measure the brain. Hence, the advances of this first stage were restricted to the psychological half of the equation that treated the details of perception and memory as a function of the nature of outside experience and remained silent on the brain's contribution to these relations.

Language, motivation, morality, emotion, personality, and mental illness were far more complicated than the ability to detect a difference in the loudness of two tones or the rate of decay in a set of recently memorized, meaningless syllables such as *cif, ris,* and *zox*. By the final decades of the twentieth century the frustration over failure to penetrate these more enigmatic phenomena could no longer be denied, and the next two cohorts took one of two paths.

American psychologists, always more pragmatic than Europeans, channeled their energies into the study of acquired behaviors in animals, because these processes were easier to measure. It was also important that the emphasis on learning new habits served the egalitarian hope that the differences in adaptation between poor European immigrants and the more affluent families whose parents were born in the United States were due primarily to experience rather than inherent constitutional inferiorities in the immigrant group. One advantage of this research was that it gave psychologists a better understanding of the robust mechanism of conditioning as a way to explain some changes in behavior. This movement produced a fair share of victories during the half-century when behaviorism, led by scientists like B. F. Skinner, Kenneth Spence, Neal Miller, and their students dominated the laboratories of many departments. The behaviorists promised to explain both the emergence of the universal qualities of each species and the variation among individuals within a species as the result of differential opportunities to acquire conditioned habits. Language, thought, intention, emotion, and morality, however, remained resistant to explanations restricted to conditioning principles. Social scientists relying on conditioning principles conducted an experiment in New York City about a decade ago that cost about forty million dollars. Youths were rewarded with money for remaining in school and passing the Regent's examination, and adults were given cash for visiting their dentist and holding down a job. The experiment was abandoned after three years because it did not work.

The Europeans, traditionally more concerned with the mind than with action, searched for a stronger set of ideas that might penetrate the mystery of human mental states. Freud thought he answered their need when he invented an initially persuasive set of interpretations that, intuitively, seemed correct to many because they supported two popular beliefs: that the events of early childhood placed serious limitations on a child's development and that sexuality played a significant role in human affairs.

Historical events supply one reason for the attractiveness of Freud's bold hypothesis that repression of sexual thoughts and feelings was the villain in all neuroses. The almost simultaneous appearance of a number of novelties, especially inexpensive contraceptives, automobiles, telephones, airplanes, and demands by middle-class women for enhanced status, generated among Americans and

Europeans a node of uncertainty over the way the world should work. Yielding to the temptation to find one cause for their inchoate feelings, a large number of adults collapsed the varied sources of confusion into a single feeling of uneasiness, which Freud located in the imprisoned wish for a guilt-free sexuality that was attainable by entering into psychoanalysis or being lucky enough to have experienced Freud's version of proper child rearing.

Psychologists nurtured for nearly fifty years the hope that the facts of conditioning and the concepts of psychoanalytic theory could somehow be linked to form a final theory, as Paul Dirac accomplished when he invented one set of mathematical equations from the different solutions of Erwin Schrödinger and Werner Heisenberg to explain quantum phenomena.

Thomas Huxley recognized that the power of science lay in its ability to slay a beautiful, but incorrect, assumption with a collection of ugly facts. It became clear by the late 1960s that a broad, integrative theory of behavior, emotion, and thought was unattainable. Many younger scholars in the next generation reacted to this insight by returning to the phenomena of perception, memory, and reasoning because they seemed more amenable to quantification. Their efforts defined the cognitive revolution of the 1980s. But the nineteenth-century commitment to discovering the events in the brain that were responsible for psychological phenomena had not disappeared. It was only waiting for bright physicists and engineers to design machines that promised to measure the brain profiles accompanying psychological phenomena. When these machines became available in the late 1970s, psychologists eagerly exploited positron emission tomography (PET), electroencephalography (EEG), magnetoencephalography (MEG), and functional magnetic resonance imaging (fMRI), hoping to gain deeper insights into the material origins of psychological events. This research promised to provide psychologists with their first set of fundamental structures that would be analogous to particles in physics and cells in biology.

This third phase in psychology's history is alive and well and recruits a large number of highly talented graduate students who hope to find the material homes of fear, joy, memory, language, mathematical reasoning, perception, and intentions to act, to name a few. This research rests on the unproven premise that specific patterns of activity in particular neuronal clusters will explain why a person in an airport on a snowy day is afraid to board an airplane.

A larger group, who either did not believe that psychological phenomena could be localized in a brain circuit or did not want to take the time to master the complicated technology, chose to study personality traits, mental illness, or the developmental history of these phenomena.

Unfortunately, these psychologists did not possess a set of powerful methods to explore their hunches, and too many settled for the traditional strategy of asking people what they felt, believed, or did. Most of these scientists denied the warnings of Virginia Woolf and Ludwig Wittgenstein that words were poor vehicles for understanding mental states. Over the past fifty years, psychologists have administered to thousands of adults a large number of questionnaires with unique names that were measuring similar phenomena. Sadly, language provides limited information on most mental states because all people have a restricted vocabulary, are tempted to conceal traits they regard as undesirable, and have no access to what their brain or body is doing when they describe their feelings or motivations. It is surprising, therefore, that the scientists who wish to locate the brain bases for traits like extroversion or the emotion of fear expect to find robust correspondences between a pattern of blood flow to certain brain sites and the answers to questions phrased in a vocabulary that everyone can understand. The fruitful concepts of vertebrate evolution would not have been discovered if natural scientists had asked the world's most experienced hunters and farmers to write down all they knew about animals.

What is missing from much research is careful consideration of the influences of the immediate context in which measurements of brain, behavior, or verbal replies are gathered. Many psychologists write as if their observations would not change much if their informants were alone, with an unfamiliar examiner or a friend, in a familiar or unfamiliar place. They also ignore the continuing influence of the differential exposure to the settings that accompany a particular social class or culture when they explore the relations among measurements. Too many papers assume that a result found with forty white undergraduates at a Midwestern university responding to instructions appearing on a computer screen in a small, windowless room would be affirmed if the participants were fifty-year-old South Africans administered the same procedure by a neighbor in a large room in a familiar church in Capetown.

This is not a new criticism of psychological practices. An eminent British psychologist, in a speech given in 1965, asked why psychologists placed humans in restrictive laboratory settings in which they could behave "as little as possible like human beings" and used the resulting evidence to make statements about human nature. Donald Fiske and Richard Shweder edited a volume of essays in 1986 that made the same claim. The fact that not much has changed over the past forty-five years implies that most psychologists do not like this message and will resist its implications as long as reviewers of research articles allow them to do so. Chapter 1, which addresses this issue, concludes that "agents in a context" should replace the current, restricted focus on the stable properties of individuals that, like their eye color, are presumably available for expression in all settings.

Discovery of a robust relation between the brain's response to an event, for example a picture of rotting food, and the feelings penetrating consciousness demanding an interpretation continues to evade the best efforts of talented investigators. The cascade of events that begins with brain activity and on occasion ends with an interpretation of an intrusive feeling defines the boundaries of the concept of emotion. Emotions in psychology play a role similar to heat in eighteenth-century physics because it seemed obvious that the intrusion of an acute emotion usually changed a person's demeanor or behavior. No one disagrees with the premise that the interpretations of intense feelings contribute to disturbances in civil harmony, impaired reasoning, and the bouts of distress that make life miserable. Equally salient emotions with a pleasant valence are the foundations of life's pleasures.

Although most investigators probe the disturbing emotions that are variations on the abstract ideas of anxiety, fear, anger, guilt, shame, and sadness, a small group of American psychologists decided about forty years ago that it was time to examine the shinier side of the penny by probing the emotions that accompany, or define, a satisfaction with one's life. Pleasure comes in three flavors. One class of satisfactions is brief and tightly yoked to a specific sensory experience, perhaps a slice of chocolate cake or a gentle caress. The second, also brief, is experienced when the person completes a task, visits a sick friend, or honors any one of a variety of private ethical standards. The third basis for pleasure is a primarily cognitive judgment that reflects the degree to which the person is satisfied with his or her entire life up to that moment. This state, called subjective well-being, is measured by replies to a small set of related questions whose core meaning is captured by the answer to the query, "All things considered, how satisfied are you with your life these days?" This notion has captured the interest of many psychologists, economists, and political scientists who assume, without the advantage of compelling logic or unambiguous evidence, that the replies to a stranger asking this question provide deep insights into the person's level of happiness and the vitality of the society in which the informant lives. This is an odd assumption. Few psychologists would treat the answers to the question, "How much do you understand about the world?" (rated on a five-point scale from very little to a great deal) as an accurate index of the depth of the respondents' knowledge. That is why we administer tests that measure a person's understanding of a particular area of knowledge. Nor would investigators assume that the replies to "All things considered, how good is your memory?" provided an accurate index of the respondent's memorial skill. It is puzzling, therefore, that psychologists are willing to believe that a verbal report of lifetime happiness, without any other information, is an accurate measure of a psychological state whose definition remains fuzzy.

A few investigators have gone further by suggesting that legislators and other government officials should rely on the average subjective well-being of their citizens to evaluate the benevolence in their society, rather than use the objective statistics on unemployment, morbidity, longevity, mutual trust, value coherence, and economic inequality. Chapter 2 examines the validity and utility of the concept of subjective well-being and arrives at the skeptical conclusion that the meanings of the verbal replies are not equivalent across cultures. Therefore, similar levels of reported well-being cannot be compared across different societies. It will prove more useful to rely on the objective features of a society to figure out the meaning of the answers its citizens give.

Chapter 3 considers the meaning of mental illness and how clinicians and investigators determine when a behavior or emotion represents a disorder rather than a normal reaction to a provocative event. These issues are of seminal concern to the public and, of course, have profound implications for the national health budget. A committee of eminent American psychiatrists, aided by some equally respected psychologists, are, as I write, working on a document called the Diagnostic and Statistical Manual of Mental Disorders–Version 5 (abbreviated as DSM-5), which in a few years will become the official handbook psychiatrists will use to decide who has a mental disorder and what disorder he or she has. Unfortunately, the forthcoming edition of this guide, like the four before it, ignores the origin of a symptom and relies primarily on the feelings and behaviors patients describe as salient in their consciousness. This definition of mental illness is flawed, because every symptom in the current handbook has more than one origin. Most of these illness categories are analogous to complaints of headaches or cramps. Physicians can decide on the best treatment for a headache only after they have determined its cause. The symptom alone is an insufficient guide.

Chapter 4 describes the varied treatments for mental disorders and documents the fact that most drugs and forms of psychotherapy are nonspecific to the diagnosed illness. Most drugs can be likened to a blow on the head, and the effectiveness of a form of psychotherapy depends on the patient's expectation that it will be helpful rather than the procedures the therapist follows. This chapter also evaluates the influence of history and cultural setting on the concept of mental disorder and suggests that a therapist's ethical preferences affect the advice offered.

I am not the first psychologist, nor will I be the last, to list the problems trailing contemporary research. Many wiser scientists have offered similar critiques in more graceful prose. But because we remain a minority, it seemed useful to restate some of the major flaws in research strategy and favored concepts. History teaches us that criticism of existing ideas or procedures, without providing constructive replacements, is rarely effective. Chapter 5 proposes a few strategies that might facilitate progress.

I urge scientists to look for patterns of measures rather than continue to relate a single causal condition to the average value on one outcome measure. I hope that lay readers will be suspicious of news reports that attribute a mental illness or unusual accomplishment to a single cause. The Nobel laureate François Jacob insisted that organizations of elements must be the targets of all analyses, no matter what the level of analysis chosen. A person's genome is a patterned organization of DNA strings; the immune system is an organization composed of many types of cells. Psychologists who study emotions, personality, and attitudes must also study patterns of evidence by supplementing verbal reports with direct behavioral and/or biological measures and looking for a meaningful organization in the set of observations.

A patient willingness to spend a prolonged time studying an important puzzle should replace the impatience of many nontenured faculty trying to publish many papers in a short time in order to be promoted. The current strategy makes it harder to make a significant discovery. Chairpersons, deans, and provosts should award less weight to the length of an investigator's publication list and more weight to the theoretical importance of the work. This change in the criterion for promotion and research awards would reduce the chronic tension felt by many young scientists who worry constantly over the number of papers they will publish during the current year.

A final plea is for a more acute awareness of the subtle influences of the psychologists' ethical preferences on the questions they ask and the solutions they seek. Two popular premises among American psychologists is that a confident posture of autonomy during the adult years requires a secure attachment during infancy and minimal stress during childhood. The evidence, however, indicates that a secure attachment in infancy does not inoculate a child against future problems, an insecure attachment does not doom the child to a failed adulthood, and some stressors have benevolent consequences.

Scientists use one of four criteria when they select a target of study: Will the results illuminate an important puzzle, be of benefit to individuals at risk, have implications for the society, or have an elegant form? Most psychologists choose either the first or second of these criteria. Investigations relying on either criterion will benefit from greater attention to the context of observation and a persistent search for patterns in evidence.

Progress in all scientific domains is facilitated by a candid acknowledgment of fault lines as well as the celebration of past victories. It was not until the end of the nineteenth century that some biologists had an initial understanding of why the mixing of female and male seed was followed, after a delay, with a newborn animal. Yet humans had been brooding on this puzzle for thousands of years. The formal discipline of psychology is less than 150 years old, suggesting that current accounts of most phenomena are bound to be crude or simply wrong. Physicists are not ashamed of acknowledging their puzzlement over what was present before the Big Bang; geneticists are not reluctant to describe the conceptual problems raised by the recent evidence on epigenetics; geologists admit that they cannot explain why our planet, which during its first two billion years had very little free oxygen, eventually became a place with abundant oxygen.

One reason psychology slipped from a position of prominence only sixty years ago to a subordinate rank in the academy was a reluctance to question popular concepts and analytic procedures. The descent in status led, inevitably, to increased numbers of talented college seniors choosing one of the natural sciences rather than psychology for a career. Denial of the unpleasant can be an effective defense in individuals, but it is toxic in the sciences. Capable youth with a passion for science enjoy solving difficult challenges. Candid discussion of psychology's problems might recruit a larger number who would like to spend their productive years illuminating the puzzles that so many brilliant scholars before them could not resolve.

Who might profit from or simply enjoy these musings? Nadine Gordimer noted, with her usual wisdom, that words are symbols with shared memories. Most readers find philosophers and physicists hard to understand because concepts like truth and ten-dimensional strings are symbols whose memories the public does not share. Hence, these terms have special meanings in the texts these scholars compose. Fortunately, the vocabulary that psychologists use are far more accessible because most adults ask the same questions, often phrased with the same words, when they wonder about their personhood and the meaning of their lives.

I thank Laura Jones Dooley for her usual careful, creative editing, Paula Mabee for typing assistance, and Richard McNally and Jay Schulkin for constructive comments on one or more chapters.

ONE

Missing Contexts

Although the public's understanding of science is dominated by images of elegant machines and useful products,
the two most basic rituals are making observations and
inventing concepts that might explain the evidence. In
1910, Peyton Rous injected cells taken from a rare tumor
of the skin found in one chicken into healthy chickens
and discovered that the animals receiving the cells developed the same cancerous tumor. After proving that the
toxic agent in the tumor cells had to be extremely small,
he suggested that a virus was the likely cause of the cancer. In time, many investigators and physicians extended
this explanation to all cancers. This belief turned out to
be incorrect. We now know that although a virus was the

cause of the cancer in Rous's chickens, viruses are not the cause of all cancers.

Every observation is made on one kind of object or process in a specific setting, usually with the help of a particular machine or procedure. Thus there is always the possibility that the same phenomenon might not be observed if the object, setting, machine, or procedure were altered. The scientist's continual hope is that the concept and explanation applied to the observations in one setting with one procedure would remain appropriate in other settings with similar procedures. If so, the conceptual name chosen for the original observations would remain valid. If not, perhaps the particular thing, setting, or procedure was essential to what was observed. Put differently, scientists want to know what exists in nature, but they must always be concerned with the reasons why they believe what they do because different procedures or settings can yield observations that change what they know.

Physicists have been the most successful at imagining concepts and explanations that apply across an extraordinary range of situations, because the major features that define the concepts salt crystal, carbon atom, and electron are relatively stable, inherent characteristics of those objects rather than their functions. Newton's famous equation stating that the gravitational force between two objects is lawfully related to their masses and the distance between them holds for the relation between the earth and moon as well as between an apple on a tree and the earth below. Any object thrown up in the air from any place on the earth will fall to the ground. Einstein's equation $E = mc^2$ (energy is the product of the mass of an object and the square of the speed of light) is a quintessential example of the physicist's search for concepts and laws that are indifferent to variations in the setting. This equation does not specify the form the energy assumes (light, heat, radiation) or the object (a kilogram of uranium or iron).

Biologists have had a more mixed success, because the defining features of a large number of biological concepts apply to a restricted number of species. More important, the features of many concepts refer to the reactions of a cell or living form, and the reactions observed depend on the local setting. The presence of one X and one Y chromosome is a defining feature of the concept *biological male* in mammals, but this feature is not the criterion for maleness in fish or birds. Female fertility is reduced during the winter months among women residing in northern latitudes characteristic of Scandinavia, where there are long periods of darkness, but is not seen among women living close to the equator.[1]

Psychologists have encountered the greatest difficulty

generating concepts that applied to settings that were very different from the one that gave rise to the original observation because most concepts refer to the behavioral or physiological reactions of animals and humans to specific situations, rather than to the relatively stable, inherent features of these agents, such as their body mass, pigmentation, or blood type. As a result, many psychological concepts refer to phenomena that are necessarily influenced by the context. The surface of the sea, compared with the sea bottom, provides an analogy. The form that the surface water assumes in any particular ten-thousand-square-foot area is influenced by the wind, the presence of ships of different sizes, whales, and in some places acres of garbage. Yet psychologists continue to search for laws that have the power of $E = mc^2$. This practice ignores the fact that a number of physical concepts are mathematical inventions that have not yet been observed and, therefore, lie far below the surface. Dark matter and the Higgs particle are two examples.

A frustrating consequence of the influence of the local context is that few psychological concepts intended to represent a person's tendency to react in a certain way apply across diverse settings, even though concepts, such as *fear*, *extroversion*, and *intelligence*, imply that they do. Most seven-month-old infants cry if an unfamiliar adult with a neutral facial expression walks toward them quickly. But few cry if the same stranger is smiling while walking toward the infant slowly. Therefore, attributing a fear of strangers to an infant depends on the context.

This fact and many others are the source of serious disagreements over the defining features of important concepts. A hand supplies a clarifying metaphor. Biologists study the stable features of the genes, proteins, and other molecules responsible for the development of a hand. Although all hands are by and large similar, the things that hands do, which psychologists measure, vary with the setting.

Physicists agree that quarks, leptons, and bosons, the constituents of atoms, are the basic elements of matter, and they describe the inherent properties of these particles. Biologists concur that genes are the foundation of all the proteins that make up tissues and organs, and they describe genes as sequences of DNA molecules. But psychologists are not even close to an accord on the biological and psychological processes that are the foundations of the phenomena they wish to understand. These include aggressive actions, emotions, consciousness, regulation, morality, stress, and reward. None of these concepts specifies the setting in which the defining information was observed or the procedure that produced the evidence. Therefore, they both imply a generality across contexts and procedures that does not always occur and generate disagreements about the defining properties of these and other popular concepts.

One investigator, for example, will attribute a state of fear to individuals who show a large surge of blood flow to a particular brain site (indicating activation of that site) when a face with a fearful expression appears on a screen. A second scientist will attribute fear to adults who display a large skin conductance reaction on the fingers when they see a stimulus that warns them they might receive an electric shock to the wrist. And a third will attribute fear to college students who report on a questionnaire that they often feel scared when they see a mouse. The problem is that the majority of individuals who display a surge of blood flow to the amygdala to fearful faces do not show a large skin conductance reaction to the threat of an electric shock, and a majority of individuals in the latter group do not say they are afraid of mice. This evidence implies that the concept *fear* has different meanings in these three settings. It would seem wise, therefore, for investigators to stop writing about "fear" in the abstract and specify the measure and setting whenever they attribute fear to a person or to an animal.

The theoretically important concept *reward* provides an illustration of the need to include the details of the setting when the concept is invoked. The term *reward* was invented originally to explain why some events had the power to increase the occurrence of a behavioral reaction that was followed by a rewarding event. The probability that a hungry rat will repeatedly strike a lever with a paw increases if food is delivered after the lever is struck. This fact is interpreted to mean that food is a reward for a hungry animal. Humans, however, find the mastery of a difficult task and the active pursuit of a goal as rewarding. The many writers, composers, and scientists who labor for years in the hope of winning recognition illustrate the wisdom of this view. The feelings and thoughts that follow the sating of hunger, however, are different from the feelings and thoughts accompanying the receipt of praise for an accomplishment. For that reason, the concept *reward* cannot refer to a single biological or psychological process. Even though one restricted set of neurons is activated by the anticipation of any desirable experience, the total pattern of brain activity is unlikely to be identical to all types of rewards. A small number of neurons in the auditory cortex are excited by music, speech, thunder, explosions, and rain striking a windowpane. But the complete pattern of brain activity, as well as the profile of associations, is quite different to each of these five events, and they therefore should not be regarded as belonging to the same psychological category.

Consider a simple example of the mistaken inference that is possible when it is based on observations in only one context. Let's assume that Mary has a strong motive to please others but a weak need to prove she is well disciplined, whereas Alice has the opposite pair of motives. Both are tested for their ability to inhibit impulsive decisions in a laboratory setting, and both women attain the same score on a measure of impulsivity. But because the identical scores are the result of different motives, the inference that Mary and Alice are equally capable of inhibiting impulsive acts in the laboratory would probably not be affirmed if the setting were a party at which friends urged each woman to stay up all night drinking beer and smoking pot.

There is a more formal way to describe this issue. A majority of psychologists begin their research with a favorite hunch and gather one type of evidence in one setting to confirm the truth of their hypothesis. They are unlikely to try to disprove the favored hypothesis by gathering additional data in different settings. These scientists assume that their hypothesis is true if the evidence they gather supports it. A second, smaller group starts with a weaker intuition about what to observe and begins by gathering a large set of observations in the hope of finding patterns that might generate a strong hypothesis. These investigators assume that what they observe will be the best source of a useful hunch. These are different strategies with different probabilities of generating true statements. The probability that Peyton Rous was correct when he wrote that a virus was the cause of the chicken's skin tumor turned out to be high. But the probability attached to the truth value of the hypothesis that all cancers have a viral origin turned out to be low.

The aims of this chapter can be stated in a few sentences. Behaviors (including verbal replies in humans) and biological responses in a setting remain a primary source of evidence for psychologists who conceive of their task as inventing concepts that will predict when a particular class of behavior will occur and to explain why it occurred. Three factors influence the probability that a particular behavior will be expressed. The properties of the brain and the individual's prior experiences are the most obvious. The structure of the human brain makes it likely that most two-year-olds will smile, speak, and reach for objects in many settings. Life histories add a host of new behaviors that would not have occurred naturally, such as sewing a button, hitting a baseball, or texting a message.

The local setting, the third influence, selects one behavior from an envelope that usually contains more than one possibility. Pedestrians holding an empty candy wrapper can throw it on the sidewalk or put it an official receptacle for rubbish. They are more likely to choose the former if they see others litter but apt to select the latter if they note that others put used wrappers in receptacles. The brain structures of modern humans, which emerged between 100,000 and 150,000 years ago, awarded our species the ability to invent a written script. But the evidence suggests that this ability was not expressed until about 8,000 years ago, when the setting was optimal for the exploitation of this competence. This talent, along with texting a message and operating an automobile, lay dormant for more than 100,000 years.

The local setting affects parents' and teachers' descriptions of the personalities of children. Parents and teachers usually disagree because the parents base their judgments on the child's behavior at home, whereas the teachers rely on behavior in the school setting. Hundreds of psychologists across the United States are involved in intervention programs designed to alter the intellectual abilities or personality traits of children from economically disadvantaged families. In most cases, the intervention occurs in a school, university, or Head Start program. Evaluations of the effectiveness of these efforts reveal that the modest changes observed in the settings where the intervention occurred did not always generalize to the home and community contexts where the parents and children spend most of their time.[2]

Each person is a member of a number of symbolic categories that usually include their developmental stage, sex, family pedigree, ethnicity, religion, class, culture, and work role. Some add their city, nation, or region in which they live. Each of these categories has a privileged link to a particular set of behaviors. The strength of a person's motives, beliefs, and behaviors varies with the categories that are predominant in a particular setting. Because each setting activates only some of these categories, the motives, moods, attitudes, or behaviors that are likely to emerge vary across settings and cultures. The person's categories for sex, age, status, and work role will be activated in male college students who, having volunteered to participate in a study in a university laboratory, meet an older woman who administers some questionnaires. A different pattern of motives and behavior biases will be activated when these same students are at home talking with an older sister. Hence, the answers to a question asking about their feelings toward their parents are apt to differ when posed by a stranger in a laboratory or a sibling at home.

Stanley Milgram attained sudden fame in the late 1970s after publishing a series of studies demonstrating that ordinary Americans would obey an experimenter who told them to administer extremely painful electric shocks to a stranger who they believed was participating in an experiment on learning whenever the stranger made an error. Actually, the stranger was a confederate and was not receiving any shocks. Although a majority of subjects obeyed the examiner and administered what they thought were painful shocks, the features of the setting affected their behavior. The subjects were most likely to administer very painful shocks if the stranger was located in a separate room, the subject could hear his simulated cries of pain, and the experimenter was perceived as a legitimate authority. The subjects were less likely to administer the painful shocks when the stranger was sitting next to them and the experimenter was either physically absent (he gave orders on the telephone) or was not perceived as an authority figure.[3]

The direction of a career is occasionally determined by the distinctive features of a city or nation during a particular era. Claude Lévi-Strauss was France's most celebrated twentieth-century anthropologist, even though he had no interest in this discipline as a young man. Lévi-Strauss had accepted a temporary position as lecturer in sociology in a university in São Paulo because he needed a job. While in Brazil he took a short trip west where he made contact with some Indian tribes, gathered photos, and collected artifacts. These scattered sources of information were greeted with acclaim when he returned to Paris because French anthropology lagged behind that in England and the French were eager to improve their competitive position. It was also relevant that French intellectuals favored Lévi-Strauss's abstract style of thought. Academic scholars in most other European nations held a more critical attitude toward this form of writing. Lévi-Strauss, who was pleasantly surprised by his unexpected celebrity, decided that anthropology might be the best route to fame and fortune. I suspect that if he had grown up in Munich, Moscow, Stockholm, or London, his brief encounters with the Brazilian Indians would not have attracted as much admiration and he would have selected a different field of inquiry that might not have brought him the international stature he enjoyed during the second half of his long life.

The young Albert Einstein was working in the patent office in Bern reviewing proposals for clocks that would more accurately record the times in different places at a particular instant. People wanted to know the precise time in Paris when the railway clock in Bern struck noon. It is easy to imagine these proposals focusing Einstein's creative mind on the meaning of simultaneity, which became the deep insight in his special theory of relativity.[4] Had Einstein secured a faculty position in Vienna or Zurich, which he preferred, he would not have been working in the patent office and, perhaps, would have turned his extraordinary intellect to other puzzles. Similar accidents of location made the distinguished careers of Ivan Pavlov and Gregor Mendel possible. Pavlov was working at the only laboratory in Russia that had the operating rooms and equipment required for performing surgery with dogs. Mendel was admitted to the only monastery in his region that had an active herbarium. A special talent, like a rare form of orchid, requires the right soil in order to flourish. The injunction of the Oracle at Delphi, "Know thyself," should be reworded to read, "Know thyself in each context."

The term *context* within psychology has both a narrow and a broad definition. The narrow meaning refers to the physical and social features of the setting, especially its familiarity, the presence or absence of others, the specific events presented, and always the procedure that produced the evidence. Each procedure imposes a unique set of constraints on the person or animal being observed, and these constraints determine what the scientist observes. Physicists appreciate this fact. If single photons are directed at a pair of slits placed side by side in front of a screen, scientists observe an interference pattern on the screen, suggesting that light is composed of waves. If, however, physicists want to measure the direction of movement of each photon, they have to add a source of energy to the apparatus. When they do, the pattern on the screen consists of single spots, implying that light is composed of particles. The message is clear. The features of each procedure intrude into and affect the observations recorded. The first naturalists who studied the sky relied on what they could see with their eyes or with the help of a crude telescope. The Hubble Space Telescope reveals observations that Galileo could not have anticipated. Each set of evidence invites different conclusions about the cosmos.

Psychologists typically rely on three distinct kinds of evidence: motor responses, verbal descriptions (in humans), and biological reactions. Unfortunately, the meanings of these observations remain controversial because psychologists do not have a strong theory that explains most actions, verbal descriptions, or biological responses. Physicists agree on the meaning of the spectrum of electromagnetic radiation emitted by a particular category of atom, and biologists enjoy consensus on the meaning of a microscopic analysis of the density of a class of white blood cells. Psychologists, however, continue to quarrel over the meaning of an increase in attention in infants, verbal replies to personality questionnaires, or an increase in blood flow to a site in the brain.

One reason for the disagreements is that each source of evidence varies in its ability to reflect particular psychological processes. Behaviors, for example, are moderately sensitive indices of intentions or motives but poor at revealing feelings. Verbal reports are relatively accurate measures of facts, such as the size of one's family, but are less accurate indices of the quality of feelings. Profiles of brain activity provide sensitive measures of level of alertness but are poor at reflecting the content of thoughts. As a result, the meaning of the concept *anxious* applied to a group of persons must specify the source of evidence that was used to make the inference.

Different biological measures often require different inferences. A team of psychologists wanted to know what emotional state to attribute to young adults while they were looking at pictures that were either unpleasant (for example, a blood-stained body), pleasant (a baby smiling), or neutral (a table). They measured three biological reactions that presumably reflect an emotion: the magnitude of the eye-blink reflex to a loud sound, the size of the surge of blood flow to certain brain sites, and the magnitude of a particular wave form in the electroencephalogram. The unpleasant pictures produced the largest eye-blink reflex. The pleasant pictures produced the largest surge of blood flow. The pleasant and unpleasant scenes evoked larger wave forms than the neutral scenes, but there was no difference between the pleasant and unpleasant pictures. Faced with this evidence, it is not clear what these psychologists should conclude about the psychological states accompanying unpleasant compared

with pleasant scenes. A similar level of ambiguity surrounded two different measures of brain activity while
adults were reading real words, strings of consonants, or
strings of geometric forms. The indices of neural activity
based on increased blood flow to a site or on changes in
the magnetic moments generated by the neurons receiving information required different inferences regarding
the brain's response.[5]

Many psychologists assume that adults who show activation of the amygdala when they see faces with fearful
expressions are in a state of fear. But a simple change in
the procedure in which scenes symbolic of fear occurred
along with the fearful faces reduced the amygdala's response to the faces. Now it is less clear that fearful faces
automatically generate a fear state independent of the
context in which they appear. Moreover, the psychological state created by seeing a static picture of a fearful face
on a man with no body is unlikely to resemble the state
evoked by actually seeing a fearful face on a thirty-year-
old man waving his arms on a city street.[6]

The popular concept *self* has at least three distinct
meanings depending on the measurement. The psychologists who believe that self has a foundation in brain
activity base their inference on the brain profiles that accompany particular feelings. Those who prefer William

James's definition record the person's verbal descriptions of their traits and social categories. Psychologists friendly to the positivism of behaviorism base a concept of self on observed behaviors. These are three different definitions of self. Three psychologists basing a judgment of self on only one of these classes of observations resemble a trio of observers standing in different places judging the qualities of a rainbow. Each will arrive at a different description of what he or she sees.

The same problem trails many conclusions about cognitive abilities. A number of experiments over the years led to the hypothesis that humans must have an intact brain structure, called the hippocampus, in order to learn and retain a new association (for example, learning that the medical term for hardening of the arteries is *atherosclerosis*). The typical procedure in these studies presents individuals with a picture of a single new object and an unfamiliar name and requires them to learn the association between the novel object and novel word. A subtle change in this procedure revealed the surprising discovery that adults with a damaged hippocampus could learn a new name for an unfamiliar object if the procedure were altered in what would seem to be a trivial way. Individuals with a damaged hippocampus, as well as normal adults, saw pictures of a familiar and an unfamiliar object at the same time, instead of seeing only one picture, as they heard an unfamiliar name. Under these conditions, the adults lacking a hippocampus were able to learn and remember the new association. Perhaps the extra mental work required when the person had to infer that the unfamiliar word must name the unfamiliar object, rather than the familiar one, recruited activity in brain sites that made the learning possible.[7]

Women perform much better on tasks requiring mental manipulation of an object in space if the form is a human body rather than a meaningless block figure. Simple changes in procedure also affect inferences regarding the cognitive capacities of infants and young children. Three-month-olds appear able to discriminate between a heavy and a light object because they hold the lighter object for a longer time. But they only do this when tested in a dark room. The infants do not behave this way in a room that is normally lit. Even a detail as seemingly irrelevant as the size of the room can change inferences about children's talents. Two-year-olds usually pay attention to a single blue wall if they are in a large, windowed room with three white walls and will use the distinctive blue landmark to find an object they had seen hidden in a corner of the room. But if the room is small and windowless, they do not attend to the blue wall and therefore fail to find the object.

Even the presence of rubbish tempts individuals with a strong need for order to think in more stereotyped ways.[8]

Contextual constraints on the generality of concepts are common in animals. High-ranking primates are stressed when the dominance structure of the group is unstable; low-ranking animals are maximally stressed when the rank is stable because they are usually in a subordinate position. Brown trout with high levels of the stress hormone cortisol are submissive when observed in a laboratory aquarium but are dominant when observed in the natural ecology of a stream. Whether one bonobo chimp dominates another depends on whether two animals are interacting or a third bonobo is present. A species of fish found near Australia's Great Barrier Reef provides a dramatic illustration of the consequences of an animal's status within a group. The basic social unit in this species is a male who dominates a harem of three to six females, with one female dominant over the others. If the male dies for whatever reason, the female who had been dominant undergoes a change in sex and becomes a biological male. Apparently, the male's presence suppressed the capacity of the female to undergo a sex reversal. One could not ask for a more persuasive example of the profound effects of the local social context on biology and behavior.[9]

The nature of the setting at Jane Goodall's Gombe Stream field station in Africa contributed to the high incidence of chimpanzee aggression she recorded. The daily portion of food that her staff put out close to the station brought baboons and chimpanzees together in a small area. This degree of crowding does not usually occur in the forest. Therefore, the exaggerated level of aggression was caused by this atypical context. It is not surprising that humans commit more antisocial acts in densely crowded urban areas than in rural communities. Young male elephants experience periodic surges in testosterone that are accompanied by increased aggressive behavior. This state, called *musth*, can last as long as six months if no adult males are present but has a much shorter duration if older males are introduced into the group of young aggressive males.[10]

Evolution provides a final example of the significance of the local setting. It appears that the emergence of our species required the ecology of Africa as the context in which relevant genetic changes occurred. An earlier human species called *H. heidelbergensis* emerged in Africa about seven hundred thousand years ago. The members of this species that migrated to parts of Europe evolved into the Neanderthal and vanished as a species about thirty thousand years ago. The members of *H. heidelbergensis* that remained in Africa evolved to become modern humans. Enough! I could cite many more examples but trust that this list is sufficient to persuade readers that it will often prove useful to restrict the applicability of many concepts to the context of observation or to very similar settings.

A broad definition of context, which applies primarily, but not exclusively, to humans who interpret the symbolic meanings of a setting, include the person's sex, ethnicity, developmental stage, social class, and cultural background. These properties affect the person's construal of the examiner, the task administered, the expectation of what might happen, and the probability of an adequate or inadequate performance, as well as many biological reactions.

Developmental stage is always a factor. Six-year-olds and adults, lying in a scanner that measured the activation of their amygdala, saw pictures of their mother with a happy or angry face and pictures of an unfamiliar woman showing the same two expressions. The children displayed their greatest activation to their smiling mother, but the adults showed their greatest activation to their angry mother because children and adults construed this unusual context in very different ways.

The populations that settled in Europe, Africa, Asia, and South America many thousands of years ago developed different genomes over time, different vulnerabilities to certain physical and mental disorders, and different patterns of brain activity to stimuli as simple as faces and houses. Psychologists should be troubled that most of the world's research on human psychological processes is conducted in English by Americans on Americans. American college students between seventeen and twenty-five years of age with a European pedigree were the major participants in more than two-thirds of the papers published between 2003 and 2007 in six leading American psychological journals. Because the genomes of Caucasians, Africans, Asians, and Hispanics vary significantly, these populations might display distinctive brain and behavioral reactions to the same event. It is not at all obvious that most of the results reported in published papers with college-age, white American participants would be the same if the same studies were implemented with fifty-year-olds from a rural village in Ghana, the center of Beijing, a New Guinea forest, or a suburb of Quito.

Moreover, the number of subjects observed in most studies is usually less than fifty, whereas particle physicists base their conclusions on at least several billion events. It is unlikely that the results found with fifty male rats from one strain or fifty American college students would be repeated if the experiment was performed on one thousand rats of both sexes and varied strains or five thousand men and women from varied class and cultural groups.[11]

Most of the research on the relation between brain activity and behavior is conducted with mice or rats. There is, however, a serious bias favoring the study of male animals. The ratio of male to female animals in research studies published in 2009 was five to one. Because male and female rats and mice differ on many biological measures, it remains possible that some of the results found with males would not be repeated with females.[12]

This serious restriction in the types and sizes of human populations studied poses a problem for the psychologists who want to believe that the observations they gathered with Americans on some aspect of morality, happiness, or the concept of time apply to all humans in all societies. Most Americans and Europeans represent time as flowing from the right side of their body to the left side. Members of one Australian Aboriginal group, however, use their position with respect to the compass directions of north, south, east, and west to represent time as flowing from east to west. Failure to acknowledge the historical changes that occurred over the past one hundred thousand years is seen in a report on contemporary hunter-gatherers in Africa. Because genetically unrelated individuals belonged to the same group, the scientists concluded that this arrangement was probably true for the original hunter-gatherers who lived in these areas so many years ago. This bold claim ignores the different contexts in which the older and contemporary individuals survived as well as the changes in knowledge, beliefs, practices, and ease of access to the wider world that transpired over this long interval.[13]

Some phenomena that are robust during one historical era become less reliable when social conditions change. In 1956, Solomon Asch published findings that were cited in every introductory textbook. American college students consciously suppressed what they believed to be the correct answer to a perceptual problem and conformed to the incorrect answers given by a group of strangers who were Asch's confederates. But the next generation of young Americans was more rebellious and less conforming. As a result, psychologists were finding it difficult to repeat Asch's result.[14] German youth born after 1935 were vulnerable to guilt or shame over their parents' or grandparents' cooperation with Hitler's demands. German youth born only twenty years earlier were proud of the dignity that Hitler was bringing to their country.

The increased specialization in the natural sciences, accompanied by the reliance on complex technologies, has led to the need for cooperation among a large number of scientists and, therefore, a sharing of recognition and fame for an important discovery. Almost 80 percent of the papers in the natural sciences published in 2000 had more than one author, and many had six or more authors.

American adolescents, however, are socialized by family and media to seek personal achievement and a celebration of the individual for any accomplishment. The heroes of youths who are interested in science are Galileo, Newton, Darwin, and Einstein, all of whom worked alone. This historical change in the conduct of science may help to explain why undergraduates in the class of 2011 took fewer science courses than the class of 1951 and why only 6 percent of American twenty-four-year-olds have an undergraduate degree in a natural science, mathematics, or engineering. If parents socialize their children to seek personal celebrity at the same time that science becomes a cooperative team effort, a career in science loses some of its luster.

I confess to being surprised by a paper in one of America's premier journals that failed to describe the ages, social class, or ethnic or cultural background of the forty-two volunteers who were asked to assume a body posture symbolic of either high or low power. Nonetheless, the authors did not flinch when they concluded that these two postures are accompanied by different profiles of hormones, feelings, and behaviors.[15] Apparently they wanted readers to believe that simply opening one's arms wide or closing them around the body produced the same distinctive consequences in any person in any place at any time. These psychologists seem to be suggesting that subjugated women living in a Taliban-controlled area of Afghanistan would feel empowered if they opened their arms wide for a few minutes each morning.

The size of a community influences the patterns of social relationships. The social patterns in a rural village of a thousand inhabitants are different from the patterns observed in cities with a million or more residents. The incidence of mental illnesses is usually greater in large cities than in rural areas or small towns because social supports are more common in the latter settings. Children of above-average intellectual ability living in small communities will have fewer peers with comparable talents and are likely to feel more confident than children with the same ability living in cities with much larger high school populations. This phenomenon is called the "big fish in the little pond effect." Even the probability that a child will be diagnosed as autistic is higher (at least in California) if the child lives within a mile of another who received the same diagnosis earlier. It is likely that a mother of a child with serious language retardation and poor social skills who knows that a child in the same neighborhood with a diagnosis of autism became eligible for special tutoring would ask her doctor whether the same diagnosis applied to her child.[16]

Haiti and the Dominican Republic occupy the same small island. But the former is poor and has an unstable government, whereas the latter prospers. It is impossible to explain the dramatic differences between these two nations without understanding their historical contexts over the past four hundred years. Haiti, which was initially governed by France, imported many slaves, had irregular rainfall, and in the twentieth century was led by a dictator who did not promote a capitalist economy. The Dominican Republic, initially governed by Spain, had far fewer slaves, more rain, and a dictator who favored business interests. A few cities possess for awhile an ambience of tolerance and respect for scholarly accomplishment that makes it easier for talented, motivated adults who belong to a minority group to attain positions of eminence. Nineteenth-century Budapest was home to a large number of such influential intellectuals, including the physicist Leo Szilard, the mathematician John von Neumann, the biologist Albert Szent-Györgi, and the writer Arthur Koestler.[17]

Adolf Hitler provides a malevolent example of the influence of a community's values. Hitler in 1918 was twenty-nine, penniless, without a steady job, and mentally unstable. Twenty years later he was chancellor of Germany. This counterintuitive rise to power required the particular social context that characterized Germany during a period that combined hyperinflation, high un-employment, anger at the nations that defeated it in the First World War, and an intense anti-Semitism among the working class.

The economy of a region establishes special contexts. The social and institutional differences between the American North and South in the eighteenth and early nineteenth centuries were due, in part, to their econo-mies. The average household in New England survived on a small landholding on which the family grew grains and raised chickens, pigs, and cows. As a result eighty to one hundred families lived in a relatively small area and could band together to build a church, school, and community. By contrast, economic survival in the South relied on tobacco as a major crop. Because a reasonable income from tobacco required four hundred to eight hundred acres, each family was isolated from its neigh-bors, and it was difficult to get one hundred families to cooperate in building a church and school.

European historians have argued that eighteenth- and nineteenth-century Germany was distinguished by a small set of unique properties. This country was located between the more cosmopolitan societies of England and France to the west (which Germans admired) and the less sophisticated Russian nation to the east (which Ger-mans derogated). This position, analogous to being the middle-born boy with older and younger brothers, may have motivated Germans to develop a unique philosophy that emphasized the centrality of *Geist*, translated as spirit, and *Kultur*, a respect for the arts and literature, which allowed citizens to feel that they had a distinctive and respected identity.[18]

One scholar has argued that the different value systems of Germans and Americans during the early twentieth century motivated German biologists to study the complex problems surrounding the development of vertebrate embryos. The practical Americans, who were more interested in finding robust, empirical facts than in illuminating profound mysteries, studied the consequences of different genes in simpler animals, especially fruit flies, worms, and bacteria.[19] Put a little too plainly, the American scientists wanted to prove how smart they were by discovering irrefutable facts; the Germans wished to demonstrate their wisdom by probing the dynamic relations in complex, mysterious processes. Decades later these national differences have just about vanished, and the American style dominates both groups of scientists.

The emotional response to a painting, play, novel, memoir, or poem varies with the person's historical-cultural setting. Most seventeenth-century Londoners watching a production of *The Merchant of Venice* were not unduly ashamed of their anti-Semitic attitudes and would have reacted to Shylock's speeches with feelings and thoughts different from those experienced by more tolerant, contemporary audiences. A metal tree placed on the grounds of an art museum is regarded as an aesthetic object. The same tree built by the same person but placed on the sidewalk in front of a first-floor window to block the view of pedestrians would not be treated as an artistic object.

The anthropologist Richard Shweder described an exquisite example of the influence of the local context. Shweder and his wife, living temporarily in the temple town of Orissa, India, where he was doing fieldwork, were entertaining three guests of different statuses for dinner. Therefore, Shweder had to guarantee that the food was acceptable to them all, and he went to a local temple to gather food others had placed there earlier in the day, because anyone is allowed to eat a food after a god has removed its essence. Some rice remained in the bowl after the guests departed, and Shweder's wife diced chicken into the bowl of rice and served it to her husband. Shweder was surprised by a sudden feeling of disgust and an inability to eat the food. Apparently, the moral standards of the temple town in which he was working had become part of his context as he sat in his temporary dining room. Shweder has no problem eating diced chicken in a bowl of rice when sitting with his wife in their dining room in Chicago.

The argument up to now claims that every observation of a human behavior or biological reaction takes place in a specific physical setting, is preceded by another event, is expected or unexpected, familiar or unfamiliar, is or is not relevant to the person's intention at that moment, and is affected by the personal properties associated with the symbolic groups to which the person belongs. The individual's understanding of his or her social class in a community is especially important because it generates particular states of mind due, in part, to variation in socialization and exposures to varied settings. Of course, the features that define social class vary with culture and historical era. In fifteenth-century Europe, status was based primarily on the amount of land the family owned. Class position in contemporary Europe and the United States, which are egalitarian, is based on education, type of work, and income. These features are supposed to be attainable by anyone. A century earlier, however, ethnicity and religion affected rank until the civil rights movement of the 1960s demoted the significance of these properties. Scholars and peasant farmers had a higher status in eighteenth-century China than merchants, but merchants in eighteenth-century England had a higher status than scholars or farmers.[20]

A ritual or personal feature can enhance a person's status when it is restricted to a small group. Wearing silk in public was permitted only for those with elite status in sixteenth-century Scotland. Two centuries later, after an egalitarian ethic pervaded the society, silk lost its symbolic significance. A degree from an Ivy League college in 1900 was, like wearing silk in Scotland, a mark of high rank. That is no longer true today. Of course, the psychological consequences of a particular class position vary with its frequency. In communities in which 60 percent live on a small income and have less than eight years of schooling, the intensity of the corrosive emotions that accompany a perception of disadvantage is muted. When only 15 percent possess these features, intense anxiety, anger, or depression can rise because a perception of difference is added to the deprivations of poverty and inadequate schooling.

The social class in which children develop affects their exposure to varied stressors, parental behavior and promotion of values, identification with a privileged or less privileged group, and a mainly unconscious recognition of one's psychological potency and acceptability to others. An adult's status relative to another can even affect voice quality. When the television host Larry King was interviewing a person of high status, for example Bill Clinton, he began to match the sound quality of his voice to that of Clinton. King did not do that with guests of lower status. The effect of social class on the growth of a child's intellectual abilities can be detected as early as ten months of age. The personality patterns that developed in a group of California children born in the 1920s were predicted by their childhood IQs and school achievement scores. Both measures were related to the child's social class. Even in the small, isolated town of San Pedro, located on the shores of Lake Atitlán in northwest Guatemala, the small number of children whose families in 1974 were engaged in commercial activity performed far better on a series of cognitive tasks than the larger group from poorer families who remained involved in small-scale agriculture.[21]

The social class of the child's family even trumps the influences of day care, preschool attendance, and peers. Less than one-third of American children under age five in 2005 were cared for at home by a parent or close relative, compared with over 95 percent a century earlier. Nonetheless, the differences in cognitive skills between children of the poor and affluent remain as large today as they were in 1905. The Polish city of Warsaw was destroyed by bombs during the Second World War; the Soviet Union, which rebuilt the city, required families of different class positions to live in the same apartment buildings and to send their children to the same schools. Nonetheless, the children reared by college-educated parents obtained better grades than those living with parents who had less education, in part because of more consistent motivation for academic achievement among the children of well-educated parents. Variation in class membership even influences the kinds of goods purchased. Working-class adults tend to buy expensive luxury items that are similar to those purchased by friends. The more affluent look for items that allow them to feel different from their friends. Advertising agencies exploit this fact by placing different kinds of automobile ads in the magazines normally read by adults from different classes.[22]

It is not surprising that class of rearing predicts a variety of psychological properties that aid or impede adaptation to a society. In the United States, these properties include IQ scores, academic grades, adult vocation, forms of anxiety, health, longevity, gambling, divorce, depression, homicides, and antisocial behavior. The financial worries of the poor often exacerbate the subjective intensity of the pain that accompanies osteoarthritis or fibromyalgia. The substantial correlations between a person's social class and each of the above outcomes cannot be explained completely by arguing that individuals from different classes possess different sets of genes. The influence of genes on IQ scores is much smaller in children from disadvantaged homes than it is in children from affluent families because most middle-class children live in settings that support cognitive skills. As a result, genes play a greater role in determining variation in IQ among privileged children than they do in children who have less support for their intellectual growth.[23]

When the differences in status are large, the less privileged are vulnerable to envy of and anger toward those perceived to be more privileged or to moods of self-doubt and depression. These emotions become especially intense when a majority of people in the society assume that everyone is supposed to possess roughly equal status. This idea has always been part of the American ideal. Given this premise, small inequalities can become major irritants because they violate a consensual understanding. The intensity of anger or distress over a position of lower status is muted when those in lower ranks accept the idea that some members of the society are inherently superior or inferior. This suggestion may be Tocqueville's most profound insight in *Democracy in America*, written on his return to France in 1832 after nine months touring regions east of the Mississippi.[24]

The increasing commitment to the ideal of equality of privilege among all humans slams against the brute fact of obvious inequality. Like two tectonic plates moving slowly toward each other, human groups that vary in privilege are vulnerable to a collision that can generate extraordinary levels of civil unrest. Two obvious examples were the slaughter of Tutsis by Hutus in Rwanda and the rebellions in 2011 by the less privileged against the elites in Tunisia, Egypt, and Libya.

Economists invented an index of the degree of income inequality in a society called the Gini coefficient. This coefficient was an excellent predictor of the prevalence of mental illness in twelve economically developed, democratic nations. The United States and England had the highest levels of mental illness and income inequality. Japan and Germany had the lowest values on both measures. The degree of income inequality is also a better predictor of civil strife than the average income. The Gini coefficient, which began to rise in the United States in the 1980s, was positively related to the murder rate in primarily Caucasian counties of the American South, as well as to the murder rate in each of ninety-two nations. The greater the range in academic achievement among urban youth in developed societies, the more frequent were acts of violence committed by the underachieving youth, who more often belong to economically disadvantaged families.[25]

Most animal species survive as populations in a particular ecological setting. Animals compete with each other for food, mates, and territory, and not all members of a population obtain the same amount of these resources. Human populations with enough food compete among themselves for enhanced status, and as with animals, only some individuals can rise in status. Even fewer can occupy positions of very high status because that number is necessarily small. This social fact guarantees conflict and feelings of anxiety, anger, envy, fatalism, or depression among those belonging to less privileged ranks. It is not uncommon for the small number of working-class students attending elite colleges on a scholarship to feel intimidated by the many wealthier students who went to private high schools and have more money to spend on luxuries.

The distinctive emotional profiles of disadvantaged and advantaged adults affect how they socialize their children. This may be the most robust fact discovered by social scientists. Readers who broke a leg or suffered from the pain of shingles for several months will remember their helplessness and compromised sense of agency. Many adults trapped in poverty and possessing no special skills feel impotent to alter their unhappy condition. Children reared in very different social-class settings resemble groups of monkeys of the same species living in distinctive ecologies separated by a range of mountains. A few hardy animals manage to find a path through the mountains and join the other group. Most do not. In the United States, changes in the economy, the nation's ethnic composition, and the quality of the public schools over the past hundred years have obstructed the easy trails through the mountains and made the probability of passage in 2011 smaller than it was a century earlier.

Most psychologists are aware of the substantial contribution of children's social class to their pattern of cognitive talents, moods, and behavioral traits. Scientists who believe that one particular condition can influence one of these properties, independent of social class or any other condition, need a way to eliminate what they regard as the unwanted influence of class. The usual strategy is to rely on a statistical procedure, called analysis of covariance. This analysis first computes the magnitude of the contribution of social class to a psychological outcome and then computes the additional contribution of the particular condition that piques the psychologist's interest, over and above the influence of social class. One team of psychologists who wanted to prove that poor-quality day care impaired adolescents' cognitive abilities adopted this strategy. Poor-quality day-care centers, however, are more likely to contain children growing up in disadvantaged families, and more of these children attain lower scores on cognitive tests whether or not they attended a day-care center. That fact leaves open the possibility that the combination of poor-quality day care and a disadvantaged class position predict the lower cognitive scores and that the quality of day care alone has a trivial effect.[26]

Unfortunately, the use of covariance to eliminate the influence of social class (or other unwanted conditions such as gender, ethnicity, or IQ score) is not always the correct solution. There are several reasons why. First, the correlates of social class, especially parental practices, quality of schools attended, frequency and type of stressful experiences, and the values of peers, are not equivalent for all children who belong to the same social class. Economically disadvantaged, homeless children living with one or both parents in a shelter did not experience the same number of prior stressful events, such as quarrelling between the parents, exposure to violence, or temporary separation from the family. The homeless children who experienced many of these stressors showed unusually high cortisol levels, but the equally disadvantaged children living in the same shelter who were protected from frequent stressors failed to show this rise in level of stress hormone.[27]

A second problem trailing the use of covariance analysis is the assumption that the variation in the predictor or the outcome is due to only one cause. This is rarely the case. Psychologists wanting to prove that boys who were victims of school bullies will find it harder to adapt to their society write as if victimization has a unitary effect on all children. This is not true because the child's social class affects the reason for being bullied. Boys from predominantly lower-class neighborhoods attending schools with youth of the same class are usually victimized for being timid sissies and failing to adopt a tough persona. Boys attending predominantly middle-class schools are bullied for being "nerds" who always get A grades and conform to all teacher demands. These two groups of victimized boys draw different conclusions from their experience. The socially disadvantaged boys envy the bullies and try to adopt their "macho" personality. Many of the socially advantaged boys are likely to conclude that brute power is morally abhorrent and are apt to invest even more energy in academic work. These are two different outcomes of being the target of bullies, and each has different implications for adaptation to American society. For that reason, it is an error to believe that statistics can remove the effects of class and evaluate only the psychological consequences of being bullied.

A third problem with covariance analysis is that it assumes that the relation between the covariate (for example, social class) and the outcome of interest is linear. Analysis of covariance is inappropriate when the relations are nonlinear, and nonlinear relations are extremely common in psychology. Adults from varied occupational statuses were asked how often they felt angry. Those in low-status unskilled jobs, as well as those in high-status managerial or professional positions, experienced anger more often than those in vocations with middle-range status. That is, there was a nonlinear relation between class and frequency of anger, probably because more in the middle-range positions were self-employed and had neither many supervisors nor many people to supervise. Under these conditions, an investigator who wanted to prove that the number of people working together in the same place predicted frequency of anger cannot use covariance to rule out the effects of the occupational status of the job.[28]

A simple example illustrates the incorrect inference that can occur when a psychologist uses covariance and assumes linear relations among the measures. Assume that a psychologist was interested in predicting the number of years of formal education a group of adults attained based on their IQ scores at six years of age and wanted to eliminate the known influence of a family's social class on the adult educational level of their children. The investigator first computes the correlation between the covariate (income) and years of schooling to arrive at an estimate of the increase in years of schooling that should accompany a given increase in annual income. The investigator then determines whether the childhood IQ scores make an additional contribution.

The problem with this strategy is that it makes incorrect predictions about number of years of schooling for those belonging to very low social class groups whose families happen to enjoy a small increase in income and those from very advantaged families who suffer a small loss of income. A rise in annual family income of $5,000, from $15,000 to $20,000, does not necessarily lead to a few additional years of schooling in the offspring. And an equivalent decrease in income from $250,000 to $245,000 is not accompanied by fewer years of schooling among the children of the wealthy. The covariance procedure makes the incorrect predictions that children from very disadvantaged families that gained a little in income will attain more years of schooling than they actually do and children growing up with very privileged families that lose a little income will attain less schooling than they actually do.

The concepts of over- and underachiever supply a second example of the problem that arises when there are nonlinear relations among the measures. Overachievers are children whose grade point average is higher than their IQ scores predict; underachievers obtain grades that are lower than their IQs predict. These groups are detected by using covariance analysis to compute the contribution of IQ to grades and then seeing if the child's grades are higher or lower than his or her IQ predicts. This definition guarantees that children with high IQs who always get A grades cannot be overachievers because an average grade of A is the highest that can be attained. And for the same reason, children with low IQ scores who typically receive failing grades cannot be underachievers. The covariance technique is informative only for children with IQs in the middle range who receive B or C grades.

It is easy to arrive at counterintuitive, and probably mistaken, conclusions when the investigator statistically controls for conditions that are essential to a causal sequence that leads to an outcome. One pair of investigators interested in the contribution of place of residence to being satisfied with one's life used covariance analysis to remove the contributions of income, age, sex, ethnicity, level of education, and employment in a sample of 1.3 million Americans. Because these six conditions make a major contribution to judgments of life satisfaction, the authors found that the residents of Louisiana were the most satisfied Americans, whereas residents of New York State were least satisfied. This conclusion is inconsistent with the fact that more Americans prefer to live in New York than in Louisiana.[29]

It is also inconsistent with the replies of a representative sample of Americans to Gallup pollsters who asked adults from every state a set of questions reflecting the level of satisfaction with their life conditions. The questions inquired about their health, diet, frequency of exercise, possession of health insurance, prevalence of crime in their neighborhood, and satisfaction with their community. The answers were averaged to create an index of happiness. The *New York Times* of March 6, 2011, reported that the happiness scores for Louisiana were among the five lowest of the fifty states. This fact provides convincing proof of the claim that conclusions based on the numbers produced by an analysis of covariance can be terribly misleading.

Readers who suspect this critical evaluation by a psychologist should read papers by eminent statisticians who warn against the danger of drawing incorrect conclusions from covariance analyses. One expert had a particularly harsh evaluation: "If [psychological] data are allowed to speak for themselves, they will typically lie to you." John Tukey, one of the world's most admired mathematical statisticians, advises psychologists to adopt the mind-set of detectives looking for hidden clues rather than automatically use the standard, approved statistics to prove a favorite idea. Most of all, Tukey warns, never bend the question to fit the most popular statistical techniques.[30] Too many psychologists who use the results of covariance analyses to make causal inferences ignore this warning.

A scientist wishing to prove that a cold temperature made a significant contribution to a snowfall and who used covariance analysis to eliminate the influence of humidity would find modest support for the assumption. But the conclusion that cold temperatures make an independent contribution to snowfalls is obviously incorrect. Snow always requires the combination of a temperature below freezing and high relative humidity.

Every justice on the US Supreme Court in 2011 spent some time as a student at either Yale or Harvard law school. This fact implies that the quality of instruction, the social contacts made in these schools, and early judicial assignments contributed to the justices' final appointment to the Court. I suggest that no statistical technique can remove the influence of two of these factors and measure the independent contribution of the third. The three conditions form a pattern that cannot be arbitrarily separated into separate causes. Nor can we separate the contribution of the sweetness of ice cream from its texture and temperature in order to understand its appeal in the summer months. Some unusually destructive storms combine particular sea and land temperatures, barometric pressure, wind velocity, and humidity to generate rare patterns, called perfect storms, that create serious havoc. An analysis of covariance would probably reveal that each of these conditions made a small, significant contribution to the storm when the other conditions were controlled. But it remains a stubborn fact that none of these conditions acting alone could create the storm. The power of each is totally dependent on their being elements combined in a pattern.

Genes, class position, cultural background, and life history combine to create perfect storms than can precipitate a mood of depression, a bout of anxiety, a criminal act, or a drug addiction. Although some investigators use covariance to evaluate the separate contribution of one of these factors, independent of the others, I remain skeptical of the conclusions based on this strategy. If this assumption were true, then most victims of sexual abuse, bullying, parental neglect, or natural catastrophe would develop some form of pathology. We know that this does not happen.

A similar debate was waged about seventy-five years ago between the evolutionary biologists J. B. S. Haldane and Ernst Mayr. Haldane evaluated the role of genes in evolution with a mathematics that assumed that each gene was autonomous and its contribution to a new trait was independent of all other genes. Haldane's mathematics assumed that he could add the independent effects of each gene. This position resembles the practices of psychologists who use analysis of covariance to prove that a single condition can contribute to a later outcome without the help of any other circumstances. Mayr, who approached the puzzles of evolution by observing animals in their natural ecology rather than relying on mathematics, criticized Haldane for ignoring the important influences the larger genome exerted on the outcomes of any single gene. For Mayr, natural selection acted on the whole animal in a setting rather than on a gene. He rejected the possibility that any gene could have an independent effect on a trait without the contribution of other genes and the ecology. A large body of research has proven that Mayr was closer to the truth than Haldane. I side with Mayr when I reject the assumption that the mathematical technique of analysis of covariance can prove that a gene or a class of experience that is only one element in a pattern can have a serious effect on a complex psychological outcome without the presence of the other conditions that comprise the pattern. I hope that future research is as kind to this position as history has been to Mayr's argument.

Biological measures are not immune to variation in contexts. The probability that adults will show greater activation of the neurons in the right or the left frontal lobe can vary with the season of testing. Individuals living in the northern hemisphere showed greater activation of the right frontal lobe when tested during the autumn but not during other seasons. Even the presence of a pet in the laboratory can influence the amount of rise in heart rate and blood pressure in individuals solving difficult arithmetic problems. The rise was smaller if a pet was present than if the person was alone with the examiner.[31]

Many psychologists rely on changes in the level of oxygenation of the blood in various brain sites (called the BOLD signal) to infer psychological states. However, the specific way the stimuli are presented can affect the BOLD signal. I noted that psychologists often attribute a state of fear to individuals who show a large BOLD signal in a site called the amygdala to aversive or threatening events, such as faces with fearful expressions. The flaw in this belief is that the unexpectedness of an event is the most important determinant of the amygdalar reaction. If fearful faces are expected and happy faces are unexpected, the BOLD signal is larger to happy faces. This fact implies that those who show a large BOLD signal in the amygdala to the unexpected appearance of fearful faces, snakes, or guns are surprised, not afraid.[32]

Every person has an implicit expectation about what might occur in the next few moments in a particular setting, and the amygdala typically responds to any unexpected event. Most adults who meet a friendly examiner who does not tell them what they might see or hear while they lie in a scanner do not expect to see pictures of bloodied soldiers, angry faces, or snakes with open jaws. These aversive scenes, as well as nonthreatening ones that are unexpected, evoke a surge of dopamine, dilation of the brain's blood vessels, and a larger BOLD signal to the amygdala and other brain sites. Even audio recordings of laughter activate the amygdala if they are unexpected. Rats, too, show a more active amygdala to an electric shock they did not expect than to one they anticipated. Monkeys need their amygdala to react with caution to a novel object but do not require an amygdala to respond with behavioral signs of fear to an object that they learned was a threat.[33] Adults expect to see aversive pictures when they are watching a horror film at home on a television monitor. If psychologists could measure their brains at that time they would discover a smaller BOLD signal than the one recorded to the same scenes when they were unexpected in the laboratory.

The BOLD signal is also affected by subtle factors that are irrelevant to the investigator's interests. These are nuisance variables. Magnetic scanners produce a very loud noise that influences the BOLD signal. Second, most adults are lying on their back in the magnetic scanner, and this posture is accompanied by a pattern of blood flow that differs from the pattern observed when individuals are sitting up. Third, participants are usually alone in the scanning room, and it is possible that their blood flow profiles would differ if a friend were in the room with them. Men asked to immerse their hand in ice water showed a larger rise in cortisol, which affects the BOLD signal, when an unfamiliar woman was present than when they were alone. Furthermore, the specific features of a particular laboratory can affect the BOLD signal. Adults were scanned in four different laboratories while performing exactly the same memory task. As expected, there was great variation in the BOLD signals across the laboratories. The evidence implies that various aspects of a setting, including the structure of the scanner, affect the BOLD signal. That is one reason why there are serious controversies surrounding the meaning of most patterns of blood flow.[34]

The psychological correlates of a particular gene are affected by the person's sex, ethnicity, and cultural background. There are often several places in the sequence of DNA molecules that defines a gene where different nucleotides (there are only four of them), or differing numbers of nucleotides, occupy the same location. These sources of variation are called alleles of the gene. One contrasting pair of alleles, called short or long because of the length of the sequence, controls the level of expression of a gene whose molecular product, the serotonin transporter molecule, affects the amount of serotonin in the synapses. Possession of the short allele, however, was associated with different psychological symptoms in different populations. The short allele was linked to criminal behavior in Chinese men, bipolar disorder in Italians, and obsessive-compulsive symptoms in educated Koreans.[35]

Sometimes the context has an exceptionally specific effect on a biological measure. The cortisol levels in pairs of identical twins should be very similar because each twin pair shares the same genes. But the cortisol values of twin pairs were similar only when the saliva samples, which were the bases for the cortisol estimates, were gathered in a laboratory in the morning. The similarity in cortisol levels was minimal when the saliva was gathered in the home in the afternoon. It is not surprising that geneticists have been unable to find specific alleles that rendered children or adults at risk for a specific mental illness or personality trait. There was not even one significant relation between the presence of any one of 360,000 alleles and variation in any of the five major personality dimensions.[36] This does not mean that genes do not contribute to personality. Rather, the correct inference is that the same gene, or genes, can lead to different personality traits in individuals from divergent sex, class, and cultural groups.

A final reason for the frustrated efforts to find relations between particular genes and a specific psychological outcome is that the consequences of an allele are influenced by the total genome in which an allele of interest is only one element. Geneticists call this phenomenon epistasis. Even the tiny fruit fly *Drosophila* has many genes that interact to regulate behaviors whose display depends on the local context. If this principle applies to fruit flies, it surely applies to humans. One example involves the concentration of dopamine in the brain, which has important consequences for behaviors and moods. A number of independent genes on different chromosomes affect the dopamine concentration that is recorded. Because any particular concentration is the result of the activity of more than one gene, it is usually impossible to know which gene or genes are primarily responsible for the concentration observed. These facts render untenable the popular belief that a particular gene might have a specific effect on one type of behavior or emotion.[37] The small number of scientists who still defend this assumption resemble the fourteenth-century Jewish scholars who believed that each of the twenty-two Hebrew consonants had only one numerical value. One could determine the meaning of a biblical passage by adding up the numbers for each of the consonants in the passage. A passage with a sum of 4,400, for example, referred to the summoning of the angel Samael.

The evidence invites one of three positions regarding the generality of a trait, emotion, or ability when the assignment is based on one group of participants and one source of information gathered in one setting on one occasion. The most popular position assumes that the person or animal possesses a particular property, even though it is not displayed in all relevant contexts. This view is reasonable for most sensory capacities and representations stored in long-term memory. If individuals can hear the tick of a mechanical clock at a distance of six feet, it is reasonable to assume they can also hear speech and music without testing them. If someone cannot remember the name of a close colleague at a particular moment, it is unlikely that the name is lost permanently. There are a few rare exceptions to this principle. A woman's ability to discriminate among the different olfactory qualities in the perspiration taken from the armpits of men was restricted to women who were not on hormone-based contraception, were in the fertile phase of their menstrual cycle, and were comparing the perspiration taken from the left, not the right, armpit of left-handed men.[38]

A less frequent perspective assumes that a trait, property, or ability possesses special features when it occurs that it does not have when it is not observed. Most four-year-olds point correctly at the cow when shown pictures of a cow, cup, and car and asked, "Point to the animal." This response implies that the children did possess some representation of the semantic concept *animal*. But that knowledge lacks many of the significant features of animals that adults possess. Some developmental psychologists assume that six-month-olds possess a concept of number simply because they look longer at four black dots after seeing arrays of two dots. These psychologists are quick to acknowledge, however, that the adult's concept of number contains many important features that are missing from the infant's representation.[39] The same is true for statements claiming that infants have an understanding of causality, fear, or animate versus inanimate objects. Psychologists should acknowledge the infant's restricted understanding of each of these concepts.

The least popular solution urges psychologists to combine every description of an agent's psychological properties with the context of observation, which should always include the procedure and the specific evidence it produced. This solution is essential when the concepts refer to emotions, values, traits, and cognitive processes because of the serious disagreements over the intrinsic features of these ideas. Indeed, it is fruitful to regard many personality traits and talents as varying in generality where generality is defined by the proportion of relevant contexts in which the trait is expressed. We say that an adult understands the rule for making a noun *plural* when he or she applies the correct plural ending in more than 90 percent of the opportunities to do so. A child who can add the numbers 5 + 4, 6 + 2, and 3 + 9 has a more general understanding of the addition of two numbers that one who is successful on only one of these problems. A person who is talkative and sociable in ten different social settings is more extroverted than one who is talkative and sociable in only three diverse contexts. Almost all six-year-olds can recognize a photo of themselves, but only 20 percent can recognize a drawing of an animal that mimics their unique drawing style. Thus, they have a partial knowledge of self's products. This recommendation to gather evidence on a trait in several contexts should replace the current practice of relying on performance in one procedure, whether a score on a questionnaire or a behavior in a single setting, to decide whether a person does or does not have a property. Psychological properties are more like a baseball player's batting average over the whole season than a skin rash.

I recall seeing a three-year-old boy in my laboratory who had been treated in a hospital for several weeks because of serious burns. He showed extreme fear when we tried to place heart electrodes on his body because this action reminded him of the painful hospital routines. But unlike most children, he displayed absolutely no fear to a long rubber snake. A psychologist who wanted to ascribe to this boy a vulnerability to fear must append a description of the setting and the incentive event.

Most psychologists agree that all feelings and emotions can be placed in one of four quadrants created by crossing the two independent dimensions of intensity and valence, where valence refers to the judged pleasantness or unpleasantness of the feeling. This solution ignores the local context in which the judgment occurs. The perceived intensity of a stimulus usually depends on the intensity of the preceding stimulus. The light from a hundred-watt bulb will be judged as more intense if it replaces light from a forty-watt compared with an eighty-watt bulb. Most of the time the perception of a light, tone, taste, or smell is affected by lingering memories of related stimuli that occurred in the immediate or distant past. The subjective intensity of the feeling evoked by a picture of a snake will be greater in individuals who felt no tension before seeing the picture than in those who were feeling tense before the snake appeared.

Contextual contrasts affect valence judgments, too. The pleasantness of a piece of chocolate is usually greater if one has not tasted anything sweet for awhile. The emotion of surprise is judged as pleasant if one unexpectedly sees an old friend at the front door but as unpleasant if the face at the door belongs to a police officer. Young women report a more intense, unpleasant tension in the presence of an anxious man than one who is not anxious because the sweat of the former has a unique chemical composition and odor.[40]

A serious problem with most English words for emotions is that they do not specify the cause or the setting. As a result, the valence of terms such as *surprise*, *sad*, or *aroused* can vary in the same individuals in different contexts. More important, the words needed to describe brain processes are not the words psychologists use to describe emotional or cognitive states. The amygdala, as I noted, is typically activated by unexpected scenes of violence but is much less active to sentences that describe violent scenes. Yet many adults will say that the scenes and sentences evoked the same emotion.[41] Because brain activity and psychological states are governed by different rules and require distinct vocabularies, scientists must specify the procedure used to arrive at a conclusion.

If the preceding argument and evidence have merit, why do so many American and European psychologists continue to make the individual's properties, rather than "the properties in a context," the fundamental concept in theory? One factor, among many, may have contributed to this bias. The celebration of each person's liberty, free of all unreasonable constraints from others, which eighteenth-century England and America promoted more passionately than other societies, may have created a metaphorical relation between the concept of political liberty, on the one hand, and each person's traits and brain states, on the other. The metaphor might read, "Each mind is a soaring eagle."

The medieval English, compared with continental Europeans of the same era, regarded the rights of the individual as having priority over the interests of the family or community. England was the first European society to allow a person, rather than a family, to own land and to sign contracts. Alexis de Tocqueville commented on America's reverence for personal freedom when he toured parts of the country in 1831. The distrust of a strong centralized government was one reason for the rapid economic development of the United States during the nineteenth century. The insistence on local autonomy made it easier to establish in many cities banks that could lend money to businessmen who did not have to be dependent on one central bank in Washington.[42]

Asian scholars, along with the social psychologists Walter Mischel and Richard Nisbett, recognized the significance of contexts and the complementary relationship between each individual and his or her collective.

Some depressed Korean and Japanese adolescents belong to Internet groups that arrange for a group of like-minded strangers to commit suicide together rather than to end their lives alone. Medieval Japanese poets usually sat together when writing because the social ambience was part of the aesthetic experience. Japanese and North Americans judged the emotion expressed on the face of a central figure surrounded by others displaying a different emotion. The Japanese, but not North Americans, often relied on the emotions of the background faces in making their judgments. The Japanese media covering the 2000 and 2002 Olympic Games often described the family background and past history of the athletes who won medals. The American media focused primarily on the athlete's talent and avoided reference to his or her family or past experience. Europeans and North Americans are socialized to be true to their private consciences, to maintain the same character and opinions across contexts, and not to worry excessively about what others think. Asians understand that a person need not be consistent across settings because one's role and actions vary with the context. A woman is a mother at home, a professional at work, a guest at a party; and the actions and opinions displayed in one setting may be inappropriate in the other contexts.[43]

The pattern of conditions that explains why Asians favor the notion of an agent in a setting or collective over an autonomous agent remains an enigma. Some have suggested that China's harsher climate, marked by frequent floods, droughts, insect plagues, and earthquakes, persuaded the Chinese to award power to nature and to place each person in a posture of accommodation to, rather than one bent on subduing, ecological forces. Traditional Chinese paintings often illustrated a few, small human figures in a scene dominated by large mountains and trees. Such scenes are rarer in European paintings. In addition, small-scale agriculture was the dominant form of economic activity in China. A larger proportion of Europeans, beginning with the classic Greeks, engaged in trade or were artisans selling their products to clients. The relation between a group of adults and the land they plant and harvest invites a psychological state of interdependence between humans and nature. The verbs employed when land is the object of a sentence are different from the verbs used when the object is a person in a commercial transaction. A person protects or cares for the land; one negotiates with or exploits a partner in a business deal. The farmer is in a symbiotic relation with the earth. He or she nurtures the land; nature cooperates by supplying sun, rain, minimal infestations of pests, and a crop. The relation between two adults in a commercial venture is marked by recognition of the separate, mutually exclusive interests of each partner. This mental set favors the honing of an autonomous individual motivated to maximize his or her welfare.

Other factors are relevant to the contrast between East Asians and Europeans. Chinese farmers relied on large-scale irrigation of the land and therefore were dependent on central control. European farmers, who could rely on rainfall, retained a freedom from central authority. Science in China was also bureaucratically controlled by a central government, whereas science in sixteenth- and seventeenth-century Europe had no government support and many European scientists, for example Galileo and Kepler, challenged the ideas of authority.[44]

The Chinese language Mandarin orients speakers to the larger context in which a foreground event occurs. Mandarin has twenty verbs to describe the specific manner in which an object is being held or carried. For example, a piece of wood could rest on a person's head, shoulder, or back or be held in both arms, one arm, or one hand. English has only the terms *carry* or *hold*. More than 90 percent of Chinese words are combinations of two or more meaningful characters, and the meaning of one character often depends on the character with which it is combined. The character for *mother*, for example, combines the character for *woman* with the character for *breasts*. The Chinese characters for a predicate often specify the agent and the outcome. Although English speakers would use the same word, *broke,* in sentences such as, "The man broke the vase," "The surface of the table broke," and "The relationship broke," Chinese has three distinct forms for *broke* in these sentences.[45] The Chinese language has few abstract terms that name essences, by which I mean the properties of a concept that are preserved across situations. There are no single terms in Chinese that refer to properties like intelligence, extroversion, or anxiety, only terms for a particular skill, trait, or worry. English, by contrast, has many abstract terms for essences ranging from anxiety to creativity that fail to denote the reason for or target of the emotion or action or the particular product that a specific audience judges creative. Chinese speakers are apt to describe a friend by specifying an act in a context, for example, "Fei hugs her friends at parties." English speakers delete the setting and are likely to say, "Mary is affectionate."

Chinese philosophers, anticipating A. N. Whitehead by two thousand years, assumed that natural events were the products of processes in flux rather than derivatives of the bounded entities with fixed features that physicists call atoms. A flowing river that is altered continually by the local topography and the weather is the most popular symbol of the Chinese civilization. The popular symbols for America—a solitary eagle, a woman holding the scales of justice, and the Statue of Liberty—are material objects with stable features that are unaffected by the local setting.[46]

The ancient Chinese nominated the complementary energies of yin and yang and the five elements wood, water, metal, earth, and fire as the foundation of natural events. No element was always dominant because the potency of each depended on the specific partner with which it was combined. Metal conquers wood when an ax chops down a tree; fire conquers metal when heat is applied; water conquers fire; earth conquers water by absorbing it; but wood conquers earth when a spade digs into the ground. No object maintains its potency indefinitely. One of Confucius's commentaries on *The Book of Changes*, written in the third century BCE, contained these lines: "When the sun stands at midday, it begins to set / When the moon is full, it begins to wane."

The intransitivity in the relative potency of objects applies to countries. England surpasses Italy in gross domestic product; Italy surpasses Russia in mean annual temperature; Russia surpasses China in oil reserves; but China holds more foreign currency than England. The economist Amartya Sen also rejects the popular economic premise that each person has consistent preferences in consumption. A person can prefer steak to fish in a restaurant but prefer fish to steak when eating at home. I prefer playing tennis to a long walk during most of the year when I am in my permanent home because I have many able partners my age and walking on the street is not beautiful. But during the summer, when I am in my small home on Cape Cod, I prefer walking to playing tennis because there are fewer partners and a long walk on the beach is unusually pleasant. The core message is that the context selects the preference that a person will express. A Japanese physicist captured the distinctive mental perspectives of West and East: "The West lives in a world separated into two terms: subject and object, self and not-self, true and false, good and bad." The East rejects this sharp dualism and prefers to think in terms of a merging of subject and object, true and false.[47]

It is not surprising that contemporary Asian psychologists study the setting in which psychological decisions are made more often than American social scientists. One team of Japanese psychologists evaluated the perception of three-dimensional objects compared with their two-dimensional appearance on a computer monitor. Another group compared the error rates of one, compared with two, individuals reading the proofs of a document.[48]

Although I have emphasized the ecological and political differences between Europe and China, it is also possible that genes make a small contribution to the divergent philosophies held by these two cultural groups. Recall the earlier discussion of the short allele of the gene for the serotonin transporter molecule that absorbs serotonin from the synapses. The Chinese population has a larger percentage possessing the short allele. But a smaller proportion of Chinese, compared with other ethnic groups, possess an allele of the gene for one of the receptors for the neurotransmitter dopamine (called the seven-repeat allele of the D4 receptor, or DRD4). This allele renders the receptor less responsive to dopamine, and as a result, there is slightly lower dopaminergic tone in the brain. Children and youth who possess this allele are a little more likely to be restless and inattentive. Experts suggest that individuals with this allele might be motivated to increase the brain's dopamine tone through the active seeking of new experiences.[49]

The nine human groups that migrated more than nine thousand miles between a thousand and thirty thousand years ago had the highest proportion of the seven-repeat allele. The Chinese, by contrast, most of whom do not have this allele, migrated less than most European populations. This observation suggests that there might be a small biological basis behind an urgently felt need for new experiences. It is probably relevant that the Americans who take many financial risks are more likely to possess the seven-repeat allele and less likely to inherit the short allele of the serotonin transporter than risk-averse investors.[50]

These observations lead to the following speculation. The semantic term *unconstrained*, or one of its synonyms, is shared by the distinctive semantic networks for: a citizen's political liberty, a person's psychological traits, and an individual's brain profiles. This linguistic overlap may have created a metaphorical relation between the political concept of liberty and the latter two ideas. Put plainly, the golden halo surrounding the ideal of a politically free citizen may have biased Western scientists to award traits, actions, emotions, beliefs, and brains a freedom implying that they, too, were minimally constrained by the context in which they occurred.

A second speculation may also be relevant. Judeo-Christian philosophy awarded a position of supreme reverence to a perfect God who created perfect things and awarded humans the distinction of being the only living thing that understood the difference between right and wrong and the only species that was free to choose between right and wrong. The Chinese, by contrast, placed nature in a position of reverence and assumed that humans were a part of, and subordinate to, nature, rather than outside and subjugating it. This philosophical difference may help to explain why physics and chemistry made major advances in Christian Europe. Newton, Faraday, Maxwell, and Lavoisier could pursue their research without worrying about its political implications for human nature or moral values.

Most contemporary Europeans and North Americans want to separate each person's character from his or her talents or accomplishments in order to avoid any hint of a critical judgment of the ethical values held by adults in these ethnically diverse societies. Excessive arrogance or rudeness in a talented athlete, scientist, or musician is supposed to be ignored because, presumably, it is completely independent of their skills. The ancient Greeks would have rejected the wisdom of separating character from ability because the two formed a whole. The evaluation of a performance included the performer's character. The Greek concept of *paideia*, which referred to the perfection of a talent, was not synonymous with winning a prize for a performance.

Although a satisfying account of the origins of the distinctive ideologies of China and Europe escapes us, I return to the contribution of climate. Loss, illness, and frustration happen to all humans in all places, and they naturally search for a reason because of a deep reluctance to attribute misfortune to chance. The ancient societies of Mesopotamia, Egypt, Greece, and Rome invented gods with the power to hurt or to help humans. But they also believed that each person's actions might affect a god's decision. This meant that each individual could affect his or her future. All four civilizations were located in warm, benign climates where natural catastrophes were less frequent than they were in China.

The harsher properties of China's climate and topography might have persuaded the ancient Chinese to award to nature a potency that the societies to the east awarded to gods. The Chinese accepted human impotence and passivity vis-à-vis nature and restricted the power of individual agency. The notion that each person is free to affect his or her future, independent of natural events, family, and community, is muted in Asian ideology. Obviously, climate cannot be the only reason for the different perspectives of ancient China and Greece, but it may have contributed a little to the decision to imagine each person as an autonomous agent or as an individual.

Most Western psychologists write as if traits, moods, and abilities that transcend settings provide the most illuminating explanations of psychological phenomena. This assumption is inconsistent with an accumulating body of evidence. It is easy to arrive at a wildly incorrect conclusion if one begins with a single false premise. Bertrand Russell provided a persuasive example:

1. Assume 3 = 2.
2. Subtract 1 from each side of the above equation.
3. Now 2 = 1.
4. The Pope and Russell are two entities.
5. But 2 = 1 as shown in step 3 above.
6. Therefore, Russell = the Pope.

My essential claim is that each agent, whether human or animal, possesses a large collection of possible brain states, feelings, motives, and actions that are ready for expression. Each type of context is associated with a set of probabilities describing the likelihood of a particular outcome. Change the context, and the probabilities change. The consequences of a gene's expression depend on the total genomic context; the synaptic connections a growing axon cone makes with another neuron depend on the local chemical environment; the activity in a neuronal cluster depends on the circuit in which it is a component; the actions of an animal or human depend on the features of the setting.

The contexts of human activity have changed dramatically over the past ten thousand years, following the development of cereal agriculture, the domestication of animals, and the establishment of stable villages. These transitions included the growth and subsequent decline of the major agricultural civilizations, followed in sequence in Europe by the dominating influence of Christianity, the Renaissance, Enlightenment, industrialization, public education, and, currently, a symbolic connectedness among almost all humans made possible by information technologies. The rapid dissemination of a celebrity's suicide, which was impossible before television and the Internet, is often followed by an increased number of suicides in the next thirty days. The decade of the 1960s in North America and Europe was marked by a critical questioning of the wisdom and legitimacy of authority by the younger generation brought on, in part, by the Vietnam war and continued prejudice against minorities and women. These events were accompanied by profound changes in the arts and the social sciences, especially a demand to add pragmatic consequences and fairness to formal elegance when judging an intellectual product and its inventor. Each of these historical changes was accompanied by alterations in the hierarchy of values that affected which groups were entitled to justice.[51]

The suggestion that each context selects one profile from a larger collection has an analogue in brain function. The human brain undergoes a significant increase in connectivity between eleven and fourteen years. As a result, fourteen-year-olds are better able than eight-year-olds to suppress inappropriate acts, plan for the distant future, and resist distraction when working on a task. But the adolescent's cultural setting determines whether the increased biological maturity will be displayed through the writing of term papers or preparing a field for the planting of maize. Neuronal clusters in particular locations are biologically prepared to be responsive to a select set of features in the environment. Humans are more often exposed to faces than to the pattern of elements on the wings of Monarch butterflies. The former experience tunes the neurons in the human fusiform area to be hyper-responsive to faces rather than butterfly wings.

These conclusions would have provoked a smile on the faces of Kurt Koffka, Wolfgang Köhler, and Max Wertheimer, who brought Gestalt theory to the United States in the 1920s. Unfortunately, these scholars were unable to compete with the behaviorists for intellectual legitimacy because American psychologists, in awe of the epistemology of nineteenth-century physics, preferred to analyze events into their elemental components and to design experiments to affirm that idea. They ignored the fact that, after 1930, physicists replaced discrete atoms with energy states being filled or realized as a function of the interactions among varied sources of energy. More than seventy-five years had to pass before American social scientists acknowledged that the ease of learning a new association to a conditioned stimulus depended on the salience of the former and that salience was influenced by the local context and the biology and life history of the organism.

The suggestion that psychologists replace the properties of an individual as the primary unit with properties-in-a-context awards equal power to genes and brains, on the one hand, and to culture, historical era, social class, and the local setting, on the other. My seminal plea to psychologists asks them to reflect before writing statements with the following form: "Individuals with the short allele of the serotonin transporter gene who experienced past stressors are at risk for developing an anxiety or depressive disorder," when this relation has not yet been demonstrated in both males and females from different class, ethnic, and cultural groups with objective proof of the type and frequency of the early stressors. This abstract statement burdens readers with the task of figuring out who the individuals were, the quality and severity of the stressors, the form of the anxiety or depression, and the evidence used to infer their risk for either disorder. Instead, psychologists should compose sentences that have the following form: "Women with a European pedigree who inherited the short allele of the serotonin transporter, were sexually abused during childhood according to official records, grew up in an economically disadvantaged home, and are living alone in a large city are at risk for developing the symptoms of an anxiety or depressive disorder based on information gathered in a face-to-face interview with a trained examiner who asked about current moods and memories of past traumatic experiences."

This longer conclusion is in closer accord with the evidence and has the advantage of allowing other scientists to compare their evidence with different information on populations with different features. The history of the major advances in biology contains the clear message that nature pays extremely close attention to the details. It is time for social scientists, who study functions rather than things, to pay homage to this deep truth.

TWO

Happiness Ascendant

Scientific concepts come in three major varieties. Most are invented to name a new or unexpected observation. The concept *prion* names a class of irregularly shaped proteins capable of damaging healthy proteins in the body. A smaller number of concepts name events that have not yet been observed but, if they existed, would explain a large body of known facts. The concept of *gene*, posited to explain why offspring resemble but are not identical to their biological parents, was invented fifty years before Crick and Watson discovered the structure of the DNA molecule that is the constituent of all genes. The third type, far more frequent in the social than in the natural sciences, names events that scholars would like to believe exist because they are more beautiful or in accord with the society's favored ethical premises.

Most scholars can be assigned to one of two groups. One group holds an idealistic conception of how things should be. Goethe, Marx, and Freud are members of this group. Copernicus, too, was an idealist, for he assumed that the earth's orbit around the sun had to be circular because the circle was an aesthetic form and therefore God would have preferred it. Kepler denied Copernicus his beautiful wish because later, more exact, evidence indicated that nature preferred an elliptical orbit. The second group rejects the notion that natural events honor any of the ethically desirable ends that humans invent. They simply want to know the structure of natural phenomena and do not expect that what is true in nature bears any similarity to what humans believe ought to be true. Darwin, who never claimed that birds were "better" than snakes, is often cited as the prototypic member of this group.

A number of social scientists, but not all, belong to the first group of idealists, because they hold strong beliefs about what human nature should be and about the experiences that create the best humans. The concept of *subjective well-being*, and its synonym, *lifetime happiness*, is an example of an ideal psychological state in the minds of North American and European social scientists and the residents of their societies. But the meaning of this idea in our culture is not similar to the meaning understood by the residents of many other cultures. For that reason, it is a cultural concept, not a biological one. The quality of the taste of a ripe fig, however, is a biological concept because it is the result of a set of biological processes possessed by all humans.

Subjective well-being, which I shorten to well-being, is a private judgment reflecting the degree to which a person believes that the totality of his or her actions and varied life experiences are congruent with a private understanding of the meanings of the words *worthy, good,* and *virtuous.* Well-being is close to synonymous with the ancient Greek concept *eudaimonia.*[1]

Unfortunately, despite millennia of thought, there remains serious disagreement over the definitions of a worthy, good, or virtuous life. Agreement would be easier to attain if these terms referred to specific actions or experiences. Sadly, that is not possible. The judgment that one has led a good life and is a good person is based on an evaluation of the degree to which the person believes he or she has honored the seminal ideals that were established during childhood and adolescence. Montaigne called virtue the "nursing mother of human pleasures." Although these ideals vary both within and across cultures, the size of the contemporary list is not unwieldy. Most adults would nominate loyalty and kindness to select others, the respect of and affection from select others, the perfection of a talent, a significant accomplishment, wealth, loyalty to a spiritual commitment, or meeting the local standards for one's gender, religion, or ethnic group. The Romans would have added the trait *verecundia*, defined by the combination of a concern with one's status in social interactions and the display of behaviors that are appropriate to one's role.

The ideals in every collection exist in a hierarchy with some more important than others, and the hierarchy varies across persons. The judgment that one has led a good life requires individuals to believe that they have come close to honoring, or have honored, the ideals that happen to be in the top positions in the hierarchy. The eleventh-century Catholic crusaders who killed infidel Muslims in Jerusalem and the Shiite suicide bombers who killed Sunni worshipers would have decided that they were good persons who lived a virtuous life if they believed in the validity of their religious commitments. Americans might declare that both the crusaders and suicide bombers committed amoral acts, but the private definition of a good act, life, or person need not correspond to the definition understood by others. That is why there is a contentious debate over the meanings of *virtuous, moral,* and *good.* The meaning of life satisfaction, or well-being, does not escape this ambiguity.

Most adults who have sufficient food and shelter and are free of serious chronic illness rely on a judgment of the ethical quality of their lives when they answer the few questions that define *well-being:* "How satisfied are you with your life?" "Have you gotten most of the things that you wanted in life?" and "All things considered, how satisfied are you with your life these days?" The judgments of individuals from diverse societies would change only a little if the question were: "All things considered, have you lived the life of a good person?" However, because the semantic networks for *good* vary across historical eras and cultural settings, the meaning of a low, moderate, or high level of well-bring must also vary. Put simply, individuals who report the same level of well-being could have behaved in different ways, achieved different goals, held different values, and experienced different feelings over their lifetimes.

North Americans and Europeans place a high value on states of moderate excitement attained through action and personal achievement. Not one of the seven greatest pleasures listed by one American writer, Willard Spiegelman, referred to acts that helped another. Asians, by contrast, celebrate states of serenity, the quality and obligations linked to personal relationships, and social harmony. Identical levels of well-being reported by Americans and Asians need not have the same meaning. More generally, individuals vary in the balance they maintain between two desires: maximizing personal pleasures and regarding the self as fair, loyal, and kind with others. Two people with different balances of these two urges could report the same degree of well-being.[2]

The social scientists who study well-being appear to assume that, if most people say that all they want in life is to be happy, it must be true that "happiness" exists in nature as a unitary state. A majority of sixteenth-century Italians would have said that they wanted to please God, but Galileo did not spend time trying to measure signs of God's presence. No scientist has found a behavioral or biological measure of lifetime happiness that colleagues agree captures this state. All the evidence consists of verbal statements declaring that the individual is happy. Since many scientists and nonscientists do not assume that God exists because millions say that they believe in God, perhaps we should apply the same criterion to reports of lifetime happiness.

A judgment of well-being is, of course, qualitatively different from the experience of pleasant sensory states, such as sweetness or orgasm, because the latter do not require the person to compare their current feelings with those of the past or with their knowledge of others. A high level of well-being, however, does require individuals to compare their current state with their past or the imagined states of others. No one can know how satisfied they are with their lives without making one or both comparisons. And informants have a choice of four comparisons. They can compare their current state with their state years earlier, with the states of their friends, with their understanding of the state of a majority in their society, or with their judgment of the states of all other humans in their age category. Each comparison will yield a different answer. Unfortunately, social scientists ignore this fact and appear to assume that all respondents are using the same comparison. The well-being judgments of residents of Great Britain appear to be based primarily on a comparison of their income relative to those they regarded as an appropriate reference group, rather than on their absolute income.[3]

The penetration of radio, television, cell phones, and the Internet into most communities has created a historically unique condition in which residents of towns and villages in less-developed societies have become aware of the material resources and living conditions enjoyed by those in wealthier nations. As a result, a fair proportion of the five billion humans in Africa, India, and East Asia, who might have regarded themselves as very happy in earlier centuries when they had little or no information on Europe and North America, might decide that they were less happy because of their new appreciation of the material conditions enjoyed by the approximately 1.5 billion residents of Europe and North America. Many Afghans who might have been satisfied with their lives in 2000 would have suffered a loss in well-being after American troops entered their country. And contemporary Americans and Europeans, aware of the economic disadvantages and corrupt politics in many parts of Africa, Latin America, and Asia, report high levels of well-being, in part because they compare their conditions with others.

Denmark enjoys one of the highest levels of personal income and health of all nations, and not surprisingly, its citizens report a high level of well-being. But let us suppose that Danes were told that that their average income and health placed them in the bottom 25 percent of all nations. I suspect that now their average well-being would fall substantially. If this prediction were affirmed, it would prove that judgments of life satisfaction not only depend on the respondents' personal history, circumstances, and society but are also affected by their understanding of the differences between life conditions in their society and comparable conditions in other societies. The comment of the eleventh-century Chinese scholar Shao Yong affirms the role of comparison in judgments of well-being: "I am happy because I am a human and not an animal, a male and not a female, a Chinese and not a barbarian, and because I live in Luoyang, the most wonderful city in the world."[4]

A majority of the 1.1 million adults from forty-five different societies varying in income and health reported being satisfied with their lives, and less than 3 percent said they were unhappy. Since many of these "happy" individuals came from impoverished societies with high levels of illness, unemployment, corruption, crime, and obstacles to improving one's circumstances, it is unlikely that the criteria they used when reporting their high level of well-being were the same as those used by the Swedes and Danes who offered very similar answers.[5]

If social scientists asked adults, "To what degree do you believe there are witches in your community that can cause harm?" the replies of Haitians, many who believe in witches, would not have the same meaning as the answers of Americans. Simply because adults will answer a question posed by a stranger does not necessarily mean that the replies have a transparent meaning. Most individuals would give an answer if asked, "All things considered, what has been your level of confusion over your lifetime?" even though they had never posed that query to themselves. And psychologists would disagree on the meanings of the replies. Many individuals have not asked themselves how satisfied they are with their lives, and psychologists should also be uncertain of the meaning of these answers.

One of the beliefs defining the movement called modernism, which emerged in nineteenth-century Europe and grew in strength over succeeding decades, is that any statement believed to be true in one era is always subject to revision. This assumption bothers many individuals who would like to believe that a few ideas are always true. The advocates of modernism substitute legitimate procedures for permanent truths. The decisions of the US Supreme Court are accepted by a majority of Americans because they regard the Court as appointed by and adhering to legitimate procedures. If the gathering of scientific evidence follows legitimate procedures, most are prepared to accept as true the summaries of these observations. Hence, if a number of academically respected psychologists declare that gathering answers to questions posed by a stranger is a legitimate way to evaluate what people think or feel, and a representative sample of a hundred thousand Americans say they enjoy a high level of well-being, it seems reasonable to conclude that most Americans are happy with their lives.

It is chastening, however, to recognize that no contemporary psychologist would assume that the Devil was a natural phenomenon if an archaeologist discovered a document in Latin indicating that 52 percent of a group of ten thousand fourteenth-century Europeans who were asked, "How often during your lifetime have you felt that the Devil temporarily occupied your body?" reported they experienced this feeling at least once. This evidence does not require us to assume that their answers mean that the Devil existed at that time or that all who answered affirmatively had the same psychological state.

I invented this example to make a critical point. The fact that two billion humans might declare "I have had a satisfying life" does not prove that the concept of *well-being* has an unambiguous meaning and refers to a single psychological state that can be observed in phenomena other than a verbal answer to a question. A large number of adults would tell interviewers that knowing their astrological sign helped them adapt to life's demands. Furthermore, the societies with a large proportion of their populations holding that belief probably had economies and standards of living that differed from those that had few residents believing in astrology. Humans are able to report a great many beliefs that, if pressed, they could neither explain nor defend. Sissela Bok arrived at a roughly similar conclusion in her scholarly review of the idea of well-being in her book *Exploring Happiness.*[6]

We cannot understand the meaning of well-being judgments across different societies without asking additional questions. Nations with similar levels of well-being might be differentiated if scientists asked a complementary question: "What are the most important things in your life that you wanted but have not yet attained?" The answers to this query would help psychologists separate Sweden from Israel. Both nations had equally high levels of life satisfaction and economic productivity in 2007. But Israelis, who want to be free of the chronic worry associated with the anger of their Palestinian neighbors, would offer replies that differed from Swedes, who have no current threats to their existence. The mean levels of well-being from 1995 to 2007 in Guatemala, Colombia, and Venezuela were equivalent to the values for New Zealand, Norway, and the United States. This evidence implies that the citizens from the former societies, which have large numbers of poor peasants and high levels of crime and corruption, enjoy the same degree of satisfaction as those in the latter societies. This conclusion is difficult to accept.

The interpretation of the meaning of reports of well-being is ambiguous because most informants do not know how to attain this beautiful state. Most desired goals are linked closely to the actions required to attain the goal. A hungry person knows he or she must find food; one who is lonely needs to acquire friends; someone wanting to be wealthy has to make money. Many who wish for a feeling of well-being, however, are not sure what they should do to command that state. *Happiness,* like the concept *good,* is an open term that assumes different meanings and is attained in a variety of ways. Perhaps that is why Kant wrote, "The concept of happiness is such an indeterminate one that even though everyone wishes to attain happiness, yet he can never say definitely and consistently what it is he really wishes and wills."[7]

Most Europeans born before the Industrial Revolution placed survival, loyalty to family and community, and obeying God's commands as the primary imperatives that would bring happiness if honored. Montaigne, born at a time in the sixteenth century when illness and premature death were common, wrote that freedom from illness was the primary cause of a feeling of well-being. The proposal to replace survival, loyalty, and piety with well-being required a sequence of historical events that made the earlier gratifications either irrelevant, ethically neutral, or too easily attained. The declaration that every person has a right to be happy, or at least the right to pursue this state, did not emerge in Europe until the late seventeenth century, and many societies of the same era did not hold this premise in high esteem.

Residents of the United States are especially receptive to the notion that happiness is life's preeminent prize because it is in accord with the egalitarian ethos that has permeated this society since its inception. This idea was present when the nation was established, was enhanced by the Transcendentalist movement during the opening decades of the nineteenth century, and reached maturity after the civil rights legislation of the 1960s. Most Americans want each person's satisfaction with self to be based on character and life achievements rather than on family pedigree, ethnicity, gender, religion, occupation, or years of education. Americans insist that the most important gratifications should be attainable by any individual who obeyed the law and expended the effort necessary to attain the legitimate goals each sought. Everyone should be able to decide, at the end of a life, that they had a "good run."

Most scholars who thought they had discovered life's primary purposes usually projected their personal biases on their society or, in some cases, on all humanity. Plato and Aristotle were certain that quiet contemplation in the service of acquiring wisdom was the primary satisfaction. Thousands of miles to the east at roughly the same time Lao Tzu celebrated the absence of desire and a posture of submission. Hindus favored minimal attachments, selfless duty, and expenditures of effort with no concern for the outcome.[8]

Many contemporary American psychologists would agree with Carol Ryff's suggestion that well-being requires autonomy, social relationships, the ability to cope with life's demands, an openness to new ideas, the belief that life has a purpose, and an acceptance of self's limitations.[9] These traits are concerned only with the individual, and none refers to the welfare of others or obligations to kin, friends, and community. Equally wise commentators from other cultures, old and new, would question the universality of the above quintet as the ultimate secret to a satisfying life.

The Marquise du Châtelet, Voltaire's eighteenth-century mistress, may have come closer to the truth when she suggested in a letter to a friend that to be happy, "We must be susceptible to illusions for it is to illusions that we owe the majority of our pleasures. Unhappy is the one who has lost them." The twentieth-century poet Wallace Stevens endorsed the marquise when he wrote, "The final belief is to believe in a fiction, which you know to be a fiction, there being nothing else. The exquisite truth is to know that it is a fiction and that you believe in it willingly." Stevens suggests that each of us must invent some ethical ideals and pursue them with a passionate commitment, even if we recognize that our selection might be idiosyncratic. The persistent pursuit of these constructed ideals permits a feeling of satisfaction with one's life.[10]

I suspect that Stevens may have read a short story written decades earlier by the Swedish novelist Pär Lagerkvist. The leader of an infinitely large collection of dead souls approaches God to ask what purpose He had in mind when He created humans. God's terse reply was, "I only intended humans would never be satisfied with nothing." This insight, which can be freeing, exacts the price of acknowledging that one's deepest assumptions of what is true might be idiosyncratic inventions. The late Loren Eiseley, an anthropologist, recalled in a memoir the remarks of a black girl he met on Bimini: "Those as hunts treasure must go alone, at night, and when they find it they have to leave a little of their blood behind them."[11]

The popularity of the concept of *well-being* reflects a more general preference among American and European social scientists for extremely abstract terms that collapse diverse phenomena into a single idea. Many psychologists, for example, assert that *positive emotion*, usually assessed with a questionnaire, is a useful concept. This claim assumes that it makes no difference whether the positive feeling is the result of completing a difficult project, caring for an infant, having many close friends, going on a holiday, enjoying a meal, engaging in sex, possessing a large bank account, deceiving a client, planning a murder of infidels, or outcompeting a rival for a better position in a corporation. Freeman Dyson divides scholars into two groups. The birds soar above the variety of events on the ground and ignore the details. The frogs muck around in the messy particularity of a Vermont pond. René Descartes and Sigmund Freud were birds; Francis Bacon and James Watson were frogs. The advocates of well-being are high-flying birds. More seriously, because psychologists cannot agree on what an emotion is, it is odd that some argue for the existence of positive emotions.

Altruism, a second abstract idea popular among many biologists and psychologists, is defined only by the outcome of an action rather than by a set of inherent features. This is a dangerous strategy in the life sciences. A popular definition of *altruism* treats the behavior of worker bees in a hive and humans donating blood to a stranger as examples of the same concept. This decision should provoke some skepticism because bees do not reflect on the implications their actions have for their virtue. Human altruism is defined by intention, not by outcome. A man who jumped into a cold lake to save a struggling child and drowned both the child and himself committed an altruistic act even though the child received no benefit from the man's action. Physics is the only natural science in which similar consequences are a profitable basis for a useful concept. This criterion has rarely proven useful in biology and psychology. If similar consequences were a sufficient basis for fruitful concepts in psychology, the actions of a suicide bomber and a physician with permission from kin to withhold treatment from a terminally ill patient belong to the same category.

Most biologists are more suspicious of overly abstract concepts. That is why they regularly parse an initially broad concept into a number of categories that share the same origin and features. Novel observations forced geneticists to invent the concepts *exon, intron, promoter,* and *enhancer* as more accurate ways to understand the older, more abstract concept *gene.* If biologists were studying well-being, they would gather extensive biological, psychological, and historical information on groups who reported the same levels of well-being in order to discover the different types of people who offered identical judgments. Unfortunately, the social scientists who study well-being reject this fruitful strategy. They are fond of abstractions that ignore the varied bases for the same verbal judgments and treat identical verbal replies as if they had the same meaning.

The history of the natural sciences teaches the incontrovertible fact that surface phenomena rarely reveal the invisible processes responsible for the observed events. Should this principle apply to psychology (and there is no good reason why it should not), the answers to questionnaires or interviews inquiring about well-being, or any other emotional state, will not tell social scientists what they should want to know—namely, the specific biological profiles, actions, beliefs, feelings, and motives that lie behind a particular verbal statement. The meaning of a person's verbal reply to a question about his or her psychological state is a puzzle to understand rather than an answer to an important unsolved problem. But this procedure is loyal to the most important imperative in science: all evidence must be objective and free of the investigator's subjective judgments. If a woman living in a Bogotá ghetto who has no schooling and no steady source of income says that she has lived a satisfying life, we must accept that reply as a true reflection of her state, even if the interrogator believes she has led a miserable life.

The habit of comparing easily gathered judgments of well-being from adults in various cultures, based on the assumption that the answers have theoretically important and unambiguous meanings, ignores the wisdom on a sign in Einstein's Princeton office that read, "Not everything that counts can be counted, and not everything that can be counted, counts."

Scientists can adopt one of two stances when evaluating a person's verbal descriptions of their psychological states. On the one hand, they can assume that statements with the same surface meaning reflect the same or very similar psychological states. This assumption is reasonable when the statement refers to the physical features of an event anyone could observe: for example, "I saw a large yellow bus," or a distinctive sensation anyone could experience:

"The ice cream tasted sweet." But this premise is vulnerable when the object or event that the word names is ambiguous, and in addition, the reply rests on fallible recall of the past and engages notions of how one ought to feel. All three of these features affect judgments of well-being.[12] Therefore, scientists must be concerned with the relation between the judgments and the pattern of sociological, psychological, or biological events to which the judgments presumably refer.

Bertrand Russell and Alfred North Whitehead disagreed on the ambiguity of a word's meaning. Russell regarded words as names for things that could be observed. Words were clearly demarcated bullets. No one would confuse the meaning of *bulldozer* with the meaning of *broccoli* or *bun*. Whitehead acknowledged the different networks a particular word can evoke in different people, called its sense meaning. A word in Whitehead's understanding resembled a pot of warm taffy. Russell had great difficulty understanding the argument of his mentee, Ludwig Wittgenstein, who wrote that the meaning of a word is defined by how a language community uses it. I side with Whitehead and Wittgenstein and cite the words *fuzz*, *cool*, and *gay* as examples.

It is relevant that two molecules with exactly the same atoms in the same locations can assume different spatial arrangements in their crystalline forms. This difference often has important consequences. The same is true for identical answers to the same question. The amygdala is a major origin of the feelings that are the basis of an emotion. But adults with a damaged amygdala typically offer the same verbal descriptions of their emotional states as normal adults with an intact amygdala. Because these two groups cannot have the same feelings, it is clear that surface similarity does not always imply complete identity.[13]

The meaning and validity of a person's verbal descriptions of their psychological states or traits have been the subject of many reviews. The evidence reflects an emerging consensus that there is a minimal, or at best a very modest, relation between what people say about themselves, on the one hand, and descriptions of them by friends or, better yet, direct observations of behaviors or biological processes that should correspond with the verbal replies, on the other. Surprisingly, there is only a very modest correlation (only 0.20) between adults' answers to surveys asking them how often they used sunscreen at a swimming pool on a particular day and an objective measure of the presence of sunscreen based on swabs of the skin.[14]

The answers to questions can vary with the specific words used, the way the question is posed, the questions that preceded it, the gender, age, ethnicity, and cultural background of the informants, and always the

social appropriateness of the reply. On some occasions,
even the time of day has an effect. Most adults report
being happiest between 11:00 a.m. and 2:00 p.m., when
their core body temperature is high. Adults between the
ages of thirty and fifty report being less satisfied with
their lives than most sixty-to-seventy-year-olds because
the younger adults are raising families and working under stress to ascend in status and gain financial security.
Therefore, societies with a large proportion of older
residents should have a higher average well-being score,
independent of the economic productivity or political
structure of the society. Americans living in different
regions of the country describe themselves in distinctive ways. Citizens of the plains states say they are more
extroverted and agreeable than those living in New England or on the West Coast. But that does not mean that
if we observed a thousand adults in North Dakota and
California we would see more extroverted individuals in
the former state. Instead, it means that North Dakotans
have a stronger desire to believe that they are extroverted.
Adults with strong religious affiliations typically report
higher well-being than agnostics and atheists. However,
religious Americans are more likely to live in rural or
suburban communities in the Midwest or South than in
large cities on the East or West coasts. Therefore, a reli-

gious affiliation and place of residence can contribute to reports of well-being.[15]

Human languages were invented primarily to communicate information about things in the world and to remind others of their obligations. Most words were not intended to describe private psychological states, in part because people want to hide feelings of shame, guilt, anger, envy, pride, lust, fear, disgust, and deceit. *Disgust* is not easily translated into a single term in Mandarin, because the Chinese language has several words that reflect different aspects of the experience, especially the difference between the feeling evoked by vomit, feces, or rotting food, on the one hand, and the state that pierces consciousness when one learns of the immoral behavior of another person, on the other. The English term *satisfied* is not easily translated into a single word in all languages. Moreover, some adults interpret the word *satisfied* to mean pleasant bodily feelings, whereas others assume that the term refers to a judgment of how much the self has accomplished in life.

Most adults in all cultures automatically impose an evaluation ranging from very good to very bad on many objects and events. But the complete semantic network for the abstract term *good*, which has well-being as an element, is not the same in all language communities.

Among English-speaking Americans, nice, sweet, and helpful are the dominant features of good things. Among the Hong Kong Chinese, lovable and respectable are salient referents for good. And among Italians, Turks, and Lebanese beautiful is an essential feature of good objects and people.[16]

Most words for psychological states fail to capture the subtle gradations in the quality and intensity of happiness, as well as the many blends separate emotions can form. English has no single word to describe the blend of shame and joy felt by a woman unable to conceive naturally who has learned that one of her eggs was fertilized in a laboratory dish. Americans use the phrase "I love you" more frequently than those in most societies, but it lacks the emotional significance that it has for others. Fewer than 2 percent of the 6.4 million words found in eighty-five thousand messages sent to text pagers in the United States following the terror attacks on September 11, 2001, could be coded as describing feelings of anxiety or sadness.[17] But it would be an error to conclude that a majority of the authors of these messages did not experience one or both emotions simply because they failed to use words that could be construed as reflecting these emotions.

The philosopher Ludwig Wittgenstein was profoundly depressed and anxious during most of his life, failed to put down roots in any one place, was estranged from his brother Paul, had several older brothers who committed suicide, and wrote in a notebook that he could not imagine a future that contained any joy or friendship. Although these facts imply that Wittgenstein did not have many moments of happiness, nonetheless, minutes before he died he told a visitor, "Tell them I've had a wonderful life."[18] It is not at all clear how we should interpret his final verbal report.

English contains a large number of verbs and adjectives that provide little information on the context or target of an action or the intensity of an emotion or strength of a belief. This feature is not a characteristic of all languages. The words for *emotion* in Persian acknowledge the differential statuses of the individuals in a setting. English does not provide this information.[19] The verb *running* can apply to a boy fleeing a large dog, a girl racing toward a friend, or water flowing down a mountain.

Moreover, many scholars of language have noted that the meaning of most sentences depends on the network of related propositions in which the spoken sentence is only one component. The meaning of the sentence "A bachelor is an unmarried male" depends on networks that specify whether a gay man lives in a state or nation that does or does not regard gay couples as legally married. Only English-speaking psychologists would ask adults from varied cultures to name a large number of color chips, each presented with no background, and expect universal consensus on the relation between what is perceived and the verbal answers. Many members of the Lele tribe in the African country of Chad did not know what to say when asked to name the color of a chip painted blue, red, or green because, in their culture, colors acquire their names from the objects in which they are a primary feature. The word for the blue of blueberries is not the term used to describe the color of a cloudless sky.[20]

Adults are not even accurate when they describe how they behaved in a group discussion that occurred minutes earlier when films of that discussion were coded. Their reports were distortions of what the films revealed because the adults were biased to describe their behavior so that it was in closer accord with their understanding of how they should have behaved. Self-descriptions of conscientiousness reported by adults from various societies were highly correlated with the person's understanding of what was normative for their society but were not related to actual observations of acts reflecting conscientiousness in that community. This fact has implications for interpreting well-being judgments. If most Americans believe that, compared with most of the world, a majority of their fellow citizens are satisfied with their lives, we would expect them to attribute to themselves the very same state and also report a high level of well-being.[21]

Furthermore, subjective reports of the level of auto-nomic activity experienced to laboratory stressors did not correspond to objective measures of activity in rel-evant targets gathered at the same time. And some adults consciously falsify what they know to be true. More than 25 percent of parents lied when they told an interviewer that their child had attended a Head Start program. Even some patients who are paying a therapist for help lie to them on occasion. If adults distort what they know to be true when talking with a person they have come to for help, it is reasonable to question the assumption that most of the answers to questions posed by a stranger on the telephone or printed in a booklet represent an accurate picture of what the informants believe or feel now or in the past, even when they believe they are telling the truth.[22]

Readers familiar with Jonathan Swift's *Gulliver's Trav-els* will remember that the eighteenth-century writer satirized those who argued that language is capable of describing nature accurately. Swift described two phi-losophers scheduled for a debate who brought large sacks filled with the objects they planned to use to make their communications unambiguous. This cumbersome strat-egy works if one wishes to communicate the meanings of bricks, beets, and balloons but fails miserably if one wants to describe psychological states such as life satisfaction. Psychologists who study human psychological states have an exaggerated respect for words when they should be examining each word's identity papers.

Psychologists of the 1940s and 1950s shared this skeptical view of verbal evidence. That is one reason the Rorschach ink blot test and the Thematic Apperception Test, called projective techniques, became popular ways to detect the motives, emotions, and personal traits that most people would not, or could not, describe in words. Unfortunately, several decades of inquiry revealed that these measures were also insensitive indices of private states. This conclusion left psychologists in the uncomfortable position of needing a procedure to evaluate personality traits and emotions but having none with a proven validity. Forced to decide, most returned to the practice of the 1930s by relying once again on questionnaires refreshed with new items and given new names but providing the same superficial, contextually restricted, ambiguous information. These scientists failed to follow Samuel Beckett's advice to examine with great care every statement "until what lurks behind it—be it something or nothing—begins to seep through."

In light of the evidence, it is appropriate to ask why social scientists continue to rely only on verbal reports to measure well-being in individuals from cultures that hold unique understandings of this English term. They would benefit from reflecting on Saint Augustine's insight in

Confessions, "I cannot totally grasp all that I am . . . my mind, questioning itself upon its own powers, feels that it cannot rightly trust its own report." One reason for the unquestioning acceptance of these on-the-spot judgments is a reluctance to expend the energy and time required to develop more sensitive measures, which would include behavior and biology along with the verbal report, either because they do not believe that this information is relevant or, more likely, they doubt that the effort will be successful. This skepticism is unwarranted. Recordings of a person's blood pressure added information that illuminated the meaning of well-being judgments.[23]

A second reason grows out of the frustration among political leaders and economists over the rising level of income inequalities in some developing nations, such as China and Brazil, and the widespread anger at an unrestrained market economy that cares only about profit. Replacing gross domestic product with well-being removes some of the pressure from political leaders who find it difficult to improve the living conditions of their many poor citizens. If an impoverished mother in Nicaragua says she is "happy," perhaps it is silly for political leaders to worry about her hunger or lack of access to good schools for her children.

A third basis for the romance with judgments of well-being is that psychologists are reluctant to abandon a pretty idea, even when they recognize the difficulty in measuring it accurately. That is why concepts like *love, attachment, self-esteem,* and *consciousness* remain popular. Investigators of well-being simply deny the criticism that verbal replies have neither a transparent meaning nor validity and suppress their recognition that all adults who tell their partner they love them do not experience the same feelings or act with the same degree of loyalty toward the beloved. A research strategy that ignores reliable facts is not a recipe for theoretical progress. The assumption that the same levels of well-being reported by adults from different cultures and social classes have comparable meanings and reflect similar psychological states reminds me of Confucius's insight that it is difficult to find a black cat in a dark room, especially if there is no cat.

An abundance of evidence reveals that annual income or accumulated wealth is a modest correlate of life satisfaction across societies with a broad range of incomes. Adults from less-developed societies with limited annual incomes report lower levels of well-being than those from developed nations with higher incomes. There is, however, little or no relation between level of well-being and absolute income in societies where a majority have annual incomes greater than $25,000. But this outcome is found only when income is measured in absolute terms. An annual increase in income of $10,000 is perceived as less valuable to those earning more than $200,000 than it is to those making less than $50,000. For this reason, it makes better sense to measure incomes proportionately (by using the log of income). For example, a doubling of income from $20,000 to $40,000 is equivalent to an increase from $50,000 to $100,000.[24]

When we make this adjustment, there is an almost linear relation between income and well-being. Most countries in western Europe and the United States had the highest well-being; India and China had middle-level values; and many African nations reported the lowest levels of well-being. No country with a gross national product per person in 2007 of $20,000 or more had a low level of well-being, but some Latin American societies with low national incomes did report high levels of well-being. The correlation between well-being and mean income across 132 different societies during 2005–2006 was relatively high, but the correlation within any single society was much lower. This observation implies, as I indicated earlier, that within a community people rely more on their income relative to others in the society than on their absolute income.[25]

Average well-being in the United States has decreased a little over the past fifty years, in part because of the increase in crime, divorce rate, and income inequality, as well as the diminished moral authority awarded to traditional elites. These social changes have led to increased ambiguity regarding the status of many social positions, vacillation over the vocation one should choose, and uncertainty over the ethical standards one should use to guide a life. Humans dislike the uncertainty that grows, Medusa-like, from unresolved ambiguity.[26]

The conditions that usually have the highest positive correlations with well-being among those with sufficient income, food, clothing, and shelter are a perception of good health (but not always a physician's judgment); many close, trusting relationships; meaningful work; a religious affiliation; being married rather than single; and minimally corrupt governmental and judicial systems. Although a perception of good health has the highest positive correlation with well-being, not having a job has the largest negative correlation.[27] These two conditions are correlated with well-being for different reasons. Because most adults under age sixty-five believe they ought to be working, being unemployed implies that they have failed to meet an ethical imperative of their society. A perception of good health reflects the absence of physical distress rather than the failure to honor an ethical ideal.

One scientist has argued that a combination of average longevity and well-being should have a privileged position when judging which societies are better now than they were in the past.[28] Other commentators might nominate low levels of economic inequality, crime, rape, addiction, pollution, and feelings of distrust as far more important than longevity when judging a society's progress. Americans enjoy a longer life span than residents of Botswana but live with much higher levels of crime, rape, drug addiction, and distrust of neighbors.

Because a variety of social conditions can have equivalent correlations with life satisfaction, it is not clear whether one factor is more critical than others or, what is more likely, a combination of conditions that form a pattern is responsible for the well-being judgments. Most adults with a professional degree are likely to engage in meaningful work, enjoy better health, and have higher incomes than those who did not graduate high school and work at boring jobs. Hence, a correlation between income and well-being within a society may not be independent of the associations with the income, education, religious commitment, vocation, and health of the informants.

The mass media and, on occasion, scientific journals announce in bold headlines that happy people live longer, implying that happiness makes a causal contribution to longevity. The more reasonable interpretation of the modest correlation between well-being and longevity is that adults with any chronic illness report being less happy than those with no illness. The presence of the illness is the more critical reason for the lower well-being and the shorter life. Indeed, individuals residing in the northern hemisphere who were conceived in the fall months, when the pregnant mother is secreting higher levels of the molecule melatonin, are at a slightly higher risk for not surviving the first year as well as for a variety of adult diseases. It is likely that these individuals would report a lower level of well-being, too.[29] The declaration that happiness leads to a longer life is yet another example of the temptation to assume that two valued phenomena must be causally related. I suspect there is a modest relation between the size of the home in which children are reared and their IQs. But I trust that no magazine or newspaper would tell American parents that they might consider building a larger house if they wanted their child to have a higher level of intelligence.

Although each person's life history and social circumstances (especially their income, education, and health relative to others) are the major determinants of well-being judgments, inherited temperamental biases make a small contribution. Identical twins report more similar well-being than fraternal twin pairs, implying a small genetic contribution to life satisfaction. About 10 to 20 percent of Caucasian adults were born with a biology that rendered them vulnerable to unpredictable surges of uncomfortable feelings of tension that interfere with chronically high levels of happiness, even if they lived under objectively benevolent conditions. Leonard Woolf, an accomplished writer with a distinguished career in British politics, had such a dour personality, for he confessed in a memoir written when he was 88 years old, "I achieved practically nothing. . . . I have therefore to make the rather ignominious confession to myself and to anyone who may read this book that I must have in a long life ground through between 150,000 and 200,000 hours of perfectly useless work."[30]

A larger proportion of Caucasians, perhaps 30 to 40 percent, inherit a temperamental bias that makes it easier to experience frequent moments of happiness and serenity, even under objectively stressful conditions. Adults who laugh easily and frequently, partly due to their temperament, have a healthier cardiovascular system. The twenty-one-year-old women who smiled broadly in the photographs of a college yearbook reported greater well-being when interviewed thirty years later. Two Holocaust survivors living in Israel reported opposite moods. One felt continually sad; the other felt happy because her current life was so much better than it had been in the past.[31]

A large sample of middle-class, Caucasian adolescents

had been classified at four months of age as possessing one of two temperamental biases, based on a combination of high or low levels of distress and motor activity to unexpected events. The infants who cried and displayed lots of limb movement, called high reactive, were more timid and fearful as preschool children and more dour and socially anxious as adolescents compared with those who were quiet and lay still, called low reactive. It cannot be a coincidence that the Hawaiian infants described by their mothers as cuddly and easy to care for became eighteen-year-olds with the fewest psychological problems. Yet one-third of the high reactives at age eleven described themselves as "happy most of the time." This fact implies that the meaning of a verbal report of happiness does not always have the same meaning across individuals.

More high- than low-reactive eighteen-year-old boys reported bouts of depression and social anxiety and had a more active frontal lobe in the right hemisphere, whereas most adolescents and adults have a more active frontal lobe in the left hemisphere. The right hemisphere makes a stronger contribution to anxiety and depression than the left. A majority of adults with an extremely active right frontal lobe reported lower levels of well-being. Moreover, accident victims who suffered damage to the right frontal lobe, which should have been accompanied by a reduction in worry and sadness, reported greater well-being than those whose damage was confined to the left hemisphere.[32]

The human groups that migrated to Asia, Africa, Europe, or Latin America and remained there for at least four hundred centuries differ in many genes that might influence their temperaments. Asians and Caucasian Europeans, for example, differ in about one of every four alleles in regions of the DNA sequences that control the expression of genes responsible for a variety of protein products. I noted earlier that two alleles control the expression of the gene responsible for the serotonin transporter molecule, which absorbs serotonin from the synapses. Some individuals possess an allele with a shorter DNA string; others inherit a longer string. It turns out that Asians have the highest prevalence of the short allele, Africans have the lowest prevalence, and Caucasians are in the middle. Individuals with the short allele have a chronically lower level of serotonin activity in the brain because of adjustments induced by the prolonged presence of serotonin in the synapses. As a result, they are likely to have a more excitable amygdala than those possessing the long allele. It may not be a coincidence that residents of Japan and Hong Kong, societies that enjoy a large gross domestic product and good health, report slightly lower levels of well-being than expected given the economic prosperity, good health, and longevity in their societies.

It will prove useful to add individuals' biology to their current circumstances, life history, historical era, and culture in order to understand the meaning of their judgments of well-being. The modest influence of temperament on well-being is one reason why some ancient scholars, and even a few modern ones, claim that a sustained mood of happiness requires some measure of good luck.[33] The Old English term *happ* means luck and is the root of the modern English word *happy*.

If reports of high, moderate, or low well-being across different cultures have an elusive meaning, an alternative strategy is to assess a person's feelings at a particular time in a particular place. Daniel Kahneman and his colleagues, who are also skeptical of the validity of well-being judgments, asked informants to record the events during a particular day and later rate the valence and intensity of the feelings they remembered having experienced to those events. Not surprisingly, this index of happiness (or unhappiness) had a minimal relation to income, education, or life satisfaction, because the events described as unpleasant were typically those that occur when individuals are pursuing a goal that is worthwhile or required for economic survival (for example, studying for an examination, caring for a child, or commuting to work).[34]

Other scientists claim that a person's judgment of their unhappiness at a particular moment, caused by a stress, pain, frustration, or loss, is a psychologically significant state. Alan Krueger invented an equation presumed to reflect the mean level of unpleasantness in a population. The index of unpleasantness would be higher in portfolio managers who are under continued stress for most of the day than in unemployed Mexican adults. Many poor Mexicans, however, are eager to immigrate to the United States, where they might become portfolio managers or at least secure a good job. Not surprisingly, American women experienced a significant increase in the unpleasantness index after 1965 when many entered the workforce, but I suspect that a majority of these women wanted to go to work.[35]

Feelings of satisfaction usually emerge at the end of a period of effortful activity, whereas most bouts of unhappiness do not require a long period of preparation. An illness, loss of money or a job, or the death of a relative usually occur suddenly. Therefore, moment-to-moment assessments of pleasant feelings during the current or previous day do not lie on a continuum with feelings of unhappiness, and neither state is correlated with well-being judgments.[36]

If equivalent judgments of well-being have different origins and meanings, are minimally related to sensory pleasures or daily moods, and are influenced by the informant's age and culture, it is reasonable to be skeptical of the popular belief that the average well-being level in a society has important implications that might provide a useful guide for presidents, prime ministers, or legislators. The Nobel laureate economist Amartya Sen agrees with my claim that the bases for life satisfaction judgments are enigmatic, and he too questions the wisdom of using this information to evaluate a society or to guide its political leaders. The author of a review of several books on this concept concurs: "There is more to life than subjective well-being . . . and happiness . . . as defined by happiness studies offers little guidance on many of the choices that matter most."[37]

I suspect that one reason social scientists continue to gather this evidence across societies is the implicit assumption that the average level of happiness in a society reveals something important about the vitality of that society that is not captured by a combination of more clearly defined objective features. The most relevant are average income; percentage employed; percentage without chronic or infectious diseases; average life span; degree of agreement on basic values; percentage reporting they would open the door to talk with a stranger; low density of population; small magnitude of income inequality; and a small percentage incarcerated in jails or prisons. The values on these nine desirable, objective measures are highest in Denmark, Switzerland, and Norway, whose residents report the highest levels of well-being. The values on these indices are very low in Cambodia, Zimbabwe, and Bangladesh, whose citizens report low levels of well-being.[38]

These conditions also predict the variation in the average level of happiness among Americans. I noted in chapter 1 that the Gallup organization calls 300 to 2,000 Americans each day and asks them about their health, freedom from stress, job satisfaction, quality of diet, exercise, satisfaction with their community, physical safety at night, and possession of health insurance. The average of the replies to these questions is treated as an index of happiness, which is similar, but not identical, to subjective well-being. The five happiest states in 2010, which had low levels of income inequality, low unemployment rates, small percentages with nonwhite residents, low crime rates, and low population densities compared with the other states, were North Dakota, Wyoming, New Hampshire, Vermont, and Alaska. The five states with the lowest happiness scores, all in the South (Louisiana, Arkansas, Kentucky, West Virginia, and Mississippi), were characterized by a much larger proportion of African Americans or Hispanic immigrants, a larger number of Evangelical churches, lower levels of consensus on ethical values, higher levels of income inequality, higher crime rates, and a larger proportion with annual incomes below the official definition of poverty. This evidence supports my suggestion that scientists would profit from measuring the nine objective indices I listed rather than restrict their conclusions about a society's well-being to verbal reports. Social scientists have the cause-effect relations backwards. They should use the objective conditions in a community to understand the meanings of well-being judgments rather than use the judgments to evaluate a community or society and explain its vitality.

The same principle applies to interpretations of the answers to personality questionnaires. The traits called conscientiousness and agreeableness increase steadily from early adolescence to age sixty-five.[39] The most reasonable interpretation of this fact is that older adults are working and raising a family and these responsibilities require greater conscientiousness and agreeableness. The answers to the personality questions are determined, in part, by the person's life conditions, and psychologists can understand the meaning of these verbal reports by finding out each respondent's work and family responsibilities rather than assume that the answers reflect a fundamental and stable property of the person.

The biology humans inherit creates four seminal concerns. Each person will be concerned with survival,
avoiding pain, and seeking sensory pleasures and will
want to regard the self as good and virtuous. Because
this quartet of biases leads to social problems when large
numbers in a society have less power and less access to
valued resources, humans invented institutions whose
primary function was to find a balance among the desires
of the individual, on the one hand, and the harmony of
the community, on the other. Unfortunately, these institutions have been unable to maintain harmony for long
periods of time, in part because individuals were reluctant to worry too much about their community. That is
why the responsibilities of governments are often inconsistent with the wishes of the majority.

Benevolent political leaders in this century assume
they have an obligation to maximize employment and
provide adequate education, health care, and equal justice
for all citizens. The feelings of the majority are not always the wisest guide to the legislators who have to worry
about the entire community. Socrates died in 399 BCE
because he challenged the Athenians' belief in the gods
and the wisdom of the democratic majority. Many of
America's statesmen who helped write the Constitution also worried about the election day decisions of the
many who had no property. National polls revealed that

a large number of Americans opposed the federal health care reform bill of 2010, and many continue to oppose the legalization of gay marriage. It is worth noting that most Germans would have reported greater well-being in 1940 after Hitler assumed power than in 1930 when inflation was rampant and the citizenry despondent. Most Southern plantation owners in the years before the Civil War would have reported high levels of well-being. Many Afghans are frustrated by the current level of corruption under the Hamid Karzai regime and the presence of foreign troops, and I suspect that a fair proportion were more satisfied when the harshly restrictive practices of the Taliban were controlling large parts of the country. These facts suggest that a high level of well-being, or a rise in a nation's well-being, does not always mean that the society is more vital, more productive, or more just.

Scientists conducting research on well-being in order to advise governments should reword their usual question and ask instead, "How satisfied are you with your society?" If they did, they would discover less optimistic replies among contemporary Americans. The United States has greater income inequality, less effective public schools, more homicides, a larger proportion diagnosed as mentally ill, and a larger percentage in prisons than most societies that have comparable democratic institutions and national incomes.

Many Americans have begun to question the reassuring belief held by a majority of Americans only sixty-five years ago that their country was the most moral, democratic, industrious, classless, and tolerant of all the world's nations. These Americans were permitted a feeling of pride in country because they were taught about Washington's victory over the British, the Louisiana Purchase, the Emancipation Proclamation, the bravery at the Alamo, and the American contribution to the defeat of Germany and Japan in 1945. Those born after 1950 were reminded of the dark underside of the penny that included the harsh treatment of the antebellum slaves, the slaughter of Native Americans, the lack of empathy by the nineteenth-century robber barons for the poor immigrants huddled in tenements, the dropping of the atom bomb on Hiroshima, and the killing of innocent civilians in Vietnam. These images evoke a feeling of shame. The diluted pride in country over the past four to five decades, compared with the extraordinary pride felt at the end of the Second World War, has been accompanied by a conscious anger toward elites and politicians and a partially conscious guilt over allowing their leaders to engage in wars that killed thousands of innocent civilians and ignoring the conditions that led to schools with high school graduates who cannot read the newspaper, adolescent girls performing oral sex on boys they met a few hours earlier, marginalized youth murdering peers, doctors taking large fees from drug companies in exchange for touting the miraculous qualities of the firm's medicines, and priests abusing children. And their elected representatives in Washington gave billions of dollars to banks and automobile companies to rescue them from the consequences of the extremely risky decisions their corporate leaders made but did little to save the millions of poor families who lost their homes because they too assumed the risk of buying a house they could not afford. Even four-year-olds have a tantrum if a parent violates their sense of fairness by awarding an undeserved privilege to a sibling.

All these events coalesced to create a storm of hostility directed at the villains that Americans believed robbed them of every ideal they had been protecting since childhood and to nurture the hope that new leaders would bring back a past they had idealized. It was easier before 1940 to name a particular businessman as a target for anger. John D. Rockefeller and William Randolph Hearst were popular villains. As historical events created international conglomerates, it became harder to specify a particular person as responsible for acts of injustice or greed. Most people find it more satisfying to rage against a person rather than a corporation. It is not surprising that the public selected members of Congress as targets for outrage and voting them out of office had to be gratifying. Although most pundits blamed only the high unemployment rate in 2010 for the Republican victories in the midterm elections, the vast majority of Tea Party members and independents who voted against Democratic incumbents held secure jobs and were in no danger of losing their homes to bank foreclosures.

The reaction among a small proportion of younger Americans was more self-destructive, but its seeds can be detected in J. D. Salinger's 1951 portrayal of Holden Caulfield in *Catcher in the Rye*. The difficulty in finding an ethical standard so sacred that it could not be abrogated has generated in some youth (fortunately a small minority) a demonic urge to destroy any remaining illusory beliefs in sacred rituals, sacred persons, sacred words, or sacred events. These young adults seem to be saying, "You may think you understand what betrayal means, let me show you what it really means." All sexual intimacies between romantic partners are nothing but carnal, physical acts. All authorities are corrupt and narcissistic. Thanksgiving and Christmas are occasions for family quarrels and jealousies. The Fourth of July and Veterans Day are days you do not have to work. This level of masochism makes clinical descriptions of men asking women to whip them a fairy tale.

Humans behave irrationally when a belief in their privileged status, values, or virtue is challenged. The status of the traditionally elite families in old Salem, Massachusetts, in the seventeenth century was threatened by a group of newcomers living in a different part of the town. The former reacted to their loss of dignity and injured pride by accusing some of the newcomers of witchcraft. The Japanese attacked the United States in 1941 because they regarded themselves as a superior race and wanted revenge for the humiliation of being treated as an inferior "yellow race" by white Americans and Europeans. The acts of terrorist aggression by extremist Muslim groups are fueled by a similar desire to right the perceived wrongs perpetrated by the medieval Crusaders and the European and American exploitation of the Middle East over the past two hundred years.

Humans must act and need to believe that the actions they choose are ethically worthy. All but the most seriously demented appreciate that, on occasion, they have the opportunity to decide what to do that day, the following week, the coming year, or during the next few decades. These choices were far more limited for the humans who inhabited the planet for the first 140,000 years of our existence as a species. The major imperatives for these populations were to find food, protect self and family from the weather, predatory animals, and illness, and to care for young children. These demands kept most adults busy most days. When these concerns were muted among eighteenth-century Europeans with adequate incomes, citizens looked for another ideal goal to pursue. A majority chose freedom from authority as the prize, and a century later, after most Europeans and North Americans had achieved political liberty, the abolition of slavery became a prized goal. Once that ideal had been gained, public education for all children and a woman's right to vote became sacred pursuits. It is probably not a coincidence that research on well-being began about forty years ago when the American economy was healthy, civil rights had become law, most youths had the opportunity to attend a college, and many younger Americans were rejecting the fixed features of family pedigree, attendance at an elite college, occupation, ethnicity, and gender as bases for a privileged rank. Hence, a new goal was needed, and lifetime satisfaction seemed to be the appropriate prize that everyone ought to try to attain.

Some social scientists in addition sensed the increased cynicism that became more prominent in America during the 1970s and were dissatisfied with the psychiatrists' preoccupation with anxiety and depression. They decided that each person should celebrate the pleasures of life and seek private states of happiness rather than invest so much energy trying to regulate anxiety and depression.[40] These goals, which define the movement called positive psychology, assume that each person's "happiness" has priority over the welfare of one's family, community, or nation. This premise, which is in accord with the tenets of evolutionary theory, has a firmer foundation in North America and Europe than in Asia, Latin America, and Muslim societies in the Middle East, Africa, and Indonesia.

Insightful observers who have grown up in one culture are usually sensitive diagnosticians of the values of a different culture. Nadine Gordimer, who lived in South Africa, captured five distinguishing features of contemporary Americans: the celebration of youth, material success, personal freedom, patriotism, and being in love with a good person.[41] The events of the past few decades have tainted the formerly unblemished sacredness of some of these ideas among a reasonably high proportion of Americans. The high rates of adolescent pregnancy, crime, and drug addiction, the frequency of divorce, the callous greed of bankers and corporate executives, the increased inequality in wealth, a volunteer army that protects the sons and daughters of wealthy families from having to defend their country, the intrusiveness of government into the definition of marriage, and the spread of pornographic films into homes and hotel rooms informing romantically attached couples making love that all they are doing is fucking are new social facts that make it more difficult to sustain the belief that one is leading a satisfying life.

In addition, information technology has made it possible for one culture to appreciate that other cultures hold distinctive moral premises. Because the demand for tolerance requires Americans to withhold criticisms of actions and beliefs they regard as amoral, for example, a father killing his daughter because she had been raped, youth find it hard to find an ethical standard their heart tells them must be honored. It is not surprising that American adolescents questioned in 2006 reported more cynicism and less trust in others than the adolescents assessed in 1976.[42] A cartoon in the *New Yorker* illustrated a cat, a woman, and a man who says, "It's odd that you're so dull and I'm so boring, and our cat is, for all we know, plaster of Paris."

A spate of books on the American Revolution published in 2010 has even tainted the halo that most schoolteachers and history textbooks place on the brave colonists who won our independence. These authors suggest that greedy Boston merchants were responsible for a paranoia that infected the masses during the decades before the Declaration of Independence and led to the rebellious acts that brought British troops to Boston and eventually to the conflicts at Lexington and Concord. In these reform narratives, the idealistic colonists who were fighting for independence are robbed of their heroism by being portrayed as duped pawns of selfish New England businessmen.[43] The resemblance to the actions of Wall Street bankers in the years leading up to 2007 appears to be intentional.

Humans have a need to believe in a few absolute truths, but modern life has made it hard to maintain an uncritical faith in that idea. The next best substitute is the opinions of authorities who follow legitimate procedures in arriving at temporarily true conclusions. Early generations of Americans had been willing to award this halo to judges, clergy, writers, philosophers, and scientists. Indeed, less than a century ago many respected commentators announced that the ideas and vocabulary of science would unite the peoples of the world in a community of shared understandings that were free of prejudice and superstition. Few would make that claim today. All we expect of scientists is that they find ways to cure our afflictions and make our lives easier. When many began to question their prior faith in the authority figures occupying these roles, as well as their institutions and procedures, youth were forced to cope with the uncertainty of not being sure what was true or good other than their immediate feelings and thoughts. If nothing is absolutely profane, it is difficult to find something that is permanently sacred.

The history of the developed world is marked by a gradual disappearance of sacred acts, objects, people, or feelings as nature replaced God, scientists replaced priests, reason replaced piety, and unhappiness replaced the guilt that followed a sin.

The following lines from "Petrifying Petrified," by the Mexican writer Octavio Paz, capture the mood of a fair proportion of Americans.

> We have dug up Rage
>
> . . .
>
> The lovers' park is a dungheap
> The library is a nest of killer rats
> The university is a muck full of frogs
> The altar is Chanfalla's swindle
> The brains are stained with ink
> The doctors dispute in a den of thieves
> The businessmen
> fast hands   slow thoughts
> officiate in the graveyard.[44]

A decrease in well-being usually emerges when a society's demography, laws, or institutions prevent large numbers from pursuing their ethical ideals or when historical events have created conditions in which the ethical standards held by a majority have lost some power to award a feeling of virtue to those honoring them. Many middle-class Europeans were propelled into a state of melancholy during the opening years of the nineteenth century because their hope that the French Revolution would be followed by a long period of fraternity and liberty was not realized. Many poets, including Words-worth, Shelley, and Keats, called their era "maladie du siècle" (sickness of the age). A similar mood was present in Europe during the years following the armistice that ended the First World War, because many thought that this war would end all wars. When Mao Zedong's revolu-tion, which promised to raise the happiness level of mil-lions of poor peasants, turned into a totalitarian regime that murdered dissidents and led to famines, the next generation of Chinese turned excessively cynical.

Ben Bradlee, editor of the *Washington Post* during the Watergate era, reflected on his period of service in the Pacific during the Second World War, "It may sound trite to modern ears, but those really were years when you could get involved in something beyond yourself— something that connected you to your times in ways that no longer seem so natural, or expected." Many contempo-rary twenty-year-olds are deprived of this feeling. Adults from twenty-one different language communities rated 620 common nouns naming very familiar objects (for ex-ample, pot, arm, child, woman, battle) on fifty scales that represented opposite properties, such as good to bad, fast to slow, strong to weak, or colorful to colorless. Across all the languages the good to bad dimension made the largest contribution to the ratings of the nouns. Air pollution, anger, cheating, crime, debt, divorce, greed, noise, murder, and war were among the objects given the most extreme ratings on the bad end of the scale. These are the events that dominate the media, and their frequency has increased over the past fifty years. It is no wonder that many Americans are in a despondent mood. The suicide rate among Americans aged fifteen to twenty-four doubled from 1950 to 2000 from 4 to 10 per 100,000. It may not be surprising, although it is sad, that a 2006 survey of American adults revealed that 31 percent of white Americans, almost forty million, told an interviewer they do not believe that they are full and equal citizens.[45]

Three factors contribute to this unhappy state. The first is the broad dissemination of the premises of evolutionary biologists and economists, which award priority to acts that benefit only the self. The second is the absence of a small number of values that a majority agrees are always good and a small number of other values that are absolutely bad and must be defeated. The third is our culture's habit of relying only, or primarily, on the amount of economic gain or loss to decide on the correctness of a life decision or government program.

A team of social scientists who had a rich corpus of

psychological and health information on more than seventeen thousand British adults who had been evaluated as children and adolescents restricted their analyses to one outcome—the person's income as an adult. An essay in the December 18, 2010, issue of the *Economist* suggested that twenty-year-olds planning to work five or six years for a PhD degree should reconsider their decision because they will only earn 3 percent more than those with a master's degree. There was no discussion of the psychological satisfactions a historian, anthropologist, linguist, philosopher, biologist, or mathematician might enjoy because each decided to pursue a life of intellectual inquiry.

Some students at Rutgers University who learned in 2011 that Toni Morrison would receive thirty thousand dollars for giving the commencement speech that year might reason that if Morrison's visit to their university was a "gig" for a handsome fee, perhaps they were guests at a fancy hotel rather than youth awarded the privilege of exposure to adults and information that might provide answers to their most pressing questions. It is not surprising that the young are confused. Tony Judt recalled, "For thirty years students have been complaining to me that it was easy for you: your generation had ideals and ideas, you believed in something, you were able to change things. We (the children of the eighties, the nineties, the aughts) have nothing."[46] This may be one reason increasing numbers of couples in developed nations are wondering whether they should bring a child into a world they believe is careening toward calamity.

Humans cannot resist inventing goals they believe they should attain. Their families, life experiences, and culture persuade them that the attainment of a few select prizes will allow them to whisper to themselves at the end of a day, decade, or life, "Well done." The historical and empirical evidence imply that most people feel satisfied with their lives when they believe they have met, or are making progress toward meeting, the values they chose as deserving loyalty.[47] Most adults remain happy as long as their pursuits encounter only brief interruptions that they sense can be overcome. The function of governments with benevolent intentions is to find a balance between imposing minimal restraints on the variety of individual pursuits while increasing the social harmony of the larger community and the health of an increasingly polluted planet that will soon host seven billion egos eagerly pursuing their diverse dreams.

Judgments of well-being, made in less time than it takes to thread a needle, reflect various combinations of four conditions: a personal evaluation of the ethical integrity of one's life, inborn temperamental biases, an estimate of the wealth, freedom, and opportunities enjoyed by the respondent's society compared with those in other nations, and the natural tendency to deny unpleasant facts in order to persuade the self that it has all it wants. Since it is impossible to know the differential contribution of each of these conditions to a single judgment of well-being, or to the judgments of a thousand persons, we should question the practice of treating these reports as profound insights into the minds and hearts of a society. An exchange between the two tramps in Samuel Beckett's 1956 play *Waiting for Godot* captures my skeptical evaluation of the usefulness of the evidence on well-being.

> Vladimir: Say you are, even if it's not true.
> Estragon: What am I to say?
> Vladimir: Say, I am happy.
> Estragon: I am happy.
> Vladimir: So am I.
> Estragon: So am I.
> Vladimir: We are happy.
> Estragon: We are happy. What do we do now, now that we are happy?
> Vladimir: Wait for Godot.[48]

THREE

Who Is Mentally Ill?

The number of adults diagnosed with a mental illness has been growing steadily over the past fifty years and absorbing a larger share of the health budgets of many nations. The physicians in some countries have invented what seem like new illness categories. Swedish psychiatrists decided that "burnout" was a mental disorder.[1] Actually, this category is not novel but the return of a popular nineteenth-century belief that the increased pace of modern life, which required long hours of work, excessive pressures for meeting deadlines, and mastering unfamiliar technologies, was causing a serious loss of bodily energy. This loss led to the symptoms of fatigue and insomnia called neurasthenia.

Experts estimate that about one-fourth of Americans older than age eighteen (close to sixty million) had at least one bout of mental illness during the previous year. It is important to note, however, that only 10 percent of this group (about six million) had symptoms so disabling they required professional help. Most of the sixty million were coping with their responsibilities in a satisfactory way.[2]

The current psychiatric handbook, the *Diagnostic and Statistical Manual of Mental Disorders*, abbreviated as DSM-IV, describes more than three hundred mental illnesses, which is more than three times the number found in the first handbook, published in 1952. This increase would not be a problem if the larger number was the result of reliable research revealing that each illness had a distinctive biology and/or life history. Unfortunately, the list of illnesses is based on the majority opinion of experienced psychiatrists and psychologists who debate the validity of each diagnosis while sitting around large tables.

More important, most of the illnesses are defined primarily by the patient's verbal descriptions of symptoms that cause intense personal distress or interfere with the ability to meet the day's responsibilities. Psychiatrists rarely include behaviors observed in the patient's life settings or biological measures as essential elements in the diagnosis. A few personality profiles are called illnesses simply because a majority of Americans regard the traits as violating their ethical notion of what is appropriate. Psychiatrists invented the category "narcissistic personality disorder" to describe adults who are interested only in their pleasures, are unusually arrogant, and need reassurance from others affirming their superiority. I know several successful men who fit this description. But none regard themselves as unhappy, all cope adequately with their responsibilities, and they would be insulted if told that they were mentally ill.

Most physical diseases are defined by the biological processes that produced the symptoms rather than by the complaints patients report to their physician with the limited vocabulary characteristic of daily conversation. Although the official definition of a mental illness is supposed to be indifferent to its frequency, it is usually the case that a minority satisfy the criteria for a disorder.[3] This is not true for physical diseases. If 60 percent of the adults in a particular region of a country had the HIV virus and the early symptoms of AIDS all would be classified as ill, independent of their feelings or daily functioning. If 60 percent of Americans reported in 2011 that they felt anxious over the current economic recession, warming of the oceans, and the threat of another terrorist attack, most clinicians would regard them as responding appropriately and would not classify them as mentally ill.

When social conditions create a sharp increase in despondency or worry among many members of a society, which occurred in America during the depression of the 1930s and the threat of nuclear destruction during the cold war, most commentators regard the society as sick. This was the theme of Philippe de Broca's popular 1966 film *King of Hearts*, which portrayed the lighthearted mood of a group of mental patients housed in an asylum in a small French town who were simultaneously shocked and saddened by witnessing the mutual destruction of platoons of French and German soldiers during the First World War.

Whenever historical events disrupt social arrangements that have existed for many generations, uncertainty penetrates the moods of the populace, and many look for a scapegoat to blame. The persecution of witches from the twelfth to fourteenth centuries is a classic example. During this period the church had become corrupt and full of dissension, the feudal estates were being replaced with nation-states, and urban groups were challenging the power of the rural gentry. Satan was charged as the culprit. Those who were different from the majority were accused of being possessed by Satan and plotting malevolent actions against innocents. Today, increasing economic inequality, religious and ethnic diversity, radical Islamic groups threatening random bombings, and always the danger of a nuclear explosion have raised the level of distress among citizens in many developed nations, but genes and early experience, rather than social conditions, are nominated as the villainous causes of these moods.

Worry, sadness, guilt, shame, frustration, and anger are frequent experiences among humans in all societies. Fear assumed special prominence during the medieval era, when anxiety over God's wrath was a preoccupation. Augustine regarded anxiety as adaptive, for it motivated greater civility. A thousand years later, John Bunyan affirmed that a fear of God was a blessing because it facilitated a love of the Deity. Contemporary experts are certain that chronic fear is an abnormal state that restricts the ability to love. These facts invite a closer examination of the meaning of an abnormal psychological state.

A majority of psychiatrists contend that the brain states, emotions, and actions that define a mental illness are abnormal, meaning that they reflect processes nature did not intend to be a general human characteristic. A mental illness is assumed to be analogous to malaria. If, however, most humans experience at least one serious, although temporary, bout of depression or anxiety during their lifetime, it is not obvious that these states reflect abnormal brain profiles produced by deviant genes. Gregory Miller, a respected scientist working in this area agrees, "We must be vigilant against indefensible but popular . . . claims that most illness is simply a brain disorder, a chemical imbalance, or a genetic problem." Samuel Beckett had one of the characters in his play *Endgame* remark, "You're on earth, there's no cure for that."[4]

Adults who become depressed, irritable, and insomniac because the person they loved rejected them are not experiencing "abnormal" emotions that are unusual in our species. Michelangelo Antonioni's 1957 film *The Outcry* portrays a mechanic, Aldo, who is deeply in love and living with a woman whose husband had deserted her. When news of the husband's death arrives, Aldo anticipates the joy of marrying the woman and becoming the legitimate father of a preadolescent girl their union had conceived. The woman's unexpected rejection of Aldo precipitates a year of wandering the countryside marked by deep despondency, irritability, and insomnia. At the end of the film Aldo returns to the village where the woman lives hoping for a reconciliation, sees through a window that she has a new infant, goes back to the refinery where he used to work, and climbs to the top of one of its tall towers. The woman had caught a glimpse of Aldo when he peeked in the window and follows him to the refinery. She yells to him as he stands on the top rung of the tower, he waves to her, begins to sway back and forth as if he has lost his balance, and falls to his death.

Aldo meets all the psychiatric criteria for a diagnosis of serious depression. The question is whether his symptoms are abnormal products of a biology that is unusual among members of our species. If most humans are capable of becoming as despondent as Aldo after losing a cherished goal they had idealized, whether a love relationship, child, prize, or position of high responsibility, and I suspect this is the case, it is necessary to separate the concept of *depression* from the concept of *illness* or *disease*. Psychiatrists are treating these two ideas as synonyms. Almost all humans develop one or more painful dental cavities during their lives. Neither dentists nor patients regard tooth decay as an illness that requires an abnormal biological vulnerability that only a few individuals possess. It is probably true that, during their lifetime, 25 percent of Americans have suffered at least one serious bout of depression or form of anxiety that interfered with their functioning. Scholars who study the semantics of language can debate whether this means that 25 percent of Americans had a mental illness! Eighteenth- and nineteenth-century social scientists expended extraordinary energy gathering national statistics on birth, death, and marriage rates. Today, experts add documentation of the rates of mental illness. Both groups assumed that the numbers reflected important laws governing human nature.

Intense personal distress is the criterion psychiatrist use most often to define most mental illnesses. A woman who cleaned her home daily, washed her hands frequently, checked all doors twice before leaving the house, and saved every elastic band might not be diagnosed as mentally ill if these habits were not bothersome and she was effective in her marital, parental, and occupational roles. A woman with exactly the same traits who was distressed by her persistent urge to implement these rituals would be diagnosed with a mental disorder. The same is true for the many wives who do not have a frequent desire for sex with their husbands. The only women who would be regarded as mentally ill are those who were upset because they believed their weak libido was abnormal. Many contemporary Americans, especially older adolescents and adults under age fifty, find it hard to inhibit an urge to check their cell phone, Blackberry, or laptop computer for an incoming message or to send one. This behavior meets the criterion for a compulsive ritual. But few who engage in this behavior are bothered by this practice; indeed, most enjoy it. Hence, this habit is not yet regarded as a sign of an obsessive-compulsive disorder.

The authors of DSM-IV confessed that their definitions of most mental illnesses were not clear enough to allow experts to discriminate perfectly between those who were ill and those were not. They were aware of individuals like Aldo and wanted to exclude intense emotional reactions that were appropriate or typical reactions to a situation. Treating prolonged bereavement following loss of a beloved spouse as an illness is tantamount to reducing the dignity of a broken heart to a biological abnormality requiring medicine.[5] This decision, however, opens a Pandora's box containing a host of ambiguous cases. A youth encouraged by his peers to murder a member of a rival gang acted in accord with the mores of his social setting.

Psychiatrists wriggle out of this dilemma by arguing that the symptom has to reflect a "dysfunction" in the person's biology. Unfortunately, the meaning of *biological dysfunction* is ambiguous, leaving the boundary between mental illness and normality fuzzy. Richard McNally's elegant summary of the research on mental illness arrives at the same conclusion. The current list of mental disorders composed by a committee of psychiatrists and a few psychologists sitting in hotel rooms arguing about the criteria for each illness might resemble the list composed by a committee of gods on Mount Olympus who, having watched humanity for eons, arrived at a consensus on the discontents that plague this species.[6]

The problem with a heavy reliance on the opinions of experts is evident in the judgments of twenty-five eminent American sociologists who, in 1916, ranked the major ethnic and national groups on a variety of psychological traits. Not surprisingly, white Americans who emigrated from Germany or England were classified as possessing the highest intelligence and the best ability to control impulses. The experts ranked Slavs, southern Italians, and Negroes the lowest on these qualities.[7]

This chapter and the next make four major points. First, most, if not all, current DSM-IV categories for mental illness have more than one origin in patterns of biology, experience, and social circumstances. The conditions that contributed to each symptom profile should be added to the patient's complaints. The addition of this new knowledge would result in new illness categories that combine symptoms with their origins. Patients who are perfectionists and anxious with strangers but free of depression because they possess one pattern of genes and life experiences should be assigned to a category different from the one assigned to patients who combine social anxiety with depression but possess no signs of perfectionism because they possess a different pattern of genes and life experiences. At present, both patients are typically diagnosed with "social anxiety disorder" because that is the salient symptom and because health insurance companies require one standard diagnostic label before they will pay the doctor. Current categories for mental illness can be likened to the arrangement of foods in a supermarket where pragmatic considerations determine the location of a product. Cheese, milk, yogurt, and steak, with a common origin in cows, are found in distinctive places to make the shopper's task easier.

Second, I describe the attempts to find inherited features that are not symptoms but predict symptoms. These features are called endophenotypes, and their discovery will hasten important advances, even though many problems trail this effort. My third aim is to summarize the evidence pointing to an absence of specificity in the treatment of mental disorders with a drug or a form of psychotherapy. Finally, I suggest that clinicians and investigators will profit from reflection on the cultural and historical contexts in which symptoms appear. The meanings of reports of worry or apathy are more susceptible to cultural and historical influences than complaints about the chills and fatigue accompanying an infection with the malarial parasite. I do not deny that a great many children and adults suffer from intense worry, sadness, guilt, frustration, anger, or loneliness. No one quarrels with that fact. The critical questions center on the best categories for these states, their origins, and the most effective ways to treat them.

The most serious problem with current diagnostic schemes for mental illness is that almost all of the categories have more than one set of causal conditions.

There are at least four reasons why about 3 to 5 percent of American adolescents willfully inflict harm on their bodies, often by cutting, scratching, or burning their skin. Most engage in this behavior to distract themselves from intrusive feelings of guilt, sadness, or anxiety. Others do so as a way to announce their need for help. A third group feels guilty over some action or thought and the self-imposed harm is treated as a punishment. Last, some who are deeply apathetic cut their skin to generate some feeling, even if it is unpleasant.[8]

The features of each current disorder are analogous to the pain of a headache that can be the result of a variety of distinctive conditions.[9] The contemporary concept of cancer provides a better analogy. Only fifty years ago most physicians mistakenly believed that all cancers had a viral origin. Contemporary experts agree that cancer refers to a large number of diseases, each with a distinctive biological origin and physiological pathway and often influenced by events in the environment. A tumor of a particular organ, say the prostate gland, can arise from different biological conditions. Even ancient Greek physicians distinguished between the madness caused by divine intervention and similar forms of frenzy due to environmental events, such as the bite of a rabid dog or a loss of wealth.

Psychiatrists have been reluctant to acknowledge the complexity in the origins of mental illnesses. A large number regard all disorders as the outcomes of deviant genes whose products produced abnormal brain states. Although uncommon, some symptoms result from an abnormal physiology in sites outside the brain. An overactive thyroid gland or an autoimmune disease can occasionally produce the symptoms of a psychosis. Americans with schizophrenia usually die earlier than expected because of a cardiovascular problem.[10] Communities isolated from the facts of modern medicine, including small towns in Mexico and an Ojibwa tribe in Manitoba, classify a number of diseases by their cause. A bout of diarrhea followed by eating a certain food is awarded a name different from the name given for the same symptom if it follows an emotional stress. The second-century physician Galen, as well as Robert Burton in his classic seventeenth-century treatise on melancholy, acknowledged that many conditions, including diet, climate, season, lifestyle, and the balance among the four humors, can lead to symptoms of melancholia and believed that the treatment should be based on the presumed cause.[11]

The main historical trend over the past two thousand years has been a replacement of the broad concept of *madness*, understood to have different origins, with an increasingly large number of illnesses based only on presenting symptoms. This decision was necessary because psychiatrists are not paid by insurance companies if they do not arrive at a diagnosis that other experts would agree on. They cannot include the origin of the symptom as part of the diagnosis because no one understands the complex interactions of biological and experiential conditions that can precipitate any current disorder.

Paul McHugh tried to find a balance between these two perspectives by proposing four families—or generic categories—of mental illness that include presumed origin as a seminal feature of the category. Although each family contains varied illnesses with distinctive causes, the illnesses belonging to the same family share a few critical features, especially the conditions that are the origins of the symptoms.[12]

McHugh made three assumptions. First, each family contains different combinations of biological vulnerabilities, past histories, and current circumstances. Second, a form of anxiety or depression can be present in any of the four families. Third, some individuals develop symptoms as a result of their life history and/or current challenges and need not possess a special biological vulnerability. Clinicians born after 1970 may not appreciate that during the first half of the last century most professionals believed that the seeds of most adult illnesses were detectable in childhood. Close to one-half of American cities established child guidance clinics between 1909 and 1932 with the responsibility of detecting and treating deviant childhood moods and behaviors in the hope of preventing serious adult pathology. While a graduate student I worked part-time at the major child guidance clinic in New Haven in 1953. The experience that year strengthened my resolve to become a child psychologist because I had concluded that crooked thoughts, not deformed genes, were the foundations of most cases of unhappiness.

I add four premises to McHugh's reasonable trio. First, a precipitating event, which can be a change in one's circumstances, is usually necessary to transform a vulnerability into the symptoms of a mental illness. Filipino-Americans who have immigrated to San Francisco are at a higher risk for abusing alcohol than members of the same ethnic group living in Honolulu because the former have too few Filipino-Americans available for social support. First-generation Latino immigrants who have lived in North Carolina for a brief time are at a higher risk for an anxiety or depressive disorder than Latino immigrants who have lived in the same region for a longer time because the former feel marginalized in the community.[13]

Extremely shy individuals who feel anxious with strangers are likely to experience frequent distress if they take a job in a bureaucratic institution where they must interact with others continually. Equally shy individuals with the same biology who are scholars on a university faculty or writers working at home are better able to control their social contacts and are protected from frequent distress. The physicist P. A. M. Dirac, the biologist Rita Levi-Montalcini, and the writer T. S. Eliot, all Nobel laureates despite their chronic social anxiety, were able to mute their discomfort because they could remain apart from others for long periods. An adolescent with a genetic vulnerability for a callous attitude toward violating community norms requires a group of like-minded peers to commit acts of gang violence. An adolescent with the same vulnerability who lives in a small, rural community without gangs is far less likely to engage in these behaviors. Most research designed to discover the predictors of conduct disorder or criminal activity ignores the person's current life setting.[14]

Genes alone cannot explain why, during the past forty years, the risk of imprisonment of American white males who did not graduate from high school was twenty-eight times the risk of white males with a college degree nor why the likelihood of imprisonment in America was six times the rate in Canada, seven times the rate in France, and ten times the rate found in Sweden.[15] The youth of my generation, born during the second and third decades of the last century, did not have easy access to cocaine or guns and there were few cases of cocaine addiction or school massacres. There were, of course, angry or marginalized youth, but they expressed their anger by bullying timid classmates. They did not murder peers they did not know.

The brain and psychological states created by genes and early history limit the number of possible psychological profiles that might develop, but a large number of alternatives remain, and as I noted in chapter 1, the person's current setting selects one set of symptoms from the larger collection. A painter's initial brush strokes on a fresh canvas restrict the number of final products but do not determine only one final, aesthetic form. The photons that emerge from an excited atom were not in the atom but were created when the atom's state was altered. Analogously, a symptom is not inherent in a gene or brain profile but emerges when individuals with a certain vulnerability encounter obstacles they cannot overcome.

Second, the patient's interpretation of events and the feelings that follow, not the events that a camera would record, are primary causes of most symptoms. The victims of war, crime, rape, earthquake, or a hurricane are likely to develop the insomnia and anxiety that define posttraumatic stress disorder (PTSD) if they interpret the disaster as implying that they are partially responsible for their distress, are vulnerable to a further catastrophe, or regard the trauma as having significance for their personhood. Those who experienced exactly the same disaster but regarded it as a chance event with no implications for their virtue, future safety, or identity are usually protected from PTSD symptoms.[16]

Religious Israelis living in areas vulnerable to terrorist attacks were less likely to develop posttraumatic stress disorder than non-religious Israelis residing in the same dangerous locations. It is rare for both the wife and husband who were injured in the same serious automobile accident to develop an anxiety disorder. Dangerous storms, deaths of relatives, illness, and rejections by friends are common experiences. If a woman rejected by a formerly close friend felt that the rejection did not diminish her sense of self, or she decided that she did not need the friend who snubbed her, the risk of developing symptoms would be small.[17]

A diary entry by the German writer Thomas Mann recorded when he was fifty-eight reveals the power of private interpretation to mute the seriousness of bouts of melancholy. Mann had experienced frequent depressive episodes and had attributed them to overwork. On the morning of March 15, 1933, he wrote, "This morning . . . I was free of the morbid dread that has depressed me for hours on end these last ten days. . . . It is a fear-ridden, intense melancholy such as I have previously experienced

. . . when parting from material things. It is clear that what is involved is the pain of leaving a long-familiar situation. . . . I must find a new basis for my existence. . . . I view this necessity as spiritually beneficial and I affirm it." Mann sought an explanation for his past bouts of depression, and the one he chose made him feel better.[18]

If, however, individuals believe that they made a willful contribution to their unhappy condition, they can become vulnerable to a corrosive guilt that can precipitate the symptoms of a mental illness. The dramatic rise in suicides among Japanese adults from 1993 to 2003 mirrors the rise in unemployment across the same interval because the men and women who lost their jobs blamed themselves for their precarious financial position and inability to contribute to the support of their family.[19] Most Americans who lost their jobs after the economic crisis of 2007 blamed banks, mortgage companies, their employer, or the government. Some blamed all four.

The events psychologists call life stressors have two different definitions. The one that is popular, because it is easier to measure, is based on the objective event, such as storms, assaults, or loss of a parent. An alternative definition places the meaning of a stressor in the person's interpretation. The definition of art provides an analogy. Most art critics prefer to classify an object as art by its intrinsic features. A minority share Marcel Duchamp's opinion that the creator's intention determines which products are art. If Duchamp built a urinal with the intention of displaying it in a museum, it would be art. If he planned to sell the same object to a plumber, it would be a urinal.

Not only are private interpretations of stressful events the critical elements in the causal cascade that leads to the symptoms of many mental illnesses, but they are also the basic elements in psychological theories of human functioning. The symbolic networks that comprise interpretations are as fundamental in psychology as quarks are in physics and genes in biology. Because personal understandings of experience are invisible, they are analogous to the missing fossils of animal forms that Darwin believed had to exist in order to explain how some invertebrates evolved into vertebrates.

One measure might reflect some aspects of meaning making in the brain. Whenever the meaning of an event violates the one expected, the brain generates a wave form about four-tenths of a second later. The magnitude of that wave form mirrors the severity of the violation of meaning. A woman I shall call Mary Jones, who believed she was unlovable, would show this wave form if she read on a screen, "Mary Jones is liked by all her friends." And a woman named Alice Smith, who was certain that all her friends loved her, would show the same waveform if she read, "Alice Smith is not liked by any of her friends." Although interpretations are accompanied by, and emerge from, brain activity, they cannot be translated into sentences that only describe neuronal activation.

Third, the unexpectedness of an experience enhances the intensity of the emotions that contribute to a symptom, in part because unexpected events are usually accompanied by the secretion of brain chemicals, such as dopamine and norepinephrine, that activate many sites contributing to emotions.[20] A marital quarrel is far more distressing for a child in a family where such quarrels are rare than for a child who has become accustomed to frequent quarrels between the parents. A majority of contemporary middle-class Americans born after 1960 enjoyed lives that were generally free of major stressors. They did not have to worry about food, shelter, polio, tuberculosis, or premature parental death and, unless they enlisted in the armed forces, never suffered the wounds of war. Against this gentle background, the emotions that follow the loss of a friendship, rejection by a college or professional school, or failure to be promoted will be more intense and distressing than they would have been in the adults born between 1915 and 1925, who lived through the depression of the 1930s and served in the armed forces during the Second World War. I suspect that the so-called epidemic of anxiety and depression among middle-class Americans under fifty is due, in part, to the absence of serious trauma during their earlier years, which generated an exaggerated reaction to frustrations and losses that are common human experiences.

Fourth, the belief that one can do something to alleviate distressing symptoms is always relevant. A bout of anxiety or depression is always more disturbing if individuals believe they are unable to deal with the crisis responsible for their emotions or cope with the intrusiveness of the feelings. Depressed British patients were far more likely than other English citizens to suffer from a variety of chronic physical ailments, including ulcers, asthma, thyroid deficiency, obesity, or hypertension. These illnesses, which are difficult to cure, contribute to a mood of despondency that the patients feel impotent to alter.[21]

McHugh's first family of illnesses is defined by serious deficits in attention, memory, reasoning, language, regulation of emotion, or states of consciousness that are usually due to genetically based abnormalities in brain anatomy or chemistry. These symptoms have always been regarded as signs of a serious disorder, which earlier generations called insanity. A majority of these patients inherited one of a large number of alterations in their genomes. A decade ago most experts believed that each of these illnesses was the result of one or more mutations in a nucleotide that was part of a gene (for example, the nucleotide guanine was replaced with cytosine). Research has suggested that this type of change is less likely than changes in which a number of nucleotides are either deleted or repeated. These changes are called copy number variants. These modifications can affect brain development in the fetus as well as brain function after birth. Although these illnesses have the highest heritability of the four families, their prevalence varies across cultures, due either to the use of different diagnostic criteria or the presence of distinctive genes in the human populations residing in different regions of the world.[22]

The symptoms of this family can, in a smaller number of cases, be the product of prenatal, perinatal, or postnatal events that are not strictly heritable but nonetheless affect the brain's integrity. These conditions include an infection, metabolic disease, or serious stress to the mother during pregnancy or an autoimmune, inflammatory response in the young infant's brain. Pregnant mothers who were exposed to intense hurricanes that struck Louisiana during any year from 1980 to 1995 were a little more likely to give birth to children who would later be diagnosed with autism.[23]

The age when symptoms appear might be a clue to the origin of the illness. Most patients with bipolar disorder, defined by alternating cycles of depression and manic excitement, experience their first symptoms of serious depression during adolescence. A smaller number do not display any symptoms until their third decade. The illnesses in these two groups might be due to different causes. The same is true for many cancers. Cancers that emerge before age fifty have a stronger genetic origin than those that occur after age sixty-five because the latter are affected more by lifestyle and continued exposure to carcinogens in the environment.

Most family 1 illnesses are more common in males, are the most difficult to treat, last the longest time, have the lowest prevalence of the four categories, and their frequency has changed the least over the past century. I suspect, but cannot prove, that their frequency has remained relatively constant for centuries. These patients, which make up less than 5 percent of all mentally ill patients, excluding the diseases of aging, such as Alzheimer's disease and senile dementia, are usually diagnosed as having schizophrenia, psychotic depression, bipolar disorder, or autism.

There has been a dramatic rise over the past decade in the diagnoses of the last two disorders in children. The increased prevalence appears to be due to changes in the criteria used in making the diagnosis. Some children who are very irritable and prone to temper tantrums are being diagnosed with bipolar disorder. This decision is probably incorrect for most of these children do not develop the symptoms that define bipolar disorder in adults. The symptoms that lead to a diagnosis of autism can result from a variety of conditions. When I was a student, most of these children were called "minimally brain damaged." Rather than diagnose all these children as members of an autistic spectrum, which implies a common origin, it is more fruitful to discover the distinctive origins of these symptoms and assign patients to distinct categories based on the causal conditions. This suggestion is affirmed by the fact that children with fragile X syndrome, who are members of the autistic spectrum, possess a brain anatomy than differs from the anatomy of the majority classified as members of an autistic spectrum.[24]

The failure to find a consistently sensitive biological predictor or marker of schizophrenia, autism, or bipolar disorder, despite more than a hundred years of scientific inquiry, suggests that the symptoms that define each of these categories have distinctive origins. For example, the manic phase in bipolar disorder is typically more intense in men than in women, implying the possibility of different origins in males and females. Abnormal levels of dopamine may characterize some cases of schizophrenia but not all.[25]

Some psychiatrists, reluctant to accommodate to these

facts, defend the notion that schizophrenia, autism, and bipolar illness are each unitary diseases with one fundamental cause. This belief rests, in part, on the fact that these illnesses run in families. But that fact does not always guarantee heredity. The incidence of the brain disease called *kuru* was very high in a small number of families in New Guinea villages, leading experts to conclude initially that it was inherited. It turned out, however, that kuru was caused by a virus. The disease ran in families because the close relatives of a victim of kuru ate small pieces of the deceased victim's brain in order to partake of the person's spirit and, in so doing, ingested the virus and came down with the disease.

The attraction to a single cause for each of the current family illnesses may reflect a hidden desire among psychiatrists to make their profession resemble the more respected natural sciences. Physicists claim that there was a singular moment, the Big Bang, that evolved over eons of time to become the current universe. Biologists, following Darwin, believe that the rich diversity in contemporary living forms originated in a single organism that was the first example of life. I cannot inhibit an association to the Judeo-Christian assumption of God as the origin of everything. It may be true that all life did spring from a single form, but I am certain that future research will show that there is not one cause of each of the three profiles currently called schizophrenia, bipolar disorder, or the autistic spectrum.

Membership in McHugh's second family is defined by chronic or acute bouts of intense anxiety or depression that often originate in specific, biologically based temperamental biases that generate either apathy, on the one hand, or chronic vigilance, on the other. Some individuals experience both feelings. The adolescents who had been high-reactive infants were at risk for either or both feeling states. These eighteen-year-olds possessed a chronic vigilance toward any unexpected event and displayed this property to unfamiliar people and objects when they were only fourteen months old. Apparently they preserved this trait for more than seventeen years, because when they were placed in a magnetic scanner that recorded blood flow to the brain but were not told what they might see, they showed a large surge of blood flow to the amygdala to the first presentation of photos of faces with an angry expression. Most high reactives who had not developed a depression or social anxiety, as well as the youths with a low-reactive temperament, did not show this reaction because their amygdala was less aroused by the unexpected appearance of the angry faces.

The private interpretation of either apathy or vigilant tension, however, depends on the person's current circumstances, life history, and always the perception of its source. The patients in this second family are usually diagnosed with depression, a phobia of a specific animal, event, situation, or object, social anxiety disorder, post-traumatic stress disorder, panic disorder, general anxiety disorder, obsessive-compulsive disorder, anorexia, or bulimia. Patients with social anxiety disorder worry over how to behave with a stranger and how the stranger will regard them. The feeling of anxiety in most individuals with a phobia of spiders, cockroaches, or mice reflects a fear of harm or contamination. These are two different states of anxiety.

The symptoms in this second family belong to more than one illness category. Even among patients with a specific phobia, those who are afraid of snakes and those who fear visits to a dentist show very different brain profiles to the target of their fear. The same is true for patients diagnosed with obsessive-compulsive disorder. Specifically, patients whose diagnosis was based only on obsessive thoughts of being contaminated and a cleaning compulsion had an allele in the gene for one of the receptors for estrogen that was absent among adults with other compulsive symptoms. This evidence points to the need to create finer categories based on particular symptom patterns. A phobia of heights or of blood may be exceptions to this rule. A large proportion of the former suffer from a compromise in vestibular function that renders them vulnerable to unpleasant feelings when they look out from a tall building. Many blood phobics have low heart rates and blood pressures and hyperventilate when they see blood or are about to receive an injection. As a result, they feel faint or actually faint for a brief interval. These individuals can become anxious if they do not understand the reason for their bodily reactions. But the origin of their symptom is a compromise in a biological system that is not primarily a brain abnormality or the product of stressful life experiences. These patients should be assigned to a category separate from the ones assigned to patients with one of the other anxiety disorders.[26]

Most, but not all, of these diagnoses are more frequent in females than in males, perhaps because the sexes possess distinctive neurochemical and hormonal profiles. Most scientists assume that the symptoms associated with a specific neurochemical pattern are due to the current actions of the molecules. This is the most reasonable explanation. But nature does not always conform to what seems reasonable to human minds. There is initial evidence suggesting that, in some cases, distinctive neurochemical profiles in adults reflect processes that operated when the fetal brain was developing and these processes altered the brain's anatomy. In these cases, the adult symptoms are partially the result of events in the womb that altered brain functioning in ways that contributed to the later symptoms.[27]

A completed suicide is one of the few symptoms in this family that is more common in males, in part, because men have an easier access to guns and successful suicides require the person to suppress the natural fear (or anxiety) associated with a physically aggressive act. Equally relevant is the fact that a suicide by an American or European does not imply, as it does in Japan, that the person is acting heroically.[28]

The family 2 illnesses are more prevalent among white Americans than among Hispanic, African, or Asian Americans. This fact does not mean that African American males without a college degree and a secure, well-paying job don't experience low levels of anxiety or depression over their disadvantaged status. Rather, it means that most members of this group would not tell an interviewer conducting an epidemiological survey that they possess the features defining these diagnoses. Depressed Chinese Americans regard their mood as especially stigmatizing and, therefore, report bodily symptoms rather than apathy when they see a physician or are interviewed as part of a survey.[29] Hence, population estimates on the prevalence of depression imply that depression is less frequent in Chinese Americans.

Although most family 2 disorders probably have an origin in specific imbalances in brain chemistry, there is considerable variation in the genomes, neurochemistry, brain function, and experiences within any one disorder. Patients with depression display a resting profile in their electroencephalogram that is different from the profile shown by patients with posttraumatic stress disorder. Moreover, the social class of depressed patients affects the pattern of symptoms.[30]

The relatively high prevalence of depression across the world is probably due to the extraordinary diversity in the reasons for a depressed mood. A sudden or chronic illness, disease or death of a loved one, many young children to care for, loss of a gratifying social relationship, poverty, prejudice, task or occupational failure, lack of social support, disappointment in grown children, and frequent marital quarrels are common precipitants of a bout of depression. The heterogeneity in the origins of a depression means that it will be difficult to find a particular gene or set of genes that predict a diagnosis of depression. This expectation is affirmed by the evidence gathered thus far.[31]

Over 40 percent of New Zealand adults who were assessed regularly from childhood to age thirty-two reported at least one bout of depression during one of the assessments. This percentage is much higher than the prevalence of lifetime depression based on the usual method of relying on the individuals' memory of their past moods. The majority of adults who experienced an episode of depression after the loss of a spouse or parent (almost 90 percent) did not meet criteria for this disorder eighteen months later. This observation implies that an episode of depression lasting a month or two, provoked by illness, loss of a job, death of a loved one, or a broken social relationship, is a normal human reaction and perhaps should not be classified as a mental disorder. Eighteenth- and nineteenth-century poets and novelists described moods of melancholy more often than anxiety, and physicians were more concerned with depression than with any other distressing mental state.[32]

A critical feature in most family 2 illnesses is an abnormal level of excitability in a circuit that connects the amygdala with numerous sites in the prefrontal cortex. This circuit renders the person vulnerable to a surge of bodily activity and a vigilant state whenever an unexpected event occurs. Over time, many of these individuals learn to fear the sudden occurrence of these sensations, a feeling that one is losing control or appearing anxious with others. This trait, called anxiety sensitivity, is present in about 15 percent of Americans who become frightened when they feel their heart beating fast, have difficulty breathing, or experience unusual bodily sensations. Since the experiences that can provoke these bodily reactions are common—for example, a power failure, a severe storm, a sudden illness, or lost keys—these individuals can become increasingly tense and defensive over time. This profile captures the personality of Felix in the film *The Odd Couple*.[33]

Historical era and culture, however, can influence the symptoms that emerge from this hypervigilant state. Americans and Europeans would be diagnosed with obsessive-compulsive disorder if they could not inhibit an urge to wash their hands every few hours or take two hours to bathe each morning. Adults with the same risk genes living in adobe homes in desert regions of Arizona two hundred years ago, without easy access to water, would have displayed different rituals that might not have interfered with daily responsibilities as seriously as frequent hand washing or prolonged bathing.

The family 2 patients who starve themselves are diagnosed as anorexic. The increased prevalence of anorexia over the past fifty years has been restricted mainly to adolescents and young adults living in economically developed societies that have a surfeit of food and celebrate the desirability of being thin. The descriptions in historical archives of adolescents or adults starving themselves indicate that this behavior did occur in earlier centuries, but the causes of the restricted eating remain unknown.[34]

Most adolescents who become anorexic have an unusually strong need to be in control of all aspects of their lives. They become anxious if they sense that this control has been compromised, and restricted eating is one way to prove to the self that a measure of control has been regained. One anorexic patient described how she felt when she began to starve herself: "I finally felt as though I was in charge of my own welfare. It was strange but wonderful . . . a sort of powerful feeling." Adolescents or adults with the same need for control, and the same biological vulnerability, born six centuries earlier in Catholic Europe might have joined a convent. Thus, anorexia is only one of several reactions to the same biological conditions. Analogously, the anxiety provoked by a rape, natural catastrophe, or serious accident can be followed by the symptoms of posttraumatic stress disorder or depression, depending on the person's life history and culture.[35]

Reports by experienced clinicians, as well as autobiographies, imply that a small number of patients in this family inherited a special neurochemistry that created a rare feeling tone that the poet Anne Sexton described as hollow or empty when she met with her therapists. One apathetic British woman described her mood: "The sun is shining brilliantly . . . [but] it is cloudy and dark in my inner world and I do not have the energy to construct a bridge which I can cross into this bright parallel reality. . . .

I crave silence and space unmarred by noisy crowds."[36] Individuals with the same neurochemistry, but residing in other cultures, might impose different interpretations on the same bodily sensations. These interpretations could include the belief that one had displeased God, dishonored a deceased ancestor, been a victim of a witch, was possessed by the Devil, was a target of bigotry, possessed a bad Karma, suffered from a disturbance in the body's supply of wind, or had a compromised heart.

Patients diagnosed with obsessive-compulsive disorder often experience intrusive, often amoral, thoughts that include worry over being contaminated, making a mistake, or noticing a disruption in the order or symmetry of their books, furniture, or clothing. Each of these concerns is closely associated with a good-bad evaluation. Blasphemous thoughts, being dirty, making a mistake, and a disordered bedroom can evoke anxiety, shame, or guilt because each violates an ethical imperative. Violations of a moral standard are usually remembered for a longer time than pleasant experiences. Adults asked to recall an early experience to a series of words were likely to remember events that occurred twenty or thirty years earlier when the word implied a moral violation. They remembered more recent events when the words were symbolic of pleasant experiences.[37] My two earliest memories are of moral misdemeanors that occurred when I was between four and five years old. The first involved violating hospital policy by hiding inside my father's large winter coat so that I could visit my mother on the maternity ward. The second was the intention to disobey my father's desperate plea from thirty yards away that I not jump from a small boat trapped in weeds in a region of deep water on a large lake. I did not jump.

One of the most critical unresolved questions is whether a person with a particular genetic vulnerability could develop any one of the family 2 disorders depending on his or her life history and current life conditions or whether each illness category requires its own unique set of risk genes. If the latter were the case, patients with obsessive-compulsive disorder would be unlikely to develop posttraumatic stress disorder if exposed to a serious trauma. If the former were true, a person could develop either or both symptoms depending on his or her life experiences. This question remains unresolved, but the first alternative seems more likely.

McHugh's third family includes patients with a temperamental vulnerability for brain states that are likely to lead to an addiction to drugs, alcohol, or gambling, difficulty inhibiting sexual or aggressive urges, or an inability to sustain attention in situations where concentration is required. E. L. Thorndike categorized these individuals as impulsive types in his 1907 textbook. Between 10 and 20 percent of Americans are assigned to one of these symptom groups, but most meet criteria for more than one diagnosis. For example, close to 40 percent of American children diagnosed with attention-deficit/hyperactivity disorder (shortened to ADHD) also met criteria for conduct or oppositional defiant disorder. Thus, the clinician could have awarded one of these diagnoses rather than ADHD.

These disorders are more frequent in males than females, as well as in youths and adults from less well educated families, and are likely to have a partial origin in compromised functions of the prefrontal cortex. The patterns of genes, molecules, and receptors that affect the prefrontal cortex differ from those that influence the amygdala and its circuitry. The distinction between the illnesses of family 2 and 3 is supported by studies of more than two thousand Norwegian twins. The drug Ritalin (methylphenidate) aids concentration in some ADHD patients because the drug binds to the transporters for dopamine. As a result, dopamine remains in the synapses of the prefrontal cortex for a slightly longer time and facilitates enhanced control, sustained attention, and inhibition of distractibility.[38]

A careful study of more than 4,300 white British seven- and eight-year-olds reveals how difficult it is to find a robust relation between a gene and a diagnosis of ADHD. A molecule called COMT degrades dopamine and norepinephrine in cortical synapses. When one of the alleles of the gene for COMT contains the amino acid valine in a particular location in both copies of the gene, dopamine and norepinephrine are degraded more rapidly. About 25 percent of this group of British children possessed this allele, which is regarded as a risk factor for ADHD as well as for conduct disorder. Unfortunately, 98 percent of the children with the valine allele had neither ADHD nor conduct disorder, implying that this gene is not a very sensitive predictor of either diagnosis. By contrast, both diagnoses were predicted with moderate accuracy by asking the mothers if their child was aggressive with others and showed minimal concern with the feelings of their victims. Similarly, the best predictor of delinquent acts among Russian adolescent boys was their exposure to violence and lax parental supervision. Even though these antisocial boys were more likely than others to possess a rare allele of a dopamine receptor, the genetic information did not add a great deal of predictive power over and above the psychological evidence.[39]

The prevalence of family 3 disorders is susceptible to historical events that affect a community's moral values. The vote by a committee of psychiatrists in the 1970s deleting homosexuality from the list of mental disorders because of protests by gay rights advocates is an example. Supporters of the temperance movement in America assumed that alcoholics were moral failures, not mentally ill. Acts of violence were far more common in sixteenth-century England than they are today. Men who attacked another person, often over property, were fined but were not considered criminally insane.

Contemporary clinicians following DSM-IV guidelines claim that adults who cannot inhibit urges to gamble or engage in sexual behavior may have a mental disorder requiring treatment. Nineteenth-century American physicians would not have regarded gambling as a mental disorder, nor would experts in many non-Western cultures treat frequent sex as the product of abnormal brain activity. Brazil, which holds a relatively permissive attitude toward gambling, had a high level of unemployment in 2010 among young men who had not attended college. These men had a lot of free time, and many turned to gambling instead of crime or watching television to fill the hours of the day. Frequent gambling in this cultural setting might be an adaptive trait.[40]

Uneducated mothers in San José, Costa Rica, with no special skills have two ways to support their family. They can become domestic servants, which pays little, or sex workers, which earns far more money. Although these women are aware of the social stigma attached to their choice, they rationalize their sex work by reminding themselves that the money they earn allows them to be good mothers who are concerned with their child's welfare. Because sex workers are not arrested by the police, they avoid the intense bouts of shame or guilt that occur in settings where prostitution is a serious crime and uneducated women can find other forms of employment.[41] Behaviors that evoke symptoms in one society because they are stigmatized fail to produce symptoms in places where local conditions reduce the stigma because these actions are required for survival. The National Film Guild of Canada made a film in the 1980s portraying a husband who regarded his wife's earnings as a sex worker as an honest way to contribute to the family's finances. The film portrayed the couple so sympathetically that it might have changed some viewers' attitudes toward prostitution.

Each important class of phenomena usually has a salient feature that provides a key to its understanding. The frequency spectra of the energy emitted by a heated atom was a key feature that led to major advances in understanding matter. The helical structure of the four nucleotides that comprise DNA was followed by extraordinary advances in biology. Each of McHugh's first three families has a salient property. A serious loss of reason and logic is a seminal feature of the illnesses in the first family. A chronic mood of vigilance is salient in family 2. An inability to inhibit behavioral expression of strong urges is a defining symptom of family 3.

The symptoms of family 4 disorders resemble those of families 2 or 3, but in these cases the distress or maladaptive actions originated primarily in the patient's life history and/or current social conditions, rather than in the biological vulnerabilities possessed by the patients in families 2 or 3. Persuasive support for this claim comes from the two temperamental groups of infants called high and low reactive. The former were more likely than the latter to be fearful, shy toddlers and introverted young adolescents. A trained clinician who did not know their temperaments administered a standard psychiatric interview to these youths when they were eighteen years old.

Although more high- than low-reactive adolescent males were given diagnoses of social phobia, general anxiety disorder, or depression, the prevalence of these diagnoses was similar for high- and low-reactive females. However, the high reactives who received one or more of these diagnoses, both males and females, were clearly different from the anxious low reactives as infants, toddlers, and adolescents. Specifically, the high reactives had more arches of the back at four months, were more fearful to unfamiliar rooms, people, and objects at fourteen months and, at age eighteen, showed greater activation of the amygdala to the first appearance of a face with an angry expression. In addition, the high reactives maintained activation of the amygdala to repeated sets of incongruous scenes (for example, an infant's head on an animal's body). Many of the anxious low reactives showed arousal of the amygdala to the first appearance of the novel pictures, but their amygdala became nonresponsive to the repeated appearance of the novel scenes.

These facts support McHugh's rationale for family 4. Many of the low-reactive adolescent girls given a diagnosis of social anxiety or depression were dealing with a number of stressors. They were worried about their grades, gaining admission to a good college, and the loyalty of their friendships. Thus, it is not surprising that some reported bouts of depression or anxiety. But these symptoms were not due to the temperamental biases of the high reactives with the same diagnoses who were dealing with similar stressors. Because the low reactives who received the same diagnosis of a family 2 illness as high reactives were behaviorally and biologically different from the high reactives as infants, toddlers, and adolescents, we have to conclude that individuals with very different biological properties can develop the same symptoms for very different reasons. It is likely that the most effective treatment for patients with one or more of these symptoms will depend on the origins of their symptoms.

Many family 4 patients experienced chronic stress in the past and may be encountering stress in their current life circumstances. These events can induce temporary or, in some cases, long-lasting changes in genes and brains. Mice subjected to the stress of repeated defeat by a larger, stronger mouse developed alterations in their DNA in regions controlling the expression of a gene that was part of a cascade leading to increased levels of a stress hormone.[42] This important observation implies that the experiences associated with economic disadvantage might affect genes that, in turn, influence brain sites that influence behaviors and moods.

Family 4 disorders are more common in every society among the economically and educationally disadvantaged, and especially if they occupy a marginalized social position. The 1 percent of Americans who reported a serious gambling problem, as opposed to occasional gambling, were most likely to be African-American men who did not attend college and abused alcohol. Interviews with more than thirty-four thousand Americans revealed that about 10 percent of adults with incomes less than $20,000 (a value that represents the income of the lowest 25 percent of the population) had a greater prevalence of social phobia, posttraumatic stress disorder, general anxiety disorder, or depression, compared with only 5 percent among adults with incomes greater than $70,000 (the top 25 percent). The suicide rate among native American adolescents is three times higher than it is among other ethnic groups or the white majority.[43]

The influence of social class is even present in adults who lived for years in the war zones of Bosnia, Croatia, and Serbia. The increase in the number of Americans diagnosed with a mental illness over the past twenty-five years is correlated with a parallel increase in the magnitude of income inequality between immigrants to the United States from Latin America, the Caribbean, and Asia, on the one hand, and white Americans born in this country, on the other. A similar rise in the incidence of mental illness occurred in the 1870s following the arrival of large numbers of poor immigrants from Europe. A longitudinal study of more than six hundred children born in 1954 on the Hawaiian island of Kauai affirmed this relation. The children born to parents with low incomes and less education, most often Hawaiian or Filipino rather than Caucasian, were at the highest risk for a mental illness at eighteen years of age.[44]

The increased prevalence of depression or anxiety in college students over the past twenty-five years is due, in part, to the enrollment of many more youth from working-class families for whom a college degree has become the only path to higher status. Current economic conditions have led to more intense competition for high grades among the large number of youths seeking admission to a prestigious law, business, or medical school. The harshness of this competition was diluted before 1945 when fewer working-class youth attended college and the implicit understanding among students from wealthy families, who were the majority attending our best colleges, was that gentlemen should be satisfied with grades of B or C. Only poor students on a scholarship had to work for A grades. Today, all students, rich and poor, feel an intense competitive pressure that makes them less willing to offer help or support to their rivals for admission to professional schools. It is not surprising that these new social conditions have been accompanied by a rise in suicides, bulimia, anorexia, and anxiety over failure and social isolation.

The effect of social conditions is not restricted to college students. Young adults in rural China who were not members of the Communist Party were at a higher risk for suicide than those who were members. Adults belonging to a minority group in an urban area of England were more likely to have a mental illness if they lived in a neighborhood where very few belonged to their minority category. Mississippi has a greater proportion of minority adults living in poverty than North Dakota, and the incidence of depression in Mississippi is three times the rate in North Dakota.[45]

The effect of a disadvantaged social status shares features with later-born children in a family. The position of being a younger boy with an older brother creates a special form of psychological disadvantage because the former often feels less competent than the older and is certain that he enjoys fewer privileges within the family. These beliefs often engender jealousy and envy of the older sibling and anger at the parents for seeming to favor the firstborn. It is not surprising, therefore, that there are more later-born than firstborn men who have been imprisoned for a serious crime, even when the social class in which they were reared is the same. The chronic feeling of inadequacy among many later borns often motivates high-risk behaviors as a way to prove that they are competent. Crime is one form of risky action. A form of this trait can even be observed in professional sports. When two brothers were both major league baseball players, the later born stole more bases than his firstborn brother.[46]

In general, the more typical a "symptom" is within a particular class, ethnic, or sex category, the less likely it is due to the genes that are causal for family 2 or 3 disorders. Conversely, the less typical a symptom, the greater the influence of genes. Crimes of violence, especially murder, are least common among upper-middle-class women. The small proportion of upper-middle-class Swedish women who committed a violent crime were most likely to have other family members who committed a similar crime. This relation was not true for lower-class women who committed equally violent acts. The heritability of anxiety or depression is typically greater in adults with higher annual incomes than it is among the poor. Whenever social conditions, such as poverty, have the power to create a symptom, the influence of genes is usually smaller.[47]

A disadvantaged social class position is more often associated with the physical abuse or neglect of children, family violence, and parents who neither encouraged academic achievement nor discouraged aggression in their children. There was moderate continuity of social class position across three generations of Iowa residents, and modest relations between the social class of the grandparent generation and the incidence of problem behavior in the grandchildren. About 2 percent of Swedish children reared by adoptive parents developed a form of schizophrenia in adulthood. The risk was highest, however, among children whose adoptive parents also belonged to a disadvantaged class. Not surprisingly, the sharp rise in mental asylum patients in America following the end of the Civil War, which alarmed many citizens, included an excess of poor immigrants. Although immigrants made up only 15 percent of the population from 1865 to 1885, they constituted over one-third of these asylum patients.[48]

Many cultures designate a small category of bad things to contrast with a larger number classified as good. The former include the Devil, criminals, and addicts. In fourteenth-century Europe, Jews and infidels were contrasted with the pure Christians. The poor and uneducated are a minority in the United States, Canada, and most of Europe, and youths growing up in these families are aware of their deviant, undesirable properties. Most adolescents identify with their parents, family pedigree, and social class and find it easy to conclude that some of the qualities that distinguish their groups from others might also apply to them. When these qualities are a basis for prejudice, derision, and a feeling of shame, youths are apt to come to the conclusion that their hopes are burdened with a handicap. African American women seeing pictures of suffering Africans showed greater activation of brain sites that mediate empathic identification with a person in pain than did white women looking at pictures of whites in pain.[49]

A small proportion of youth who are identified with a group that the majority regard as less virtuous develop a strong desire to prove their worth and nullify their shame through extraordinary accomplishments. The eminent Polish writer Witold Gombrowicz confessed to an identification with his native Poland that he regarded as less sophisticated than the cosmopolitan societies of western Europe. The acclaimed writer John Updike was ashamed of his father's compromised occupational status in his small Pennsylvania town. In his memoir, *Self-Consciousness*, Updike wrote of his adolescent feelings: "I would avenge all the slights and abasements visited upon my father—the miserly salary, the subtle tyranny of his overlords at the high school, the disrespect of his students, the laughter in the movie house at the name of Updike."[50]

On the other hand, youths with a parent or close relative who had a reputation for unusual bravery or accomplishment are tempted to assume that they, too, have a potential for greatness. Jean-Paul Sartre recalled his exhilaration when, as a child, he was told that the volumes on a shelf in the home were written by his grandfather: "How proud I felt! I was the grandson of a craftsman who specialized in the making of sacred objects."[51] Thomas Hunt Morgan, born in Kentucky in 1866, became the first geneticist, and the first citizen of Kentucky, to win a Nobel Prize for discoveries with the fruit fly *Drosophila*. It is probably not a coincidence that, as a child, Morgan was reminded continually of an uncle celebrated by his family and community as a Civil War hero who showed courage, daring, and gallantry. This knowledge often motivates a child to aspire to an equivalent greatness in some domain. Sometimes an identification with an elite family generates an exaggerated self-confidence that leads to unfortunate decisions. If the actor John Wilkes Booth, a second born with an older brother, had not belonged to a family of celebrated actors, he might not have felt that he had a right to assassinate Abraham Lincoln a week after his beloved Confederate armies surrendered.

The failure to measure a person's pattern of identifications is retarding progress in the search for the processes that lead to a mental disorder. This indifference stems, in part, from the fact that a pattern of identifications is the invisible product of symbolic interpretations of elements in a life history. Natural scientists dislike invisible mechanisms. The unseen, less than rational identifications that each person possesses lie outside the sphere of influence of any gene. The resistance among scientists to award influence to unseen forces is why the world had to wait until 1857 for Louis Pasteur's intuition that invisible microbes turned milk sour.

The many investigators searching for the genes that render individuals vulnerable to a psychiatric illness have been frustrated because individuals given the same DSM-IV diagnosis possess different genetic vulnerabilities and life histories. A small proportion of 860,000 Danish adolescents or young adults were born to a parent with one of the family 1 disorders. Although these individuals were a little more likely than others to develop a mental illness, their symptoms covered a broad range of problems, including a psychosis, depression, anxiety, substance abuse, or a problem of adjustment. Most important, they were unlikely to develop the same symptoms as their ill parent. Even more surprising, most of the adults who sought help from a psychiatrist were born to parents with no serious mental disorder. The lack of specificity was also seen in British women who reported sexual abuse during childhood, but the women developed a variety of family 2 symptoms. Even a diagnosis of dyslexia, which is based on sensitive and comprehensive testing of the patient's reading skill, has more than one cause. A team of Swedish scientists could not find any gene shared by the many members of a six-generation family pedigree containing many dyslexics. Since a diagnosis of dyslexia is more reliable and less controversial than a diagnosis of any family 2 or 3 disorder, it is unlikely that any of these illnesses can be traced to one set of genes.[52]

These facts are not surprising because a cascade of processes occurs between a brain state evoked by a stressful experience and a symptom. The probability that one particular symptom will emerge is a function of the combined probabilities for successive phases of the cascade, from genes to brain states, from brain states to feelings, from feelings to emotions, and from emotions to actions.

Let me explain this idea by first applying it to the state of professional football on January 10, 2011. On that day the New England Patriots were a contender for winning the Super Bowl. Because they won 84 percent of their games during the regular season, the best estimate of their probability of winning the next two playoff games as well as the Super Bowl was 0.84. We can estimate the probability of their victory in the Super Bowl by multiplying the probabilities of winning each of the three games; that is, $0.84 \times 0.84 \times 0.84$. The product of these multiplications is 0.59, implying that on January 10 the odds that they would win all three games was only about 3 to 2, not 84 percent, or 8 to 2. The Patriots lost to the Jets on January 16.

We can apply this logic to the probability that a person with a genetic vulnerability for depression will entertain suicide following the loss of a close love relationship. A reasonable guess as to the probability that certain genes will create a brain state generating feelings of low energy and apathy following a loss is relatively high, perhaps 0.7. Assume further that the probability that the person will interpret the low energy level as meaning he or she is sad, lonely, and unable to alter these states is lower, say 0.5. Finally, the probability that this interpretation will be followed by thoughts of suicide is lower still; perhaps the best estimate is 0.2. We can calculate the probability of the suicidal intention by multiplying 0.7 × 0.5 × 0.2, which is .07. Thus, among one hundred persons with a genetic susceptibility to depression who have lost a close love relationship only seven will have serious suicidal ideation. The remaining ninety-three will develop either no symptom or another symptom. This argument helps to explain why the Danish scientists found little relation between the symptoms of young adults and the symptoms of their seriously ill parents.

The absence of a close correspondence between the symptoms of a mentally ill parent and those in their offspring has led many investigators to search for inherited features that are not symptoms but are part of the causal cascade leading to the symptoms and closer to the biological processes responsible for the symptoms. These features are called endophenotypes. An endophenotype can be a measure of brain anatomy or function, an aspect of the brain's neurochemistry, cardiovascular profile, or pattern of muscle activity, or any one of a large number of behaviors measured in a laboratory. Nineteenth-century European physicians and the public, including Charles Darwin, believed that some facial anatomies were sensitive signs of a mental illness, and asylum directors regularly photographed the faces of incoming patients. Today directors of mental institutions would order a brain scan.[53]

The demand that every endophenotype be part of a causal cascade for a specific disorder may be too strict a criterion at the present time because of the brain's massive interconnectivity. The brain resembles the Internet because no one site is always more influential than the others. An excited thalamus, for example, activates the frontal cortex, which in turn activates the striatum that inhibits the globus pallidus and leads to impaired control of many motor movements. These facts mean that a heritable abnormality in any site in this connected set of structures could be an endophenotype for the frequent hand washing of compulsive patients. It is not possible at present to know which structure is the more important cause of this set of symptoms.[54]

Unfortunately, some candidate endophenotypes are heritable but are not part of the causal sequence for a symptom. Blue eyes are inherited and are more common among Caucasian one-year-olds who are shy with strangers and timid in unfamiliar situations, as well as among adolescents who are at risk for an anxiety disorder. But the genes responsible for blue eyes are probably not the genes that mediate an anxiety disorder. Adult height provides a second example of an inherited feature that is correlated with some symptoms but is probably not an essential element in the causal cascade for a mental disorder. A shorter-than-average height among adult Swedish men was correlated with the probability of attempted suicide. A shorter stature, however, is also more common among individuals born to and reared by economically disadvantaged families. A prenatal infection, unskilled occupation, poor diet, and more frequent illnesses, all of which are correlated with a disadvantaged social class, are probably the reasons for the slightly higher probability of a suicide attempt among shorter men rather than their height qua height.[55]

An unusually high level of activity in a circuit connecting the amygdala with the central gray is a promising endophenotype. This circuit is essential for the display of conditioned body immobility, called freezing, in rats exposed to a signal for electric shock or in monkeys being approached by an unfamiliar human. Some of the four-month-old high-reactive infants I described earlier, reclining in an infant seat, displayed frequent arches of the back when presented with unfamiliar sights and sounds. The arching response, like conditioned body immobility in rats, is mediated by the central gray. My colleague Carl Schwartz, a psychiatrist at Massachusetts General Hospital, has found that the eighteen-year-olds who showed their largest surge of blood flow to the right amygdala to the first unexpected appearance of faces with a clearly angry expression, compared with their blood flow response to later presentations of angry faces, had been, eighteen years earlier, the high-reactive infants who displayed at four months the largest number of arches of the back. They had also showed more frequent avoidance of or intense crying to unfamiliar toys and people at fourteen months and were most likely to utter an immediate cry of fear when a person dressed as a clown unexpectedly entered the room where they were playing. These youths were also at the highest risk for social anxiety or depression. These facts imply that these adolescents had preserved from four months to eighteen years a brain state that rendered them especially vulnerable to a strong amygdalar reaction and an accompanying psychological response to any unexpected event. It cannot be a coincidence that the monkeys who freeze for a long time when a human intruder stands in front of their cage also show the highest levels of activity in the amygdala. These facts suggest that, in young infants, frequent arching of the back to unexpected or unfamiliar events might be a sensitive endophenotype for one of the family 2 disorders.[56]

The large number of possible endophenotypes, combined with the lack of strong hypotheses to guide the selection of a smaller set of markers, poses a problem. McHugh's four families might provide clues to guide this research. For example, abnormal eye movements while tracking moving stimuli, impaired hearing, the inability to identify odors, or being born to a father who had his first child after age fifty show some promise as endophenotypes for the family 1 disorder of schizophrenia.

The autistic spectrum would benefit from reliable endophenotypes because this DSM diagnosis contains a number of distinctive diseases.[57] The pattern of looking at moving geometric forms (resembling screen savers), compared with looking at humans in motion, appears to be a promising candidate for one form of autism. Forty percent of children with a diagnosis of autism, but not one child who was either normal or had serious mental retardation without autistic symptoms, spent more than two-thirds of a one-minute film (more than forty-two seconds) looking only at the geometric forms rather than spending more time looking at the film of moving children. This intriguing fact implies that the origins of the autistic symptoms in this 40 percent differ from the causes present in others with the same diagnosis.[58]

A vulnerability to excessive vigilance, tension, or anxiety to an unfamiliar challenge or situation characterizes many patients in family 2. A hyperexcitable amygdala, especially when accompanied by minimal activity in sites in the prefrontal cortex that monitor the amygdala, may contribute to the symptoms of this family. Thus, it should prove profitable to search for heritable endophenotypes that are part of a cascade that begins with an increase in amygdalar activity to unfamiliar or challenging events. Seven promising candidates include: the combination of low heart rate variability, a high heart rate, and a shorter than average interval between the first sign of the contraction of the left ventricle and the ejection of blood from this site (called PEP and measured in milliseconds), a large rise in cortisol during the first forty-five minutes after waking, large dilations of the pupil to cognitive tasks, minimal time talking when in a group, a risk-averse strategy in tasks requiring a choice between a safe alternative that pays less and a riskier one that pays more, and especially the absence of spontaneous social smiles that involve both the eyes and mouth. The variation in frequency of smiling in infants is under some genetic control, and most anxious and depressed patients smile infrequently when talking with others.[59]

Some possible endophenotypes that are more specific for depression include smaller than expected late positive waveforms in the electroencephalogram to fearful or angry faces and greater activity in the right compared with left frontal lobe or reduced activity in the left frontal area (as indexed by a comparison of alpha power in the electroencephalogram in the right compared with the left hemisphere). Moreover, depressed patients who improve on antidepressant medication are more likely to show left frontal activation and probably belong to McHugh's family 4. The patients who do not improve on the same drugs show right frontal activation and may belong to family 2. Depressives who inherit the long allele of the serotonin transporter also improve more on drug therapy than depressed patients with the short allele. Finally, the ability to detect one's heartbeat might separate depressed patients who suffer from a lack of any feeling (called anhedonia) from depressives who experience intense anxiety along with their depressed mood. The latter group is far better at detecting their heartbeat than the former.[60]

It will prove difficult to find endophenotypes for all patients diagnosed with a depression because, as I noted, the symptom of depression probably has a more heterogeneous etiology than any member of the anxiety disorders. An excitable amygdala is present in a majority of family 2 anxiety disorders, but no one has found a comparable biological feature that is shared by all depressives. Dutch patients with depression belonged to at least one of three distinct groups. The largest category combined intense melancholia with a loss of appetite, weight loss, and early trauma. A smaller group was equally melancholic but had a disproportionate number of women with avid appetites who were overweight. A third group had a milder form of melancholia that emerged later in life and lasted a shorter time. In light of this heterogeneity among depressives, it is not surprising that investigators examining a large number of genes in depressed adults failed to find a single allele that had a highly significant association with the diagnosis.[61]

Behavioral and biological signs of fear are present in many animals, suggesting that it is reasonable to assume that some of these features might be present in anxious humans. It is less obvious that all forms of human depression can occur in mice or rats, in part, because guilt over failure to honor an ethical standard, a frequent cause of human depression, is not possible in rodents. The origins of some depressions are probably unique to our species and simply cannot be found in any other animal. This possibility is supported by studies of the common bacteria called staph, which can cause serious infections in humans. It turns out that staph are more toxic in humans than in animals because of unique proteins that are present only in human blood. I suspect that the depression brought on by guilt over a serious violation of a personal moral standard is unique to our species. There cannot be an animal model for this cause of a depressed mood.

A few family 3 categories should be linked to distinctive endophenotypes. Possible candidates include difficulty inhibiting a reflex motor response (often measured by the inability to suppress the automatic habit of orienting to a sudden change in illumination), combinations of very slow and very fast latencies to respond across many trials of a task, a very low heart rate, and the ratio of the length of the index divided by the length of the ring finger (called the 2D:4D ratio), especially on the right hand.[62]

The 2D:4D ratio warrants some elaboration. Most males have a slightly smaller ratio than most females (range of 0.92 to 0.97 for males compared with 0.97 to 1.1 for females) because the distal section of the ring finger is a trifle longer in males than females. This ratio is modestly heritable in humans and other mammals, and is influenced, in part, by the amount of testosterone to which the young fetus was exposed during the first and second trimesters. Prenatal exposure to male hormone, however, does not seem to be the only determinant of the ratio. Nor has any one found a gene or set of genes associated with the ratio, leading some investigators to question the assumption that prenatal secretion of male sex hormone is the only cause of the established sex difference in the ratio.[63]

Although the magnitudes of the relations between this ratio and a variety of psychological traits are small in an absolute sense and not always consistent, there are some consistent results across a majority of studies.

Women with a masculine ratio were a little more likely to be working in a traditionally male vocation (for example, engineering) rather than at home or engaged in a traditionally feminine vocation. Some girls with autistic symptoms have a very masculine ratio. Men with very masculine ratios are taller; have broader faces, greater muscle strength, larger testicles, more sexual partners and frequent short-term romantic relationships, fewer eating disorders, and more traffic violations; regulate anxiety more effectively; and are at a higher risk for developing prostate cancer. The finger ratios in fossil specimens of earlier human species reveal more masculine ratios than those in the modern species of *Homo sapiens*. This fact suggests that modern women have more faithful lovers and husbands than Neanderthal women.[64]

The men who work on the busy trading floors of investment firms must make frequent decisions involving large amounts of money in a short time. Those who earn their clients the most money have to control their anxiety because this state can lead to vacillation or impulsive decisions. The men who earned the most money had more masculine ratios than those who earned much less money.[65] This observation implies that a masculine ratio is correlated with a resistance to experiencing high levels of uncertainty or anxiety and might be one element in a pattern of endophenotypes for illness categories characterized by risky actions, low fear, and high levels of physical endurance. These symptoms are more common among children with conduct disorder and adults with a history of criminality or gambling. Although this discussion does not exhaust the evidence on possible endophenotypes, it provides a sense of what has been learned and the much larger task ahead.

Prediction of the emergence of symptoms requires more than knowing a set of endophenotypes. One must also have information on previous life experiences that the person interpreted as stressful. Unfortunately, the evidence for childhood stressors is usually based only on the adult's memory of their past rather than on objective evidence. The reliability of early memories is questionable. First, adults vary in the accuracy of their childhood memories because of differences in the degree to which parents and siblings talked about the stressful events during the intervening years.

Second, the form in which the early experience was registered is important. A five-year-old girl could have stored the experience of genital fondling by a relative as a perceptual image without any semantic labeling or as a semantic representation of a "bad" event. The probability of experiencing guilt later in life should be greater for the latter girl who coded the sexual experience with words such as bad, disgusting, or wrong. Children vary in the tendency to register experiences with perceptually rich images or with words. The likelihood of later distortion of the original event is greater if the child used only words as the vehicle of registration because words, such as bad or wrong, have associations to many other bad things that might not have happened. Thus, the child who coded an act of sexual abuse by an uncle as bad is vulnerable to remembering incorrectly that the uncle was also cruel with animals, selfish, and uncaring. I have no concrete images of my first year in school. If asked to recall the events of that year, I would reply that they were pleasant because I registered those experiences with semantic labels.

In addition, the child's social class and cognitive talents affect the accuracy of recall of the past. Adults who had better vocabularies as young children (most of these children came from homes with better educated parents) had more accurate memories of the past. When written court records were available to confirm that a child had been abused, the memories of earlier abuse were more accurate for adults who grew up in better educated homes. Adults from disadvantaged families, who are apt to experience more life stressors, had less accurate memories of confirmed instances of childhood abuse.[66] This phenom-

enon is due in part to the fact that infrequent or unexpected events are remembered best.

Americans who are unhappy for whatever reason are
tempted to imagine they were victims of earlier trauma.
Young adults who felt they needed clinical help with a
psychological problem had the "intuition" that they had
experienced a trauma as a child, even though they could
not remember anything about the traumatic incident.
About 20 percent of British college students who were
certain that a particular event had occurred during their
childhood later learned from a parent or friend that their
memory was inaccurate. The main point is that people
are not equally accurate in recalling past stressors, and
some imagine events that did not happen.[67]

It is also likely that some individuals possess a brain
chemistry or anatomy that causes them to exaggerate the
distress of a traumatic event that most adults would per-
ceive as less disturbing. Others minimize the severity of
a stressful event that most would experience as very up-
setting. These adults often have a low and variable heart
rate, high concentrations of male sex hormone, low levels of neural activity in the medial part of the prefrontal
cortex, and greater activity in the left compared with the
right frontal lobe. These adults have the advantage of being resilient to threatening events that upset a majority

of youth or adults. The American hostages held in a large building in Tehran for more than a year were released soon after Ronald Reagan was inaugurated in 1981 and flown to an air force base in Germany for psychiatric evaluation. Although all the hostages experienced the same realistic threat to their lives, a small proportion told the psychiatrists that they never became unduly anxious and remained confident that they would be rescued unharmed. It is possible to detect some of these resilient adults in early childhood. Most four-year-olds show facial signs of disappointment when they expected to be given a toy they had indicated they liked but instead received a toy they disliked. The small group of middle-class four-year-olds who showed no disappointment displayed a low, variable heart rate at rest and were described by both parents as sociable, energetic, and able to extract a great deal of pleasure from their daily experiences. The children with this temperament are likely to become the adults who minimize the stress of frustration, loss, trauma, or social rejection.[68]

Taiwanese adults who reported many past stressors possessed the two short alleles of the serotonin transporter and higher concentrations of the dopamine transporter. Both features could enhance the perceived intensity of a stress. Individuals with high levels of cortisol at the time they recall a past experience are less accurate than others, and adults vary in their cortisol levels. Dutch adults in psychotherapy who were prodded by their therapists to remember childhood abuses they initially denied were prone to memory errors—for example, stating that they saw a word that had not been present in a list of words seen previously.[69]

It is also relevant that mildly stressful events, from the perspective of an impartial observer, are far more frequent than serious stressors, such as abuse or death of a parent. However, preadolescents did not remember feeling more intense distress to serious than to mild stressors. Because most adults experience some stressful events during their childhood years, information theory predicts that those who report no stressful experiences probably provide more information to scientists looking for the genes or brain states that contribute to or protect against pathology than those who recall several stressors.[70]

All of these observations raise serious problems for scientists who treat memories of past stressors or bouts of depression and anxiety as accurate when that is the only evidence. The fallibility of memories of the deep past invites a critical questioning of the validity of the notion of "lifetime prevalence of a disorder." If some adults forget a brief depression that would have met criteria for a disorder at the time it occurred, whereas others exaggerate a bout of past sadness that would not have met criteria for a depression, the meaning of "lifetime prevalence" of a mental illness becomes fuzzy.

There are, therefore, good reasons to adopt a skeptical attitude toward the popular belief that childhood stressors make a major contribution to later psychiatric illness, when the only evidence for the stress is the person's fallible memory of the past.[71] I am not claiming that early abuse, neglect, or maltreatment are innocent experiences. These events do raise the risk for a disorder. But I am suggesting that adults vary in the accuracy of their memory for the severity and number of past stressful events. This means that a person's memory of childhood stressors, without any corroborating information, remains a phenomenon to be understood, rather than a sensitive marker of conditions that cause a later psychological problem. This reversal of cause-effect relations shares features with Einstein's reinterpretation of gravity in relativity theory. According to Einstein, gravity is not the cause of an apple falling to the ground but the outcome of masses accelerating in space-time. Memories of childhood trauma are the outcome of a process in which a person's biological and psychological properties react to specific events and should not be treated as accurate proxies for the actual stressors that may have caused later symptoms.

The search for sensitive endophenotypes is also hampered by the fact that measures of brain function, autonomic activity, or behavior that are presumed to be endophenotypes can be influenced by a person's life history or current circumstances. Life history is more important than genes in accounting for the reactivity of the cardiovascular system to a laboratory stressor, even though cardiac reactivity is under partial genetic control. The same conclusion applies to measures of distractibility as an endophenotype for ADHD.[72] Investigators who discover that an inherited trait distinguishes a particular group of patients cannot ignore the possibility that the same trait could have been the product of life experiences.

The frustrations experienced by those searching for a robust relation between a behavior that might be an endophenotype and a gene was revealed in a careful study of more than four hundred middle-class three-and-a-half-year-olds who were observed for several hours in laboratory episodes designed to provoke smiling and interest (called positive emotion) or fear, anger, and sadness (called negative emotion). The variation in positive or negative emotion bore no relation to possession of the short or long allele of the serotonin transporter gene.[73]

It also remains possible that males and females, as well as individuals from different ethnic groups, diagnosed with the same disorder might possess different endophenotypes. The importance of sex was revealed in the discovery, in mice, that maternal genes are more likely to be expressed when the brain is being formed, whereas paternal genes are more often expressed later in development.[74] If this intriguing fact were also true for humans, investigators searching for endophenotypes for mental illness will have to be sensitive to the sex of the patient, as well as that of first-degree relatives with a disorder. Robert Burton noted in *The Anatomy of Melancholy*, published in 1621, that melancholia had different origins in women and men.

African American women generally have a lower risk of suicide than European American women and are more likely to possess the long allele for the serotonin transporter gene, lower oxytocin levels, smaller changes in blood pressure when they wake from sleep, and a distinctive body composition.[75] These facts imply that the genetic contributions to the risk for suicide might be different in women with an African compared with a European pedigree. This suggestion is reasonable because the genes that contribute to the risk for rheumatoid arthritis are not the same in Caucasians and Asians.

These facts, and others, have led a few scientists to be slightly less optimistic about finding a large number of endophenotypes that are sensitive markers of the genes that contribute to a particular disorder, at least in the near future. This more cautious frame of mind is reasonable. After all, a combination of eleven single nucleotide polymorphisms (SNPs) accounted for only 13 percent of the variation in the ability to detect subtle differences in the intensities of sweet liquids.[76] Because the heritable variation in sensitivity to sweet tastes probably rests on fewer genes than any mental illness, investigators are likely to be initially frustrated in their search for alleles that account for a significant amount of the variation in the risk for most DSM categories as they are currently defined.

It might even prove useful to study the alleles responsible for hyper- or hypo-sensitivity to sweet, sour, or bitter tastes as possible endophenotypes. Unpleasant feelings characterize the disorders in family 2. Perhaps the genes that render a person unusually sensitive to bitter or sour tastes might contribute to a susceptibility to forms of anxiety or fear. The history of science is marked by many instances in which a condition no one considered, because it seemed so distant from the phenomenon of interest, turned out to be an important cause. No scientist studying ulcers in 1950 entertained the possibility that the bacterium *H. pylori* might be a significant culprit. Nor did any geneticist in 1950 anticipate that the same gene could lead to different traits in females and males. Nature is replete with surprises, and a less parochial perspective on endophenotypes for mental illnesses is likely to be rewarding.

FOUR

Helping the Mentally Ill

Psychiatrists and psychologists have a choice when they select words to classify a patient's illness category. The noun selected can affect their decision about the best way to help the patient. Many nouns that name categories have preferentially strong associations with particular verbs naming an action. The noun *dog* is preferentially linked to the verb *bark*, but the noun *pet* is more closely linked to the verb *requires*. The three possible noun-verb pairs for cows provide a more apt example. If a cow is classified as a food, the appropriate verb is *eat*. If the cow is treated as a commodity, the preferred verb is *sell* or *buy*. If the cow is categorized as a sacred object, *worship* is the preferred verb.

Clinicians who classify their patients as having a disease, typically those with the disorders of family 1, but also some in family 2 or 3, are biased to search for a drug cure because most physical diseases are treated with medicine. Moreover, the verb *cures* in the sentence "The doctor cures the patient with a medicine" awards all the power to the doctor and the medicine. By contrast, clinicians who categorize their patients' suffering as the product of maladaptive behaviors are biased to prescribe therapies that will help the patient suppress the behaviors and substitute adaptive ones, for the noun *behavior* invites the verb *alter*. Clinicians who practice cognitive behavioral therapy adopt this perspective. *Alter* in the sentence "The doctor helps the patient alter his or her behavior" awards some power to the patient.

Least common are clinicians who categorize the patient's plight as originating in private interpretations of life experiences. The noun *interpretation* is preferentially linked to the predicate *revise,* and these therapists persuade their patients to rethink their understanding of their distress and its causes. The verb *revise* in the sentence "The doctor revises the thinking of the patient" implies that the patient must assume an active role in rethinking his or her premises. Therefore, much of the responsibility for remission rests with the client. I suspect that the clinician's categories for patients have a nontrivial influence on the therapy chosen.[1]

The assumption that most mental illnesses are the products of atypical genes that created abnormal brain states reverses the equally heavy emphasis on experience that was dominant from about 1900 to the late 1960s. The former premise gains its strength from the dramatic advances in biology that led to the discovery of drugs purporting to cure mental symptoms without requiring psychotherapy and a managed health care system that limited payments to clinicians practicing long-term psychotherapy. The use of a drug to treat Americans seeking help with a mental health problem increases in frequency each year. One of every two patients in 2007 were treated only with a pill; only 3 percent received psychotherapy. British psychiatrists are less likely to prescribe a drug as the only treatment because Britain's National Health Service encourages physicians to cooperate with social scientists and social agencies that provide psychological support to patients.[2]

Americans during the first half of the nineteenth century had greater faith in the therapeutic value of altering the person's life circumstances. For example, moral therapy, which prescribed a change in surroundings, social supports, and a religious affiliation, helped many patients.

Experts at the turn of the last century told American parents that childhood masturbation posed serious dangers for the child's health. The popular therapeutic recommendations included dressing the child in loose clothing and ensuring that the child slept on a hard mattress.

Many papers published in the *American Journal of Psychiatry* before 1960 emphasized the social conditions that could precipitate an illness and described therapies that involved changes in the patient's circumstances. These ideas were rare in the papers published in the same journal in 2010 and 2011. Therapeutic changes in the environment were ignored after biologists began to find unusually effective drug cures for some physical diseases in the late twentieth century. The experts who maintained the traditional faith in a material foundation for all natural phenomena, characteristic of Western philosophy for the last twenty-five hundred years, easily defeated the politically weaker proponents of psychological therapies who assumed that nonmaterial emotions and thoughts were the major culprits in mental disorders. In the real world, Goliath usually overpowers David.

The premise that drugs offer the best hope for remission of most symptoms may serve an implicit desire to remove some of the responsibility for an illness from the patient and his or her family and place the blame on the roll of the genetic dice. This perspective is in accord with the egalitarian ethos of Americans and Europeans. Because most mental illnesses are more prevalent among the poor than the privileged, the habit of attributing symptoms to genes has the advantage of not adding the burden of self-blame to patients who are also victims of poverty.[3]

Unfortunately, few, if any, of the currently prescribed therapeutic drugs are selectively effective with the symptoms of most DSM-IV categories. These drugs alter neuronal activity in many sites to create abnormal brain states that often reduce the severity of a primary symptom. Most of these drugs can be likened to a blow on the head and resemble the cocktail of drugs used with many cancers that kill both healthy and cancerous tissues. It is useful to remember that during the period from 1935 to 1955, many psychiatrists were certain that surgically cutting the connections from the frontal lobes to the rest of brain, or removing the frontal lobes completely, was an effective cure for the symptoms of schizophrenia or serious anxiety or depression. Thousands of such operations were performed in many countries. The man who performed the first psychosurgery, Egon Moniz, was awarded the Nobel Prize in medicine for this "discovery." By the 1960s, however, experts recognized that this operation was accompanied by too many undesirable side-effects and, like most drugs, was a "blow on the head."[4]

The unpleasant side-effects that accompany the use of many drugs is one reason why about 25 percent of patients who are taking a drug to reduce anxiety or depression stop after the first prescription is exhausted. It is not a coincidence that experienced German psychiatrists who were asked what they would do if they developed a depression said they would wait and see what happened, rather than take the antidepressants they normally prescribe for depressed patients who come to them for help.[5]

No currently prescribed drug for any mental illness is a magic bullet. Each has a weak rationale, given what we know about the brain, and they remind me of some of the popular cures ancient Egyptians used with anxious or depressed women. These physicians believed that the wombs of these troubled women had drifted from the normal position into the upper part of the body and, therefore, had to be tempted to descend. One regimen involved placing a warmed ibis of wax into the vulva, on the assumption that the fumes would attract the wandering uterus back to its proper place. The sixteenth-century French physician Ambroise Paré inserted a metal pessary in the vagina that fumigated the uterine space. Less than two hundred years ago George Burrows, one of the most respected British physicians treating mental patients, used a therapy in which the patient sat in a chair that rotated at a rate of 120 rotations a minute. Public criticism forced him to give up this therapy.[6]

The drugs most often prescribed for schizophrenics, such as Zyprexa and Risperidal, block one class of dopamine receptors in all brain areas, resulting in a slowing of all cognitive processes. As a result, hallucinations become less salient, but so do many other mental processes. Chronic use of these foreign chemicals can alter brain physiology or anatomy and produce unwanted side-effects. Four martinis each evening reduce anxiety, but they also impair motor coordination and perceptual discrimination and, if taken every day for ten years, can damage the liver.

The antidepressants Prozac and Zoloft, called selective serotonin reuptake inhibitors (SSRIs), slow the absorption of serotonin from all the synapses affected by serotonin. Americans spent more than $12 billion in 2010 purchasing these drugs. As with Zyprexa, these drugs, too, activate many sites, including those that modulate breathing, heart rate, and other functions that are abnormal in panic attacks. The SSRI drugs blunt all emotions and, therefore, mute anxiety as well as joy and excitement. It is not surprising, therefore, that these drugs increase the likelihood of suicidal ideas. A cartoon in the *New Yorker* illustrated a patient saying to his therapist,

"Could we up the dosage? I still have feelings." About 40 percent of social phobics reported some recovery from their intense anxiety after being treated with one of these therapeutic drugs, but major recovery was usually restricted to those who had suffered for a short time.[7]

More important, these drugs are often no more effective with patients who have moderate levels of anxiety or depression than a placebo or a disciplined regimen of physical exercise. Although these drugs relieve the depression of some patients, a few problems, especially insomnia, remain. One hour of intense, recreational physical activity each week reduced the prevalence of combined depression and anxiety in one group of patients from 8 to 4 percent. Few drugs can reduce the prevalence of these symptoms by one-half. Lithium may be a partial exception to the lack of selectivity of most drugs. This medicine appears to reduce the duration and severity of the manic phase in patients with bipolar disorder, although this drug, too, has unwanted side-effects and we still do not know why it works. Application of brief pulses of magnetic current to the scalp over the left frontal lobe, which alters the electrical properties of the underlying neurons, shows some initial promise as a new treatment for depressed patients who show no improvement on any drug.[8]

It is troubling that when a new drug is ready to be tested for efficacy, the drug company needs volunteers to take part in the evaluation, called a clinical trial. It is not surprising that some extremely anxious adults are less likely to volunteer because of an exaggerated concern with the possible dangers of the medicine. This means that a new drug designed to reduce anxiety will usually be evaluated with less anxious, rather than the most distressed, volunteers.

The regular introduction of new medicines for mental illnesses that can be dispensed by any physician, independent of their training or sophistication in mental disorders, tempts doctors to classify more of their clients as mentally ill. The introduction of a novelty, whether a machine, form of psychotherapy, or medicine, can lead to the invention of a new disease. The broad dissemination of inexpensive X-ray machines that measured bone density in the hand and wrist was followed by the invention of osteopenia as a disease, even though there was no evidence that the marginal level of bone thinning that defined osteopenia placed a person at risk for a hip fracture. The latter is a feature of the more serious bone thinning characteristic of osteoporosis, which is a legitimate disease.

The availability of so many drugs advertised to reduce the frequency of anxiety, depression, or distractibility has been accompanied by a sharp increase in the diagnoses of these illnesses. After the drug Ritalin became available in the 1950s, the prevalence of diagnoses of attention-deficit/hyperactivity disorder soared. The recent promotion of Cialis and Viagra has persuaded many men over age fifty, whose testosterone levels were falling for natural reasons, that perhaps they have an erectile disorder. This logic implies that 90 percent of adults over age sixty-five have one or more physical disorders for, compared with twenty-year-olds, older adults have less energy, less libido, less motor strength, less effective immunity, and compromises in a host of other psychological functions that include memory, perception, and speed of reacting to a stimulus.

A small, but growing, number of skeptics are contending that collaborations between some academic psychiatrists and the pharmaceutical industry have unwittingly foisted on the public the false belief that the current drugs for mental disorders have the same degree of specificity as penicillin with infectious bacteria. Joel Paris, an experienced psychiatrist at McGill University, has written a sensible and fair summary of our current understanding of the advantages and disadvantages of drugs. His six major conclusions are worth remembering. Some drugs are helpful with some patients, and we should not throw out the baby with the bathwater. Nonetheless, all drugs are being overprescribed; we still do not know why a drug works when it does; the pharmaceutical industry is corrupting academic psychiatry, and their statements regarding a drug's effectiveness cannot be trusted; psychotherapy is not being used as often as it should with milder cases of anxiety or depression; and a patient's initial report of improvement after taking a drug for a few months is often no different from the improvement reported with a placebo because patients who believe that a medicine will be helpful expect to feel better.[9]

The widespread reliance on drugs for mental symptoms is less than fifty years old. No medicine that was both specific for and effective with any one of the many physical diseases that have plagued humans for the past one hundred millennia was discovered in fifty years. If we arbitrarily designate Hippocrates's century as the beginning of medical therapies for physical diseases, more than twenty-three hundred years had to pass before antibiotics, such as penicillin, were discovered. Voltaire's evaluation of medicine, written almost three hundred years ago, has some relevance to modern psychiatry's romance with drugs: "Doctors . . . prescribe medicines of which they know little, to cure diseases of which they know less with human beings of whom they know nothing." More than two hundred years later, Elliot Valenstein, an eminent neuroscientist who reviewed what had been learned about the effectiveness of therapeutic drugs, reached the same conclusion: "The truth is that we still do not know what causes any mental disorder or how drugs sometimes help patients get better. . . . [The current practice] is like a ship without any navigational guidance being driven forward by a powerful motor through a sea with many uncharted reefs."[10]

One more issue warrants mention. Psychiatrists and psychologists feel an obligation to honor two tenets of the natural sciences: the treatment of mental patients should be based on empirically proven facts, and all psychic suffering, like all physical pain, is dysfunctional and compromises fitness. Most patients agree with these premises. These assumptions ignore the fact that humans try to extract some meaning from their unhappy experiences. The concept of meaning has no place in the natural sciences. The hard disc of a computer contains information, but information is not synonymous with meaning. Biologists would regard the query "What is the meaning of a chromosome?" as nonsensical. But it is not silly for a woman to wonder about the meaning of a sudden bout of depression following the unexpected death of a husband to whom she felt ambivalent. The widow might, in a less than fully conscious mode, interpret her suffering as punishment for her failure to be a more affectionate wife. If the bout of depression relieved some of her guilt, one can argue that it had therapeutic benefits.

The woman's more rational side, however, would want to relieve the discomfort of the depression and lead her to consult a psychiatrist who would prescribe an antidepressant. If the drug were effective, her suffering would be muted and the process of penance halted.

Some adolescents who cut their skin confess that they hurt themselves as a way to inflict punishment for a prior moral violation. Some young children who feel guilty for a misdemeanor that went undiscovered commit another prohibited act in front of a parent in order to receive a punishment that will reduce their guilt. This subtle and usually unconscious process can even be observed in the laboratory. College students who had first submerged their hand into ice water rated the unethical acts they had described minutes earlier as less serious than students who had placed their hand in warm water. Apparently the pain of the cold water diluted the guilt generated by writing down their moral errors. Although a small proportion of individuals possess a temperament that allows them to inflict pain and distress on others without much guilt, a larger proportion acquired their callousness because they interpreted the extreme poverty, abuse, or prejudice they had experienced as an unfair punishment that gave them the right to express hateful actions. In this metaphor, the harshness of their youth was treated as "money in the bank" that they could now spend. Shakespeare captured this dynamic in his portrayal of Shylock in *The Merchant of Venice*.

I suspect that in a small proportion of married couples who quarrel frequently, the reason is that one spouse feels guilty for not meeting the expectations, real or imagined, of the other. One reaction to the guilt is the adoption of an extremely hostile, demanding, or critical posture designed, unconsciously, to provoke retaliation in the partner. If the partner cooperates by becoming angry, the demanding spouse now has a reason for feeling less guilty over his or her failure to meet the imagined expectations.

In Khaled Hosseini's novel *The Kite Runner*, the boy called Amir is unable to excise his corrosive guilt for failing to rescue his loyal friend Hassan from a vicious attack by three bullies. In an attempt to reduce his guilt, Amir suddenly throws pomegranates at Hassan for no reason in order to provoke Hassan's retaliation. Hassan refuses to cooperate. Years later, Amir is able to appease his conscience by leaving his comfortable circumstances in the United States and risking harm by traveling to Taliban-controlled Afghanistan to save Hassan's son from a cruel Taliban leader.

I suspect that, in a small proportion of cases, the psychological suffering that accompanies a symptom has some benefit. The junior senator from Massachusetts,

Scott Brown, noted in a memoir that the psychological distress he endured as a physically and sexually abused child helped him build a shield against serious worry over criticisms of his political stances. Many years ago, when I was about thirty years old, I tore my Achilles tendon while racing back too fast to hit a shuttlecock in an indoor badminton game. While lying in a hospital bed I relived the moment of the accident, trying to figure out why it happened and whether it could have been avoided. Suddenly, a thought penetrated my consciousness which attributed the torn tendon to my excessive competitiveness. The implication was that the accident would not have happened if I did not always try to win. I took that insight seriously. I play tennis now, rather than badminton, but I do not have to win every match, I do not run for balls that are impossible to retrieve, and I have not torn my Achilles tendon again.

I am not suggesting that all psychic suffering alleviates guilt or provokes an important insight, only that this dynamic does occur on some occasions. In these instances, the clinician might hesitate before prescribing a pill and first try to determine whether the patient's suffering might be of some benefit. Psychological suffering, which is not synonymous with physical pain, can have therapeutic advantages. Therapists would serve their patients better if they were more skeptical of the twin assumptions that psychological suffering never helps anyone and all discomfort must be alleviated as soon as possible with a medicine.

The varied forms of psychotherapy are also largely non-specific for most of the illnesses in DSM-IV because the patient's expectation of remission is the critical determinant of the benevolent consequences of any form of psychotherapy. The patient's verbal report of improvement is the usual basis for evaluations of the benevolent effects of any form of therapy, whether drug or psychological. It is not surprising that patients often report greater improvement if the drug they are taking has perceived side effects because they interpret these odd sensations as meaning that the drug must be working, and therefore, they ought to feel better. Because patients spend time and money on their treatment, they want to believe that their symptoms have become less distressing and are likely to say so when asked. Most adults who spent several thousand dollars for a holiday cruise tell their friends that they had a good time, whether or not that optimistic report matches what happened each day on the ship. This phenomenon, called reducing cognitive dissonance, operates in many situations for no one wants to believe that they expended valuable resources on something that had no value.[11]

Patients who believe that a treatment regimen will be effective are more likely to improve than those who have a less sanguine view of their treatment, independent of the specific form of therapy. Chinese patients living in Singapore who consulted a shaman who shared their religious beliefs in Taoism or Buddhism reported improvement, as did natives of Ecuador who sought help from a traditional healer. South Asian women who are depressed believe that they must conserve energy. Depressed American women believe they should expend energy. Hence, therapists treating depressed South Asian immigrants residing in the United States will be more effective if their advice matches the patient's theory of cure.[12]

Well-educated Americans with symptoms are a little more likely to seek psychotherapy rather than a drug treatment because they believe in its effectiveness. Adults who have not attended college rarely request psychotherapy because they do not share that belief. Alice James, the younger sister of both William and Henry, suffered a serious depression in 1878 but she was certain that her distress was a result of her inherited biology. The writer John Cheever suffered a similar depression fifty years later but, influenced by Freudian ideas, was equally certain that his melancholy was the result of his mother's behaviors toward him when he was child. James would have sought a drug cure; Cheever assumed that psychotherapy was the preferred treatment. The evidence suggests that each would be "helped" best by the therapy they believed was concordant with their views of the origins of their illness. Could Martin Luther's anxiety, provoked by his conviction that he saw the Devil, be treated effectively by a cognitive behavioral therapist? Unlike chloride ions, which are always prepared to unite with sodium ions to form salt, life-forms vary in their readiness to be influenced by certain experiences. Some bacteria are not killed by penicillin; some children in a Head Start program do not benefit from the intervention; and not all patients are prepared to be helped by the therapy they receive.

Placebo pills can, on occasion, be as effective as a drug if the patients believe they are receiving a medicine with therapeutic effects. Improvement can occur even when the patients know that they are taking a placebo. Patients with abdominal pain due to irritable bowel syndrome were given a sugar pill and told explicitly that the sugar pill had no active medicine but did have "self-healing properties." Three weeks later these patients reported a greater reduction in distress than the patients taking nothing. It appears that it is remarkably easy to persuade patients that the therapy they are receiving is effective.[13]

The signs of remission in a distressing symptom after taking a placebo are not always only psychological.

Individuals given a placebo they believed would reduce pain showed increased opioid activity in many sites that moderate pain and a muted brain response to the painful event. It is possible, however, that a placebo more often alters the person's appraisal of the intensity of the pain rather than always suppressing the reactivity of the neurons that process a painful event. The expectation of a desired event is usually accompanied by changes in brain chemistry that, theoretically, should be accompanied by a more favorable evaluation of one's state. Parkinson's patients with tremors given a placebo they believed would be helpful secreted dopamine, which in turn affected the brain sites that control motor activity and reduced the severity of the tremors.[14]

Simply having an explanation of one's symptoms can be therapeutic because an understanding of the reason for uncomfortable feelings mutes uncertainty. A forty-eight-year-old woman experiencing intense anxiety because she did not understand why she felt like a man reported feeling better when her doctor informed her that she was born with a chromosomal anomaly (45X/46XY) that rendered her an intersex. Her sexual feelings and biology remained unchanged, but her anxiety was reduced simply by learning the reason for her troubling moods.[15]

Freud distinguished between the normal feelings of sadness following the loss of a loved one and the more chronic depression that did not always require the death of another. In his 1917 paper "Mourning and Melancholia," Freud argued that the melancholic, depressed patient had experienced the loss of a parent's love during childhood. Because the depressed person was identified with the parent, Freud argued that the person "introjected" the features of the hated parent into the representation of self. This meant that the harsh self-derogation of depressed patients was in reality a criticism of the parent who failed to provide the required amount of love. Although few contemporary clinicians, other than orthodox analysts, find this tortuous chain of logic reasonable, many thousands of students, intellectuals, and patients did during the first half of the last century.

Why did so many well-educated adults, including the writer as a graduate student in the 1950s, find Freud's theoretical account of depression persuasive when there was insufficient empirical proof of its soundness? Almost everyone can recall some occasions during childhood when a parent was less affectionate than they wished. Therefore, an interpretation by a famous theorist that nominated this experience as the reason for a melancholic mood was accepted as valid. This principle pervades every therapeutic relationship. When humans do not understand a phenomenon, they are susceptible to accepting any explanation by any expert that is coherent and does not seriously violate their preconceptions. Earlier generations accepted statements by respected authorities stating that women had less bodily heat than men, four body humors determined human moods, witches could cause illness, and savage groups with dark skins were inferior to the light-skinned persons living in the advanced societies of Europe.

These facts imply that the specific form of psychotherapy, whether psychoanalytic, cognitive behavioral, gestalt, or existential therapy, is probably less important than the patient's belief that it will be helpful because the therapist is perceived as wise, experienced, and concerned with his or her welfare. Giorgio Baglivi, a seventeenth-century Italian physician, anticipated this simple truth when he wrote that a therapist who presents a self-assured confidence is more likely to benefit the patient. Five different therapies, which included psychoanalysis, cognitive behavior therapy, breathing training, and muscle relaxation, were equally effective in reducing the anxiety of panic patients because all the treatments created an expectation that the patient would not experience a serious increase in worry when the attack began.[16]

A task force appointed by the American Psychiatric Association, the organization charged with protecting the interests of psychiatrists, concluded that many nonstandard therapeutic interventions, including exercise, acupuncture, and light therapy, appear to have some effectiveness. The National Institutes of Health have established a National Center for Complementary and Alternative Medicine because an increasing number of Americans are turning to meditation, yoga, hypnosis, acupuncture, or breathing exercises for help with anxiety, depression, or an addiction. Many patients receiving one of these therapies reported an improvement in their mood because they expected the procedure to be helpful. One form of breathing therapy advises patients to practice the following routine twice a day. The person alternates between holding one nostril closed for a few seconds and inhaling through the open nostril, then closing the other nostril and exhaling through the formerly closed nostril and repeating this ritual for ten to twenty minutes. The faith in the therapeutic benefits of this practice is reminiscent of the faith of ancient Egyptian women who believed that a warmed ibis of wax placed in their vagina would reduce their anxiety.[17]

Evaluations of close to four hundred different forms of therapy imply that, for most mental illnesses, no one regimen is clearly superior to any other and, in a few cases, the therapy is accompanied by more distress.[18] Fans of Lewis Carroll's *Alice in Wonderland* may remember that when the Dodo was asked who won the race, the reply was that everybody won, and therefore all must receive prizes.

Consider patients with social anxiety disorder who consulted therapists loyal to one of three different regimens. The psychoanalyst will interpret the patient's anxiety as due to childhood experiences and probe their memories and dreams. The behavior therapist will tell the patient that their mood is a conditioned response and try to extinguish it. A cognitive behavioral therapist will implement six routines: help patients understand their symptoms, encourage them to monitor and chart their emotions, teach them to relax, help them detect incipient anxious or depressing thoughts, correct irrational beliefs, and encourage patients to expose themselves to the situations they fear.

Readers familiar with Immanuel Kant may recall that he anticipated some of Aaron Beck's ideas about cognitive behavioral therapy by two centuries. Kant wrote that melancholics suffered from a delusion in which inaccurate, disparaging thoughts about the self intruded into consciousness. Morton Prince, one of the founders of clinical psychology in America, may have read those lines in Kant because Prince published a paper in 1913 describing how he helped a woman with a phobia of church steeples by pointing out the illogical nature of her beliefs.[19]

If patients respect their therapists and implement their advice, they often feel better independent of the validity of the interpretation offered or the therapy prescribed. The therapist's advice is helpful if patients implement the recommendations. But patients implement the advice only if they believe in the therapist's wisdom and the benefits of the prescribed therapeutic ritual. That is why experienced therapists, no matter what form of therapy they use, are usually more successful than novices.[20]

Jerome Frank anticipated this dynamic more than twenty years ago when he suggested that in many cases, but obviously not all, patients improve in psychotherapy when three conditions are met. First, the patient and therapist agree on the cause of the patient's distress, whether or not the presumed cause is the correct one. Second, patient and therapist share the same belief about the best therapeutic regimen, whether or not this assumption is valid. Last, the patient must respect the therapist, believe that the latter values the client and wants her or him to enjoy a better life, and assume that the therapeutic regimen will be effective.[21]

I add one feature to Frank's list. Faith in most therapies is enhanced when it is novel and research has not yet revealed its limitations. In one new form of therapy, patients with an anxiety disorder or hypochondriasis are treated with a series of weekly modules designed specifically for their symptoms delivered over the Internet for a ten- or twelve-week period. These clients never see a therapist or take any drugs. Yet about one in four report a significant reduction in their symptoms, compared with patients who did not take part in the program.[22] If later inquiry reveals that this form of therapy, or any other new therapy, is less effective than promised, or not effective with every patient, both therapist and patient lose some faith in the power of the regimen and the mutual commitment required for cure is diluted. This sequence occurred for frontal lobotomy and psychoanalysis and, in time, may reduce the current effectiveness of cognitive behavioral therapy. This process may have already begun.

Evaluations of the effectiveness of cognitive behavioral therapy with depressed patients, published in 2010, found an initial improvement followed by frequent relapses, which is also true for depressed adolescents treated with drugs.[23] It is probably not a coincidence that cognitive behavioral therapy is about fifty years old. Faith in psychoanalytic therapy in the United States and Europe also began to wane about fifty years after its dissemination, and the first signs of a skeptical view of the specificity of drugs are emerging about fifty years after the manufacture of the first pills for a mental illness. It is likely that by 2060 therapy by means of the Internet will suffer a similar fate.

Unlike Americans and Europeans, the Chinese were not exposed to Freud's ideas during the last century because their traditional cultural values opposed the confession of personal problems to a stranger. Psychoanalytic therapy, therefore, strikes contemporary Chinese as a novel way to help troubled adults. China has recently embraced capitalism and is moving slowly toward the competitive individualism of the West. These changes in values have created new sources of anxiety and depression, and the novelty of psychoanalytic therapy has made it attractive to a growing number of middle-class Chinese who can afford the treatment. I suspect that some troubled Chinese, like some troubled Americans in 1930, will be helped by psychoanalytic therapy simply because they are prepared to believe in its effectiveness. Jerome Frank should be smiling.

Social scientists regularly invent novel interventions designed to improve the academic skills or personality traits of children from economically disadvantaged homes. But these efforts can only be implemented with families who volunteer to participate because they believe that the program will be helpful. Parents who have little or no faith in the program are unlikely to participate. Thus, when an intervention has a benevolent outcome it is because the families or children who were changed were psychologically prepared to improve. This is exactly what happens in psychotherapy. Patients who lose faith in their treatment drop out, and those who never had faith in any form of therapy never initiate treatment.

American educators are troubled by the small percentage of college-aged women who select the natural sciences or mathematics as concentrations and, in addition, obtain slightly poorer grades in these courses. Scientists and educators are looking for inexpensive ways to reduce this gender gap. One team of investigators asked men and women enrolled in an introductory physics course to write, on three occasions during the semester, a fifteen-minute essay on values they regarded as important. A second group wrote on values they regarded as unimportant. The women who wrote about their significant values, and also reported earlier that they believed men were inherently better at physics than women, obtained higher grades on the examinations in the physics course than the women in the second group.[24]

The scientists who did this study failed to appreciate the real possibility that this intervention had a modest success because writing about one's personal ethics was an unusual assignment in a college course in physics. The novel experience could have led these women to guess that it was intended to motivate them to give up their stereotyped belief. If every college student were aware of the purpose of the writing, I suspect that the effectiveness of this intervention would gradually vanish. The phrase "Hawthorne effect" was invented to describe the benevolent, but always temporary, consequences of a novel, unexpected change in everyday routines. New forms of therapy enjoy a temporary period when they seem to be of benefit because of the Hawthorne effect. I want to be perfectly clear on this issue. Each current form of psychotherapy does help some patients with certain symptoms. But the reasons for the benevolent outcomes are not always the ones the therapist assumes are operating. Claudius Ptolemaeus, known as Ptolemy, writing in the second century CE, accurately predicted many heavenly phenomena with a theory that assumed that the sun orbited a stationary earth.

Psychologists and psychiatrists should reflect on the cultural background of a patient before deciding on a diagnosis or form of treatment. Arthur Kleinman, an anthropologist and psychiatrist, is one of many who have written persuasively on this theme.[25] A concern with the patient's cultural background enjoyed greater prominence during the second quarter of the last century when a small group of eminent psychiatrists, including Harry Stack Sullivan, argued that all psychiatrists should receive training in sociology and anthropology. Unfortunately, their voices were quieted by the increasing medicalization of this specialty and the availability of drugs for treating mental illness. I recall listening to a lecture by the chairman of psychiatry at Yale in 1951 telling first-year psychiatric residents that the major obstacle to their success as future psychotherapists was their medical school courses in biochemistry, physiology, and neurology.

The conduct of epidemiological surveys designed to document the prevalence of anxiety or depressive disorders across the world rests on the questionable premise that a report of the emotions that English calls anxiety or depression by a sixty-year-old Tibetan Buddhist monk has the same meaning, and perhaps the same origin, as a similar report by a twenty-year-old in San Francisco, even though the Tibetan language does not have terms for *anxious* or *depressed*. Eight Tibetan spiritual leaders commented on standard questions American investigators use to assess posttraumatic stress disorder. The Tibetans remarked that many questions were too simple, failed to appreciate that Tibetans neither talk about their feelings nor think about emotions as varying in intensity, and provided no opportunity to comment on spirituality and the joys of life.[26]

The biographies of Martin Luther indicate that the father of the Reformation experienced bouts of intense anxiety and depression, combined with a chronic perfectionism, which he attributed to his failure to maintain a faith in God that met his exacting standard. This reason for anxiety, guilt, and self-doubt was common in sixteenth-century Germany. The meaning of an emotion or action that modern clinicians treat as a symptom of illness always depends on the cultural context, as the meaning of a word depends on the sentence in which it appears. For reasons that are hard to understand, some investigators are insufficiently skeptical of the meanings they ascribe to the answers offered by individuals from varied cultures to queries about their emotional states.[27]

More than 80 percent of a group of middle-aged African American women who were poor, widowed, without a college education, and working as caretakers for elderly adults reported (on a popular scale for depression called CES-D) feeling happy, enjoying life, and being hopeful about their future.[28] As noted in chapter 2, the meanings of these replies are probably not synonymous with the meanings intended by married, professional European American women of the same age who gave exactly the same answers. Both groups of women may believe "they are happy" and "hopeful about the future," but the similar verbal reports are unlikely to be accompanied by the same brain profiles or conscious feelings and therefore reflect different psychological states.

If a large forest is treated as a metaphor for a society during a particular historical era, the error in hyping genes as the major culprit in all mental illnesses becomes apparent. The trees in this hypothetical forest, which has a prevailing west-to-east wind, vary in their location, annual exposure to sunlight and water, and genomes. These properties contribute to each tree's vulnerability to a host of threatening conditions, including fungi, insects, and drought. If an infestation of longhorn beetles from the west damaged 20 percent of the trees, biologists would not assume that the tree's genes were the main or only reason for their victim status but would acknowledge the significance of their location and growth history.

For most of human history, the vast majority of adults spent their lives in small groups whose main challenges were finding food, avoiding serious illness, and defending against attacks by animals, robbers, or enemies. Many scholars, including Immanuel Kant, argued that the emergence of industrialization significantly altered the living conditions of many and created the seeds for some of the psychological states called mental illnesses. One significant change was the establishment of many densely populated urban areas hosting adults who had left their families and childhood friends to live in settings that provided weaker social support. These conditions would have made social anxiety more prevalent and created individuals who felt marginalized. Swedish children, either foreign born or born to two foreign-born parents, attending urban schools with very few foreign-born peers had an increased risk of developing schizophrenia, presumably because they felt marginalized and socially isolated.[29]

The growth of the technologies that industrial economies required led, necessarily, to the expansion of formal schooling for all children. These events created conditions that made inattentiveness and restlessness a problem and generated a new basis for competition with others and anxiety over task failure. By the late nineteenth century, new scientific discoveries and changes in economic and social structures generated additional sources of worry over one's status, sexual vigor, aging, and social relationships. Unlike the biologists reflecting on the reason why some trees were damaged by the beetles, psychiatrists nominated genes and psychologists named early childhood experiences as the primary villains. Both groups ignored the person's current social conditions when they concluded that American society was experiencing an epidemic of mental disorders due to inherited abnormalities in brain functioning created by genes and/or early neglect or trauma. In less than four hundred years, about sixteen generations, a majority of humans replaced worry over bodily harm, illness to self or family, and the safety of one's property with worry over one's acceptability to others and the reasons for engaging each day. These two sets of emotional states are incommensurable. It is not possible to know whether contemporary adults are more or less anxious than those who were born the year that Shakespeare was writing *Hamlet*.

Some clinicians may be insufficiently aware of how their personal or their society's ethical premises affect the advice they give to their patients. A majority of American and European therapists, along with most citizens in these societies, believe that sustained mental health requires: personal autonomy, a readiness to be assertive, a form of personal achievement, frequent sensory pleasures, especially a gratifying sex life, many close friendships, tolerance toward those holding opposing beliefs, and minimal guilt over failing to honor obligations to family, friends, or employers if the obligations are experienced as a burden. These values ascended in prominence in Europe during the eighteenth century when Jean-Jacques Rousseau asserted that all wickedness came from weakness. Ralph Waldo Emerson declared a century later that every person should be a nonconformist. The most frequent adjectives twentieth-century Americans used with neutral nouns referring to objects, events, or people were *big*, *great*, *hard*, and *strong*. By contrast, speakers of Japanese, Bengali, or Cantonese most often used the adjectives *beautiful*, *lovable*, and *reliable*.[30]

Lao Tzu, an influential Chinese philosopher writing twenty-five hundred years ago would have disagreed with Rousseau and Emerson because he praised passivity, conformity, and moderation. Confucius regarded shame as a beneficial state because it contributed to social harmony, and many contemporary Chinese Americans believe that a person who feels shame after violating an ethical standard is more moral. Japanese and South Korean college students do not regard shyness as an undesirable trait. It is not surprising, therefore, that they also report higher levels of social anxiety and greater acceptance of shy behavior than seven other societies.[31]

Equally important, contemporary Europeans and North Americans are biased to place the blame for unhappiness on events outside their control. During the first half of the last century, improper parental treatment of the child was regarded as a primary cause of later anguish. During the past twenty-five years genes joined parents as culprits. In both cases, the suffering person is relieved of primary responsibility for their misfortune. Hindus and Buddhists, by contrast, placed the origins of unhappiness in the individual and his or her actions in a prior life, represented by their karma. Those who suffer deserve their fate because they had chosen behaviors that violated the imperative to restrain all desire. I suspect that a growing number of Americans and Europeans are attracted to explanations that assign causal power to events that are not under their control. Neither the person nor the family needs to feel responsible for moods of worry, sadness, pain, guilt, or shame.

Elizabeth Throop, an anthropologist and therapist, is also troubled by the fact that the advice many American therapists give their patients is penetrated with ethically tinged traits that are "simply dripping with moral evaluations," which include seeking frequent sexual gratification, complete autonomy, and personal achievement.[32] These ethical beliefs have no inherent place of privilege in the human genome or in the Dalai Lama's prescription for the optimal path to happiness. They do, however, have adaptive advantages in the current economic and social structures of North America and most of Europe that force each person to be more competitive, selfish, suspicious, and disloyal than he or she would like to be.

A Muslim psychologist brought up in Iran but practicing psychotherapy in the United States noted that Iranian adults are supposed to take responsibility for their family and respect authority. The wish to please others and conform to authority, regarded as immature by Americans, are viewed by Iranians as appropriate, ethically proper postures. A comparison of the differences between Christian and Muslim ethical values reveals several important contrasts: the welfare of the individual versus his or her primary reference groups, autonomy versus conformity, and egalitarian versus hierarchical relations with others.[33]

Buddhist scholars celebrate a lifestyle that celebrates dilute emotional bonds to people and things because the loss of a close relationship or failure to obtain a desired goal are major sources of suffering and all suffering should be avoided. Luis Buñuel's 1977 film *That Obscure Object of Desire* captured this idea in the portrayal of a middle-age man obsessed with making love to a young woman who suffered intense frustration and anger because his sexual desires were never gratified. Many Buddhist therapists advising clients wishing for improved mental health might tell them to practice meditation, rid the self of desires for all symbolic goals not required for survival, and avoid deep attachments.[34]

The claim by some psychologists that adults who do not have many friends suffer from an emotional "dysfunction" is an ethical judgment rather than a conclusion based on a rich set of observations gathered across time and place. Even a distinguished American philosopher has joined the bandwagon celebrating the biological necessity of close friendships. Alexander Nehemas declared, without adequate evidence or a tight argument, that friendships were required for the healthy development of a person's character and personality, independent of whether the person believed that a satisfying life required many friendships.[35] Recall the friendless Ludwig Wittgenstein telling a friend standing by his bedside moments before he died that he had enjoyed a wonderful life. In this century, loneliness is replacing overwork as a cause of a mental illness.

Historical events over the past century brought increased geographic mobility, denser urban populations, easier access to drugs, higher crime rates, more effective contraception, more permissive attitudes toward sex, enhanced feelings of anonymity, greater distrust of strangers, more betrayals by friends and lovers, and media regularly announcing to the world acts of crass dishonesty by those in positions of responsibility, abuse of children, and unprovoked cruelty against innocents.

These changes make it hard for the current generation of twenty-to-fifty-year-olds to maintain the belief that humans are basically good, most decisions by authorities are wise and just, and there are rational reasons for maintaining an optimistic mood. Humans try to resist the conclusion that they are completely impotent, and many have decided, with the support of experts, that having more friendships will alleviate a dark despondency brought on by the loss of faith in the ethics they were taught or would like to believe are valid. The Japanese have witnessed a deterioration in the mutual bond of trust between employers and workers and a penetration of Western values celebrating autonomy from the family. These events have created a new syndrome among Japanese youth, called *hikikomori*, in which adolescents refuse to attend school or get a job and live a hermitlike existence in their bedroom.[36]

The poet W. H. Auden, influenced by Freud's ideas and the increased confusion over a personal identity during the years immediately following the Second World War, wrote in 1948 that humans were living in an age of anxiety.[37] If Auden were alive today he would have written that humans live in an era of cynicism and distrust accompanied by a feeling of impotence in the face of social forces that seem impossible to change. This state is far more corrosive of vitality than anxiety over an adulterous sexual affair or confusion over one's identity. But I suspect that this dismal era will pass. Erasmus in 1507 made an equally dark diagnosis of his culture because of the widespread prevalence of vanity and narcissism. Only a century later history's muse, in a better mood, arranged a series of benevolent changes that culminated in the Enlightenment.

American psychiatrists and psychologists are exporting to the world a conception of mental illness that exaggerates the power of genes and drug cures and regards every bout of intense sadness or worry, no matter what their origin, as a possible sign of a mental disorder. Christopher Lane has described in lively prose the sequence of events that transformed the trait of shyness, found in all societies, into the disorder of social phobia. Some psychiatrists have transformed the grief following the loss of a spouse into a major depressive disorder. Although Freud recognized the distinction between these two states, a century later Peter Kramer confidently wrote that depression was an abnormal psychological state that, like polio, could be eliminated with the right combination of medicines.[38]

The committee composing DSM-5 (to be published in 2013) intends to add a dimension of intensity to DSM-IV symptom categories. For example, the tentative plan is to award a number that reflects the intensity or seriousness of the symptoms defining a category. This strategy will inevitably increase the number of children and adults with a mental illness, as the decision to make osteopenia a disease increased the number of individuals diagnosed with a bone disorder requiring medical treatment. A chronically sad mood, called dysthymia, is under less genetic control than the more serious apathy of depression, and it is probably an error to regard these two states as members of the same illness that differ only in severity.[39] Most parents lose their temper and, on occasion, may strike a disobedient child, but very few try to choke, burn, or suffocate the child, even though these harsher acts could be regarded as products of a greater intensity of anger and a more serious loss of control. If we altered the criterion for physical disability from the inability to walk a mile in sixty minutes to the inability to walk the same mile in twenty minutes, there would suddenly be a large increase in physically disabled adults. In Lewis Carroll's *Through the Looking Glass*, Alice was asked, "What's the use of their having names if they won't answer to them?" Alice's reply, which has implications for all DSM categories, was: "No use to them, but it's useful to the people that name them."

Humans enjoy a special form of satisfaction when they believe they are crusaders fighting a source of evil. A despotic leader, slavery, serious injustice, a corrupt social institution, serious restrictions on private behaviors, harsh prejudice against a class of people, and employer exploitation of workers have been significant evils that democratic societies have either weakened or, in some cases, defeated. Many are looking for a new source of evil to combat. I suggest that hyping the extensiveness of mental disorders provides for some an enemy to defeat and a source of a renewed vitality demanding action against this terrible state of affairs. The mental hygiene movement, founded in the United States as the First World War ended, was led by middle-class citizens disturbed by the prevalence of alcoholism, crime, paresis, and school failure, especially among poor immigrants. And then, as now, the toxin was located in the person rather than in conditions in the larger society. The exchange of letters between Freud and Jung from 1906 to 1914 reveals that Jung had a more sophisticated appreciation of the influence of a culture's mores and social conditions on psychological states and understood that some symptoms were adaptations to local conditions created by history. Freud rejected this idea, insisting that all symptoms were the product of repressed wishes.[40] It may be relevant that Jung spent a fair proportion of his clinical work trying to help economically disadvantaged psychotic patients in a Zurich hospital; Freud treated mainly middle-class Austrians. Their distinctive work settings, as well as their different status positions in their communities, may have contributed to their discrepant perspectives.

Clinicians and investigators in mental health envy the high status of the natural sciences, feel a twinge of guilt over their failure to discover phenomena as profound as those uncovered by biologists, and, like all humans, are vulnerable to magical thinking. As a result, they may derive an enhanced sense of virtue entitling them to more respect by declaring that there is an epidemic of mental illness that the larger society must help them combat.

Psychiatry's lack of confidence is reflected in a comment by a former medical director of the American Psychiatric Association: "Ebullience, optimism, and pride are not prominent features of today's psychiatric practitioners."[41]

Many scholars have made these arguments with greater force and often with more graceful prose.[42] But resistance to what many regard as obvious truths remains. Why? Biologists challenge false dogma when the data demand it. After Crick and Watson described the structure of DNA in 1953 every biologist was convinced that the sequence from DNA to RNA to proteins could not be reversed. But Howard Temin and David Baltimore challenged this belief, and were proven correct, when they argued that some viruses could make DNA from RNA.

The political structure of contemporary science provides one reason for the resistance to the evidence I have summarized. The natural sciences have made more significant discoveries that have contributed to human welfare than the social sciences and their concepts refer to material things, such as cells and molecules, that can be observed. It is impossible to see, touch, hear, or smell a person's feeling of self-loathing, but that does not exclude this experience from the events we call natural phenomena. Physicists do not like the concept of dark energy because they cannot measure it directly, but they accepted this idea in order to explain their evidence. Biologists are deeply suspicious of concepts that refer to invisible events. As a result, the biological sciences remain more attractive to granting agencies, university deans, and college seniors contemplating a career than the disciplines studying psychological phenomena.

It is not surprising that talented youth interested in science prefer to join groups that have more, rather than less, political power. Freud made the same decision for he, too, was ambitious for fame. Because he recognized that physiology and physics were ascending in power in the 1880s, while philosophy was descending, Freud explicitly denied that his ideas were philosophical speculations penetrated with ethical assumptions about the primacy of pleasure over virtue, the importance of reason, the primacy of freedom, and the role of guilt. He insisted that these ideas were scientifically based inferences gleaned from his observations with patients. The immaturity of sociology allowed Freud to ignore the influences of current circumstances on a person's moods. How paradoxical that Freud's ideas on the influence of childhood experiences enhanced the position of psychology and diminished the role of biology during the first half of the last century.

Extensive study of the experiential contributions to a mental illness is being neglected because of the return, a century after Freud's insistence on the influence of early experience, to a romance with genes and brains in the hope that they will supply the needed answers. But a full understanding of the causes of mental illnesses and the forms they assume requires the study of psychological processes that must be described in a vocabulary that refers to feelings, emotions, beliefs, values, expectations, and interpretations of the events that produced them. An adolescent's feeling of shame because a parent is uneducated, unemployed, and alcoholic cannot be translated into words or phrases that name only the properties of genes, proteins, neurons, neurotransmitters, hormones, receptors, and circuits without losing a substantial amount of meaning. It is worth repeating that the symbolic networks that comprise a person's interpretations of feelings and events are as fundamental to psychology as genes are to biology. The chemist's concept of oxidation cannot be translated into or replaced with the concepts of modern physics. Even the mathematician's understanding of the concept of infinity depends on the mathematical argument in which it is a term. For the same reason, the neuroscientist's concept of fear, based on the activation of a rat's amygdala to a signal of imminent electric shock, does not capture the meaning of Leonard Woolf's fear that he had wasted his life. Nor can it reflect the meaning T. S. Eliot intended when he wrote, "I'll show you fear in a handful of dust."

FIVE

Promising Reforms

It is far easier to list the problems obstructing progress in psychology than to provide the constructive suggestions that might catalyze change. This last chapter satisfies my feeling of obligation to describe a few practices that should hasten the time when some of the victories for which so many talented psychologists have labored will be achieved.

Look for Patterns

The most important reform urges a search for patterns in a body of evidence, preferably from different sources, rather than reliance on the average of a single measure as the basis for inferring or affirming a psychological concept.[1] This suggestion honors the biologists' under-standing that all natural phenomena consist of layers of organization that include the surface pattern observed and the earlier cascades of invisible events that are its foundations. The phenomena constituting each layer form unique patterns and must be studied in ways that are faithful to the organization of that layer.

The patterns of the four nucleotides that comprise the strings of DNA are unlike the patterns of proteins that are synthesized from these strings. The patterns of brain organization differ from the patterns of proteins that are their constituents. And the patterns of actions, feelings, and knowledge networks do not resemble the patterns found in the brain. Unfortunately, many mo-lecular biologists and biochemists who study the deeper layers believe that their knowledge, when complete, will be able to explain the surface layers of action, feeling, and knowledge and they have persuaded the institutions that provide money for research that they are right. As noted in chapter 1, however, because the layer psychologists observe is affected by the local context, their confidence races far ahead of the evidence.

Almost every observation in psychology (I am tempted to say all) can result from more than one set of conditions. This claim is true for verbal reports, observed behaviors, concentrations of a molecule in saliva or blood, and aspects of brain function. Talkativeness at a party can be the result of a relaxed, sociable personality or a need to control social interactions by talking most of the time. To distinguish between these two types of personalities psychologists have to gather additional information.

Consider the popular concept of extroversion, measured almost exclusively with a questionnaire. Because all persons who describe themselves as extroverts are not sociable and assertive with others, a pattern that added behavioral observations would permit a parsing of this large group into those whose self-descriptions matched their behavior and those for whom it did not. It might also be useful to measure some biological features, such as heart rate or greater activation in the left compared with the right frontal lobe. The three sources of evidence generate six patterns, or types, of extroverts if we assign each person a high or low value on each measure. One pattern is characterized by individuals who say they are extroverted but show neither the behavior nor the biology expected of extroverts. A second type is sociable and possesses the expected biology but does not describe himself or herself as extroverted. A third type possesses all three signs of extroversion. I believe that the most fruitful concepts in a future psychology of personality will be based on patterns of observations that specify a type of person based on their biology, life history, culture, and self-reports, as well as the setting where the evidence is gathered. Japanese adults who describe themselves as extroverts on a questionnaire will behave differently at a party in Osaka than American extroverts attending a party in Los Angeles. The history of advances in biology affirms this recommendation.

Some scientists who measure brain activity resist the suggestion that patterns should replace single measures. The value of looking for patterns is seen in the following example. Adults first saw a picture that was followed by a sentence (appearing one word at a time on a screen) that either matched or did not match the picture. For example, one picture illustrated a woman dressed as a gymnast applauding another woman dressed as a journalist. The sentence read either, "The gymnast applauds the journalist" or "The gymnast punches the journalist." The subject had to indicate as fast as possible whether the sentence did or did not match the picture while their EEG was being recorded. The best predictor of the time required to judge the truth value of the sentence was a pattern of three measures: the magnitude of a waveform in the EEG occurring at four hundred milliseconds, the magnitude of a second waveform at one second, and the person's ability to hold many words in working memory.[2]

The high-reactive infants I described in chapters 2 and 3 provide another example of the utility of searching for patterns. A large number of the eighteen-year-old high reactives had experienced a bout of depression or social anxiety. The best predictor of the incidence of one or both of these symptoms was a pattern of three measures: a large number of fears to unfamiliar events when they were fourteen and twenty-one months old and a larger surge of blood flow to the amygdala to the first set of faces with angry expressions than to any of the three later sets (they also saw neutral and fearful faces). This pattern was far better than any one of the measures in predicting who would suffer from a bout of depression or social anxiety.

Developmental psychologists probing infants' cognitive talents typically measure only the average duration of looking at an event as the basis for inferences about what infants know. Although investigators rarely record the brain's response, patterns that combine the infant's looking time with brain activity often require a different interpretation of what infants inferred from visual displays. The brain's response is influenced in a major way by the physical features of a display, whereas the behavioral reaction of looking is influenced more by a combination of a moderately unfamiliar stimulus and the infant's attempt to relate the event to what he or she knows. Patterns composed of looking times and brain responses are likely to lead to a more nuanced, and hopefully more accurate, inference.[3]

The brain is extremely sensitive to the spatial pattern of two or more objects. Three equally spaced objects evoke a profile of activity that differs from the profile recorded when two of the objects are close to each other and the third is distant from the pair. This fact implies that infants' attention to visual displays should be influenced by the spatial patterning of objects. This seems to be the case. Newborn infants saw a triangular-shaped frame enclosing three small black squares also arranged in one of two triangular patterns. In the first pattern, a single square was close to the narrow space at the apex of the triangle, and the horizontal pair was close to the wider area at the base. In the second pattern, the single square was at the base of the triangle, and the horizontal pair at the narrow apex. This second pattern seems less aesthetic because there are two squares crowded at the narrow top of the triangle. Most infants looked longer at the first, more aesthetic, pattern, implying that the brains of newborns are responsive to particular patterns of identical objects.[4]

Many years ago, a graduate student in the Harvard psychology department wanted to discover which features of sound were most likely to alert newborn infants. He recorded the behaviors of two-day-old infants to each of twenty-seven sounds. Each sound was composed of one of three frequencies (that is, pitch), one of three loudness levels, and one of three rise times. After spending several years gathering and analyzing the average alertness to each stimulus, he was disappointed by discovering that no particular pitch, loudness, or rise time had a special influence on the infants' behavior, and he came to me for advice. I suggested that he look for the patterns of pitch, loudness, and rise time that produced the most obvious alerting in a majority of newborns. When he did so, he discovered one pattern that combined a particular pitch, loudness, and rise time that alerted most infants. This sound bore the closest resemblance to the qualities of the human voice.[5]

The pleasant or unpleasant quality of two notes heard simultaneously also depends on a pattern based on the ratio of their fundamental frequencies. If the highest compared with the lowest frequency has a ratio of 3:2, the sound is experienced as consonant and pleasant. If the ratio is 16:15, the sound is perceived as dissonant. Infants only sixteen weeks old turn away from melodies with dissonant chords, often with a frown on their faces, but attend closely, often with a smile, to consonant melodies.[6]

One child, from the more than 450 infants my colleagues and I have been studying for many years, showed a unique pattern of behaviors during the fifteen-year-interval from eight weeks to mid-adolescence. When this boy was eight and sixteen weeks old, the muscles of his face frequently formed the uncommon pattern of a frown. At nine months, he fretted or cried during every procedure. He had several uncontrolled tantrums in the laboratory at fourteen months, prompting his mother to comment that, at home, he often walked up to visitors and bit them. When he was three and a half years old, he played with an unfamiliar boy of the same age in a large playroom with both mothers sitting on a couch in the same room. About fifteen minutes into the session, when the other child was inside a plastic tunnel, this boy picked up a wooden pole and began to strike the tunnel in the place where the other boy was sitting. As an adolescent, he had difficulty mastering his schoolwork and was rejected by his classmates. I suspect this boy belongs to a rare temperamental category that could be detected only by a pattern of measurements over time. Most sixteen-week-olds who frown frequently do not develop the unusual personality of this particular boy.

Robert Hinde of Cambridge University provided a persuasive example of the power of patterns of measures to reveal insights about aggressive behavior in children that a traditional analysis did not uncover. British mothers and their four-year-old children were observed at home, and the children were observed in their preschool setting. There was no significant relation between the mother's warmth toward or control of the child at home and the child's aggression, when each measure was treated as continuous, because the relations between the behaviors of mother and child were not linear. When Hinde examined the evidence for patterns of measures, he found that mothers who combined moderate levels of warmth with moderate control had children who were rarely aggressive. These results, like the study of newborns' reactions to sounds, required a patient search for patterns that made theoretical sense. Experts who study childhood disorders urge their colleagues to base their diagnoses on patterns of symptoms rather than the single most salient symptom.[7]

A pattern defined by the differential density of two different classes of estrogen receptors in the brain creates two kinds of biological males. One type of estrogen receptor controls the development of the male fetus's reproductive organs. The second type blocks the development of feminine bodily features in the unborn boy. This means that one category of male possesses a penis and testes but no female traits. The other category possesses male genitals together with the female features of a round, rather than a square, face, a minimally protruding chin, little bodily hair, and the slightly thicker lips that are characteristic of most females. These two kinds of men might react in different ways to the same challenge, for example, the regulation of anger. Caucasian adolescents who had been victims of childhood abuse or neglect (affirmed by court records rather than the person's memory) and, in addition, possessed a gene linked to less degradation of serotonin had the highest levels of antisocial activity. *But this relation was absent among two other groups possessing the same gene: nonwhite adolescents who were abused as well as whites who were not abused.* Discovery of this important result required examination of patterns of evidence that included ethnicity, information on childhood abuse, and possession of a particular gene.[8]

The women accused of being witches in fifteenth-century Europe typically possessed a pattern of four features: they were older, were widows, lived in a small community, and were poor. The prediction of a postpartum depression in Swedish women who had just given birth to an infant was enhanced by adding the month of delivery to other risk factors. The depression was most likely if the woman delivered during October, November, or December when the hours of daylight are decreasing and the temperature is falling. Although adolescent suicide in the United States is a rare event, the best predictor of this act was a pattern of four features: a disadvantaged social class, residence in a rural area of a western state, and a Monday during the warmer months from April to September.[9]

Creative paintings, poems, novels, musical compositions, and scientific discoveries consist of a pattern of features, whether Einstein's theory of general relativity or
Picasso's painting *Nude in a Red Velvet Chair*. The most
common pattern in the first sixteen measures of a large
number of Western musical compositions, classical as
well as jazz, was a repetition of two similar themes (AA)
followed by a third (B) that altered the theme of the first
two measures. Beethoven employed this pattern in the
opening bars of his Fifth Symphony. The brain produces
a distinct wave form in the electroencephalogram about
one-fifth of a second after a deviant sound follows two
repetitions of the same sound (that is, an AAB pattern),
but this wave form does not appear to a deviant sound
in an AB sequence. The brain needs at least two similar
events to establish an expectation of the next one and is
prepared to react if the third event violates expectation.[10]

It is not an accident that most jokes also follow an AAB
pattern by following two repetitions of a familiar idea
with a third, incongruous one—the priest, the minister,
and the rabbi. Poets, too, often employ an AAB pattern.
The first two lines of T. S. Eliot's poem "The Love Song
of J. Alfred Prufrock" end with the same sound ("I" and
"sky"), but line 3 ends with "table." Lines 4 and 5 also end
with rhyming words ("streets" and "retreats"), but line 6

ends with "hotels." The six lines of the children's poem "Jack and Jill" also follow an AAB pattern.

The mind appears to have a slight bias to treat a change that follows two repetitions of a particular theme (AAB) as more aesthetic than the patterns AAAB or AAAAB, although modern music often follows one of these less aesthetic patterns. The occurrence of B after AAA or AAAA may be too serious a violation of expectation and for that reason interferes with an aesthetic response. It is not a coincidence that infants pay the longest attention to events that are moderately different from what they expect rather than very different. Montaigne's plea, "Moderation above all," was a profound insight.

Chapter 3 described the children on the island of Kauai who were at risk for a personality problem during adolescence because of a trauma during or soon after their birth or exposure to stressful events during their first two years. A small number of children from this high-risk group did not develop any psychological problems. These resilient children combined a pattern of four features: they were firstborn, possessed a cuddly, affectionate temperament as an infant, had no or only one sibling, and were born to a younger mother.[11]

The balance among six complementary societal characteristics has cycled over the course of human history. These characteristics are: collective versus individualistic, the celebration of reason versus emotion, secular versus religious, urban-commercial versus rural-agricultural, egalitarian versus hierarchical, and hopeful versus pessimistic. Because a change in one of these dimensions is usually associated with a corresponding change in another—an increase in urban populations is usually linked to an increase in individualistic traits—it is useful to compose patterns consisting of these six conditions. A very large number of patterns can be created from the combinations of these characteristics. The changes in European society from medieval era to the present were due, in part, to the changing balances in the features that comprised these patterns.

Psychologists typically analyze the average of single measurements across a sample rather than patterns because of the statistical techniques they were taught and the demands by most reviewers of research papers. Investigators who rely on these popular statistics assume that the values that contribute to the average reflect variation in the same underlying, mediating process. This assumption is reasonable when the measure is the average weight of a thousand potatoes or the average falling times of a thousand balls dropped from the same roof. But this assumption is questionable when the measure is the average weight of all the manufactured objects in a thousand homes or the average well-being across one hundred societies varying in economy and religion. If, as I claim, most psychological and biological observations can be the result of more than one condition, the meanings of most average values for actions, verbal reports, or biological variables are ambiguous and their interpretation uncertain.

The distribution and the average of a thousand adolescent IQ scores is the result of distinctive patterns of genes, illnesses, family experience, and quality of schooling. An IQ of 85 in each of one hundred children can be due to the genetic anomaly called Down Syndrome, congenital deafness, or rearing in a poor, illiterate family. The average increase in blood flow to the amygdala to an unexpected event is influenced by many factors, and two persons can show the same increase in blood flow to the same brain site for different reasons.

Recall the earlier discussion of the temperamental groups called high- and low-reactive infants. At age eighteen the youths from these groups were shown a variety of pictures as each lay in a magnetic scanner that measured changes in blood flow to the amygdala and thickness of the ventromedial prefrontal cortex in the right hemisphere. Youths who were born with different temperaments and possessed distinctive current personalities often showed the same increase in blood flow to the amygdala when an unexpected, unfamiliar picture appeared. However, an examination of a pattern that combined blood flow to the amygdala with the thickness of the ventromedial cortex permitted a separation of the two groups. If a confident, talkative, relaxed, minimally anxious adolescent who had been a low-reactive infant showed the same increase in blood flow to the amygdala as a quiet, defensive, shy, anxious youth who had been a high-reactive infant, it is reasonable to argue that the average increase in blood flow to one site, following exposure to an unexpected event, need not reflect the same brain process or psychological state.

Apes and humans share many biological and psychological features. This fact has motivated hundreds of scientists to spend thousands of hours and many millions of dollars trying to prove that chimpanzees and humans differ only quantitatively in most psychological traits. This hope, nurtured by Darwin and evolutionary biologists, is easily dashed by watching and testing several five-year-old children and an equal number of adult chimpanzees for about one hour. No chimpanzee can infer a variety of intentions in another chimp, learn an association between two meaningless designs in a few trials, display signs of shame or guilt after breaking a vase, point to the location of a tool that will help another gain a reward, or imitate immediately a simple motor action displayed by another member of the same species (for example, touching the ground or throwing a pebble). Chimps and humans, like butterflies and bees, are discrete categories defined by distinctive patterns of genes, anatomy, brain structures, brain molecules, and behaviors.

Humans possess a pattern characterized by a distinctive head and body shape, smaller canine teeth, less body hair, a longer thumb, a prominent chin, a larger frontal lobe combined with a smaller amygdala (relative to the volume of the entire brain), a symbolic language with syntax, and a moral sense. Even though chimps and humans share close to 99 percent of the same protein-producing genes (which comprise less than 2 percent of the human genome), it is misleading to suggest that apes and humans lie on a continuum and differ quantitatively. The male sex hormone, testosterone, and the female hormone, estradiol, share 96 percent of the same atoms, but the atoms form different patterns. Triangles have three straight lines and squares have four, but children, mathematicians, and brains treat these two forms as distinct patterns.

Geneticists appreciate that the effects of a particular gene on an outcome often depend on the pattern represented by the complete genome. This principle even holds for the small worm *C. elegans*, whose biology is far simpler than any mammal. The unique spectrum of electromagnetic radiation emitted by a heated atom is a function of the pattern of energy levels in the electrons in all the orbits of the atom.[12]

Until statisticians invent methods that are sensitive detectors of patterns, psychologists will continue to emphasize the average of single, continuous measures and rely on regression analysis and covariance to control for conditions they believe are less important elements in a causal cascade but are often essential to the causal sequence. I noted in chapter 1 that psychologists are fond of proving that one particular condition, for example infant day care, parental abuse, or bullying, makes an independent contribution to a future behavior, such as aggression, addiction, or social anxiety, without the help of other conditions. The psychologists who pursue this strategy are reluctant to acknowledge that experiences associated with these other conditions, especially the person's social class, sex, and cultural background, might be necessary for the outcome. I make this suggestion because the victims of school bullies are not a random sample of all youth; the infants in full-time day care are not a random sample of all infants. These children have other properties that may make an essential contribution to an outcome of interest, and it is not always possible to remove the influences of these other properties with fancy statistics.

A pair of economists who wanted to predict adult health from life-history information controlled for the influence of the family's social class using an analysis of covariance. After examining the separate contributions of many measures to aspects of adult health, they concluded that individuals who had fewer years of formal education were at risk for becoming adult smokers. This inference tempts unsophisticated readers to assume that amount of education alone, without the contributions of other conditions associated with less than twelve years of formal education, influenced smoking at age thirty. Had they related a pattern of measures that included class of rearing, amount and quality of schooling, health during childhood, and personality traits, they probably would have discovered that the pattern was a far better predictor of smoking.[13]

A fire needs both fuel and oxygen; an embryo cannot form without an egg and a sperm. I trust that no scholar would use covariance to remove the effects of rampant inflation and high unemployment in Germany in 1932 in order to evaluate the separate contribution of anti-Semitic attitudes to Hitler's rise to power. Nor would a biologist use covariance to remove the influence of hours of sunshine to determine the independent contribution of inches of rainfall in the spring and summer to the average height in September of a hundred tomato plants in

Aspen, Colorado, compared with Gainesville, Florida. It is time for psychologists to reconsider two popular assumptions: identical values for a behavior or a biological reaction are the result of similar causes, and covariance can prove that a single condition makes a meaningful contribution to a complex outcome when it is not part of a larger pattern.

A large number of psychologists would like to solve two seminal puzzles. The first involves the causes of mental illness. Because each illness category is heterogeneous in origin, it is necessary to gather patterns of life history and biology. The second question, whose solutions will lead to major theoretical advances, requires illumination of the pattern of biological properties and experiences that contribute to the development of cognitive mechanisms and knowledge networks. Progress on this issue requires gathering more than one measurement of a cognitive ability and combining measures of the brain with the person's perception of the immediate context. Most brain profiles, including the popular measure of blood flow, can be the result of different factors and can result in more than one psychological outcome. A site in the temporal lobe, for example, is usually activated when people are using language, but this site is also active when individuals are performing a working memory task.[14]

The habit of concluding that a significant relation between a single causal condition and a single outcome is a sufficient basis for awarding theoretical importance to a construct has problems. No concept in sociology or political science represents the combination of conditions that allowed England to become the world's leading industrialized society by the early years of the nineteenth century. These included a benign climate, an abundance of coal, a single language, sea power, nobles willing to engage in commerce, the accumulation of wealth as an ethically acceptable path to elite status, autonomous universities, and a favorable attitude toward natural science. Had one of these features been missing from the pattern, it remains a possibility that England's success might have been delayed or diminished.

Verbal Reports

My argument for patterns leads naturally to the recommendation to add measures of behavior and/or biology to a person's verbal descriptions of their emotions, past stressors, and personality traits. The most popular concepts in studies of personality, temperament, attitudes, emotions, and ethical values are based primarily on verbal replies, usually to questionnaires. I noted in chapter 2 that the meaning of a verbal report of well-being is ambiguous because the same answer can be offered by informants from diverse cultures whose different childhood histories, biological biases, and current circumstances imply different meanings for the identical replies.

Consider some reasons why words and sentences provide an incomplete or inaccurate index of a person's knowledge networks, past behaviors, emotions, traits, or beliefs. The most important reason is that individuals feel a strong urge to be logically consistent in their series of spoken or written sentences. If a woman tells an interviewer that her mother is a successful lawyer who is generous with friends, she will be tempted to suppress descriptions of any of the parent's undesirable traits in order to be consistent. Feelings and behaviors, however, are not bound by a need for consistency, and the woman may feel deeply ambivalent toward her mother and show it in her actions but not express this ambivalence in her verbal replies.

A large sample of Americans, politically liberal as well as conservative, agreed that the ideal distribution of wealth should resemble the more equal distribution found in Sweden. But many of the informants who said they favored a more egalitarian distribution voted for George Bush, not John Kerry, in 2004. Their behavior is probably a more accurate index of their beliefs than their verbal replies.[15]

Second, most English words do not specify the detailed features of an experience. A man may tell an interviewer that the streets of his neighborhood are dirty, but his perceptual representations of these streets contain the specific images that allow an interviewer to know exactly how dirty and filled with what type of rubbish.

Third, the meaning of a verbal statement often depends on the larger semantic network in which a one- or two-word reply is only one element. Many years ago I presented women from different social-class backgrounds with a two-minute audio recording of an essay that described both the advantages and the disadvantages of a mother's display of physical affection toward her infant and then surprised each woman by asking her to recall all they remembered from the essay. College-educated women, many who believe that kisses and embraces are requisites for the child's psychological health, remembered more words describing the benevolent consequences of affection. Many working-class women with only a high school diploma believe that their older children must learn to cope with the difficult challenges in American society and are afraid of spoiling their young children with too much affection. These women remembered more words describing the disadvantages of too much kissing and hugging. However, both groups of women gave the same affirmative answer when asked directly whether physical affection was good for infants.[16]

Two adults who gave the same affirmative answer to the question "Do you feel tense at parties?" would have intended different meanings if the word *tense* evoked in one respondent a network referring to the anticipation of exciting experiences but provoked in the other a network linked to feelings of muscle tightness and worry. Identical twins gave similar replies to the statement "It is hard for me to start a conversation with strangers." But they gave dissimilar answers to what seemed to be a statement with the same meaning: "I feel nervous if I have to meet a lot of people." Apparently, each twin had different networks to the phrase "nervous with lots of people" but similar networks to the phrase "hard to start a conversation with strangers."[17]

Chinese adults possess strong semantic associations between *bird* and *penis* and between *frog* and *vagina* that are missing in the networks of Americans and Europeans. The network for the concept *hard* is more closely associated with maleness than femaleness. As a result, adults asked to press their pen hard when recording their answers were biased, unconsciously, to activate semantic representations linked to maleness.[18]

A fourth reason why verbal reports are misleading is that most individuals are reluctant to admit to actions, traits, or feelings that might be embarrassing or evoke a critical appraisal from the examiner. Psychologists estimate that about 20 percent of adults give socially desirable descriptions of themselves that are serious distortions of what they know to be true. Over 50 percent of adults who tested positive for cocaine or opiates denied taking any drugs, and 20 percent of registered voters who failed to vote during a particular election said that they had cast a vote.

A fifth, more serious problem is that the correlation between what people say and what they actually do ranges from negligible to modest. Adults from one of fifty-five countries filled out a questionnaire designed to measure the five most popular personality traits. The sex differences in self-reported personality were larger among adults from wealthy, egalitarian societies, such as the United States, than in poorer, traditional ones, such as Indonesia. However, direct observations of the behaviors of men and women in America and Indonesia would lead to exactly the opposite conclusion. Sex differences in everyday behavior are far more obvious in Indonesia than in America.

College students from twenty-four different cultures rated the personality traits of friends. Surprisingly, the differences among the cultures were very small. Had these same students observed the behavior of friends in natural settings, the cultural differences in personality traits would have been far more obvious. As I noted in chapter 2, one cannot even rely on an adult's report that they used sunscreen at a swimming pool on a particular day as a reliable index of the fact that they did. *If adults are inaccurate when providing information on the innocent use of sunscreen, it is unlikely that they will be more accurate when describing their personality traits, emotions, or prejudiced opinions.* That is why a number of scientists have warned against relying solely on a person's descriptions of their personality traits to arrive at conclusions with theoretical implications.[19]

Our filmed interviews of the fifteen-year-old adolescents who had been classified as either high or low reactive at four months provide a nice example of the mismatch between what people say and their actual behavior. A small number of high reactives who said that they were neither shy nor anxious with strangers often looked away from the interviewer; a few never looked directly at her. By contrast, not one low reactive who denied being shy shifted his or her gaze away from the interviewer's face. Thus, the addition of behavioral observations permitted us to distinguish between two groups of adolescents who offered exactly the same verbal description of this personality trait.

Some scientists searching for relations between genes and personality appear to be unaware of these problems.

One team relied only on the verbal descriptions of care-takers of twins, six to seventeen years old, to decide which children had the symptoms of a mental illness. The children described as having internalizing symptoms, such as nervousness, social phobia, or depression, were also described as possessing the externalizing symptoms of disobedience and conduct disorder. Because the authors trusted the accuracy of the caretaker reports, they concluded that the same genes contributed to both classes of behavior.[20] However, if direct observations of the children's behaviors had been gathered, they would not have found that most children with internalizing symptoms (McHugh's family 2) also had externalizing symptoms (family 3).

Another group of scientists examined single changes in genes. A change in one nucleotide in the DNA of a gene is called an SNP (for single nucleotide polymorphism). This team analyzed 273 SNPs located in eight genes that affect dopamine activity hoping to discover a pattern of SNPs that was associated with a psychological trait called sensation seeking, which was measured only with a forty-item questionnaire and no behavioral information. No SNP had a significant correlation with the score on the sensation-seeking questionnaire, but there were many correlations between this score and the ethnicity, sex, and age of the respondents. Had these investigators measured sensation seeking by observing relevant behaviors, they might have found more substantial relations with one or more of the SNPs. Even Thomas Achenbach, the author of a popular questionnaire for assessing personality problems in children and youth, warned, "Diagnoses based only on self reports agree poorly with diagnoses based on multiple sources of data." The likelihood that a verbal description of a psychological state or trait will accurately capture a person's past experiences or actions is as low as the probability that a person wearing leather mittens will be able to pick up a fragile crystal sculpture of a bird without breaking off any of its parts.[21]

Even the way a question is worded can affect the nature of the answer. Most individuals have a natural bias to select the middle value and to avoid the extremes when responding to a question with multiple answers. When a question about the average amount of time spent watching television each day listed two and a half hours or more as the highest value, only one of six persons selected that choice. However, when two and a half hours or more was the second of six alternatives, with four, more extreme values, twice as many (one of three) confessed that they watched television at least that long. Furthermore, the specific language of the questionnaire is always a relevant factor. Preadolescent children from Hong Kong who were proficient in both English and Chinese described their traits once using Chinese and once using English. The children described themselves as more autonomous when interviewed in English but more interdependent when asked the same questions in Chinese. American and Chinese mothers were asked to make up stories to a series of pictures and to narrate the stories to their children. The stories composed by the American mothers emphasized the psychological states of the people or animals in the pictures. The stories narrated by the Chinese mothers emphasized actions.[22]

Most psychological research is conducted in English by Americans on Americans. This practice presents a problem because most English terms for psychological states do not specify the age or gender of the person or the cause or potential target of a psychological state, and few English words name blends of emotions. There is no English word that describes the emotion generated by the combination of pleasure on learning that a disliked rival was the victim of a misfortune and the possible guilt or shame evoked by the feeling of satisfaction. German has such a term. And the German word *angst* is not synonymous with the English words *fear* or *anxiety*. Some languages do have distinctive terms for emotions that specify the cause—for example, the difference between the anger provoked when a person made a mistake (losing a set of keys) and the state created when the same person was insulted or frustrated by another. The ancient Greeks used five different terms to differentiate among the state of a person slighted by another; the emotion that occurs when the person has made a mistake; a god's anger; a chronic mood of anger; and the emotion experienced when the person feels that his or her anger is justified.[23]

Five distinctive brain and psychological states are evoked by a desirable experience that occurs unexpectedly (a larger-than-anticipated raise in salary), an aversive event that is unexpected (a good student who usually receives A grades gets a failing grade), the absence of a desired event that was expected (a friend's failure to appear at an appointed time), the absence of an aversive experience that was expected (avoiding a collision with a car or tree after skidding on ice), and an unexpected event that is neither desired nor aversive (the lights in the room suddenly go off). Yet many English speakers would use the same term *surprise* to describe their reaction to all five experiences.[24]

The English language has many words naming abstract psychological states that fail to specify the cause, the agent, or the setting—for example, *anxiety, sociability, flexibility, regulation,* and *perseverance.* Each of these terms has semantic associations with the concepts *good* or *bad.* Because most adults want to regard themselves in a desirable light, their answers are influenced by what they regard as ideal traits. More adjectives for traits that Americans evaluate as *good* are semantically closer to the concept *female* than the concept *male*. This fact is relevant to the Big Five dimensions of agreeableness and conscientiousness because females generally have higher scores than males, in part because women believe these traits are desirable female properties.[25] The replies to most questions reflect the person's understanding of what they are supposed to believe, feel, prefer, or do, and do not always correspond to their actual beliefs, feelings, preferences, or actions. The meanings of identical verbal replies resemble the identical wrappings on two boxes containing different gifts.

We should not be surprised by these facts. It took many years for Jean-Paul Sartre to recognize the flaw in his belief as a young man that the act of naming a thing was equivalent to verifying its existence. He had confused what he read in books with real events. A short story by Marguerite Yourcenar captures this idea. The emperor of a kingdom had restricted his firstborn son to a large apartment whose walls were covered with the paintings by the kingdom's most acclaimed artist. When the emperor died, the prince left the apartment for the first time to assume power. After a few months of living in the world, he asked his attendants to bring the artist to the palace. When the artist appeared, the young emperor told him that he would be shot the next day. The artist asked why the emperor had arrived at this harsh decision. The emperor explained that for his first twenty years, the artist's paintings were his only knowledge of the outside world. Because the paintings were so beautiful, the prince had assumed that this was also true of the world. After experiencing the world directly, the young emperor realized that the artist had lied, and that was why he had to die.

Some psychologists believe that when they name a set of answers on a questionnaire as reflecting high *self-esteem*, they are confirming the existence of self-esteem as a natural phenomenon. Fifteenth-century Europeans accused some adults of being witches, but that does not mean that witches existed. A scientist's guess as to the meaning of a person's verbal description of a psychological state or trait is analogous to guessing the properties of an object and the target it struck when all one knows are the quality and loudness of the sound that was heard when the object struck the target.

The interpretation of a person's description of their psychological state is usually uncertain because psychologists do not have a theory that explains why individuals chose particular words to describe their private reactions to an event. This leaves psychologists in the position of an observer unaware of the physical laws governing the refraction of light in water who sees the lower half of a pencil immersed in a glass of water as bent but perceives the pencil as straight when it is removed from the water. Does water have the power to bend pencils, or does air have the power to straighten them? A similar confusion confronts psychologists with evidence revealing that 20 percent of the adults questioned reported that they felt tense with strangers but relaxed at home. Without a theory to explain the relation between the choice of terms like *tense* or *relaxed* and the brain or mental states to which the words presumably refer, the psychologists are in the position of the observer who saw that the pencil was bent in water but straight in air. Words "bend" private psychological states into forms that are not interpretable without a theory that can account for the relation between mental states and the language chosen to describe them.

Many psychologists have written equally cogent criticisms of verbal evidence. My skeptical evaluation of the research on personality, emotions, values, and mental illness that relies only on words that a majority in the community understand is less harsh than the judgment Lee Sechrest offered at the end of a review of the research papers on personality that were published in 1975. He suggested that the field of personality reminded him of "the apocryphal jet pilot who assured his passengers that while the plane was lost, it was at least making good time." The lack of substantial progress is revealed in the fact that every one of the Big Five personality dimensions— agreeableness, conscientiousness, extroversion, openness to ideas, and neuroticism—was described in some form by Confucius, Lao Tzu, Plato, or the writers who composed the Hindu Bhagavad Gita, the Hebrew Bible, the Buddhist Dhammapada, or the Zoroastrian Avesta in the eight centuries between 1000 and 200 BCE.[26]

It is worth noting that physicists routinely make up novel names for new events, such as quark and W boson, so that no one will confuse the meaning of the new discovery with a related concept. Psychologists, by contrast, prefer to call a new phenomenon by an old, familiar name. When investigators discovered that the eye-blink reflex to a loud sound was larger if the person had been looking at pictures of dangerous animals rather than babies or food, they decided that this reaction reflected a state of fear and did not require a new name. When people learn or perform an action in order to acquire money or praise and monkeys strike a lever to get food or a brief glance at a new scene, psychologists assume that all four events are examples of the same concept of reward. Psychologists are the only scientists who habitually assign new phenomena to a small collection of old, familiar conceptual categories. This practice implies the highly unlikely possibility that, after only 150 years of research, psychology possesses most of the significant concepts it requires.

Jack Gilbert, affirming the insights of Virginia Woolf and Ludwig Wittgenstein, used poetry to convey the inherent ambiguity of language.

> How astonishing it is that language can almost
>   mean,
> and frightening that it does not quite. *Love*,
>   we say,
> *God*, we say, *Rome* and *Michiko*, we write, and
>   the words
> get it wrong.
>   . . .
>
>   What we feel most has
> no name but amber, archers, cinnamon, horses,
>   and birds.[27]

I assume that psychologists recognize that political candidates, seducers, and salespersons say things they do not believe. It is difficult to understand, therefore, why they assume that a stranger's answers to the statements on their questionnaires are by and large truthful and accurate. Of course, if psychologists were willing to restrict the generality of their conclusions to the questionnaire evidence, they would be under no obligation to gather additional evidence. But few psychologists who rely only on questionnaire evidence are willing to accept such a serious limitation.

The phenomena psychologists wish to understand lie behind a thick curtain punctuated with a large number of tiny holes. The view through each small opening in the curtain, analogous to the information provided by one procedure, can not furnish a full comprehension of the event psychologists want to know. This knowledge requires views from many holes in the curtain. Biologists continue to invent more sensitive ways to measure a phenomenon, but psychologists who rely on verbal reports resist this strategy. There may come a time in the distant future when psychological theories are sufficiently coherent and affirmed by evidence that social scientists will be able to rely on one source of evidence to affirm or refute an idea. Some physicists are in that enviable position. The observations to be made with the Large Hadron Collider in 2011 or 2012 will allow physicists to decide whether the hypothetical Higgs particle exists. No domain in any of the social sciences is at that level of maturity at the present time. I do not have a lot of confidence that this plea to supplement verbal reports with additional evidence will be heeded by those who continue to treat this limited information as the basis for strong theoretical principles. I am confident, though, that until those who currently restrict all of their evidence to verbal reports abandon this practice, little progress will occur in the fields of personality, attitudes, values, emotions, and mental illness.

The Need for Patience

Major changes in the structure and politics of science in research universities have occurred during the past half-century. The number of faculty in American universities increased by a factor of four, from about a quarter million to over one million, in the four decades from 1960 to 2000. This increase was especially dramatic in the sciences. As a result, a large number of younger faculty without tenure have to compete for a smaller number of tenured professorships. The increased number of highly specialized fields forced chairpersons and deans to treat the number of published papers in refereed journals, rather than the theoretical significance of the research, as a primary criterion for promotion. One reason was that most of the faculty in a science department lacked the background needed to evaluate the importance of a collection of studies in a narrow field of inquiry.

At the same time, research productivity became an important basis for securing research funds from a government agency or private philanthropy. Because the scientists awarded research grants bring large amounts of overhead money to their universities, grateful deans began to award enhanced status and privileges to these investigators. This pragmatic basis for ranking faculty and their departments is moving at a faster pace in Great Britain than elsewhere. The British government, which subsidizes most universities, has begun to impose strict accounting standards on scholars in all departments. Each faculty member receives a score that represents a combination of number of papers published, number and amount of research grants won, and number of students taught. This system, which is indifferent to the significance of the scholar's efforts, forces faculty to write grants that have a high probability of funding research resulting in papers that will be accepted by a respected journal. The research proposed under these conditions is unlikely to lead to original breakthroughs because the investigators know that the anonymous reviewers of a research proposal usually disagree on its quality when it involves new ideas and procedures that stray too far from what the majority are doing. The smartest strategy in this situation is to play it safe and submit mainstream research plans whose results are likely to be published by prestigious journals. This is not a recipe for discoveries that require the persistent pursuit of less popular but potentially fruitful ideas.

British scientists with ideas as bold as those of Newton, Boyle, Faraday, Maxwell, Darwin, and Crick will
find it hard to obtain support in a system that treats a
scientific laboratory as if it were a supermarket belonging
to a chain and a scientist as the manager of the market.
Although this structure has penetrated English universities more deeply than US institutions, similar trends are
present in America's research universities.

The pressures produced by the new bases for research
funding and promotion force many faculty to adopt the
risk-averse strategy of publishing as many papers as possible in the seven or eight years before their department
decides whether they are to be promoted to the tenure
rank of associate or full professor. A long list of papers
produced in a short time requires scientists to design research that has a high probability of generating a publishable result. It is too risky to pursue a theoretically more
profound question requiring many years of work that has
no guarantee of success. When an initial study fails to
affirm a hypothesis, the clever strategy is to abandon the
original query, and that is what usually happens.

Max Perutz, a Nobel Laureate in physiology and
medicine, worked for almost thirty years before he discovered the structure of hemoglobin. Georg von Bekesy,
also a Nobel Laureate, invested many years to satisfy his
curiosity regarding the processes occurring on the sen-

sory receptors of the basilar membrane of the inner ear that are required for the perception of sound. Barbara McClintock, who studied the genetics of corn, Charles Townes, who invented the basis for the laser, and Mario Capecchi, who developed the idea of "knocking out" specific genes in animals, persisted in pursuing a research question that, initially, the leaders in these fields regarded as a waste of time. Their persistence paid off, for all three won Nobel Prizes. Darwin brooded more than twenty years on the observations he gathered during his five-year voyage on the *Beagle* before he published *On the Origin of Species* in 1859. Six years later Gregor Mendel shared for the first time the results of his years of patient research on plants with an audience of forty naturalists.

John Garcia is a psychologist without a long list of publications. But his discovery, with a colleague, that animals cannot acquire a conditioned response to any arbitrarily chosen conditioning stimulus remains unchallenged and, in my view, represents a more profound contribution than many of the results reported by psychologists who had published more than a hundred papers when they were at the same career stage as Garcia when he made his discovery. Marta Kutas's persistent study of a single puzzling phenomenon she and her mentor discovered more than thirty years ago was worth the effort. Kutas, with colleagues, has illuminated the significance of a waveform in the electroencephalogram that occurs about four-tenths of a second after the symbolic meaning of a word or picture violates the meaning a person expected. I suspect, but cannot prove, that there is a very modest relation between the number of papers published during the first eight years of a junior professor's appointment and the theoretical significance of his or her body of research over an entire career.[28]

Patience is a mandatory trait for those seeking the deep satisfaction that accompanies the realization that one has made a significant contribution to a discipline. Listen to a distinguished mathematician: "The real prize is not a medal . . . but making a breakthrough on the problem you've dedicated your life to." François Jacob, who shared the 1965 Nobel Prize for discoveries on gene regulation, confessed in his memoir, "Science meant for me the most elementary form of revolt against the incoherence of the universe."[29] No scientist with that degree of passion for understanding nature would worry about churning out four publishable papers in the next twelve months. Even when prolonged inquiry ends in failure, the committed scholar can feel gratified. Gottlob Frege spent many years trying to clarify the complex logical questions surrounding the concept of *number.* Although unsuccessful, he felt that the work had not been in vain because he had learned something from the effort.

Watch Out for Ethical Preferences

The confident defense of a belief rests on one of four foundations. Natural scientists prefer correspondence between a belief and objective observations or a logical deduction from a consistent set of mathematical statements. The claim by some physicists that strings of energy vibrating in ten dimensions are the ultimate constituents of matter rests on the latter criterion. The belief that the earth was round had been based four centuries earlier on a combination of a logical argument and an inference from indirect observations until a camera in space photographed the shape of our planet and added correspondence with direct perception to the earlier rationale.

Most philosophers treat the semantic coherence of a set of sentences as a sufficient basis for correctness. Locke's famous argument that all knowledge originated in sensory input and Kant's rebuttal of this claim are two examples. Feelings supply a fourth reason for believing in the correctness of the ideas called ethical or moral truths. The statements inscribed at the oracle in Delphi—"Know thyself" and "Nothing in excess"—are moral declarations. Neither is based on an observation, a deduction, or semantic coherence. Three men from a Gusii tribe in southwestern Kenya acted on this criterion when they murdered their mothers because they believed them to be witches. Accordingly, the men were neither punished nor ostracized for their actions because they honored a seminal moral belief held by their community.[30]

It is difficult for psychologists studying human personality, values, or mental illness to avoid the ethical ideals of their society. The primary theme in a number of papers published in 2010 in the premier journal *Psychological Science* engaged an ethical quality. Most North Americans and Europeans celebrate three ethical premises: a mother's love for her young child is necessary for healthy development; personal autonomy is essential to attaining optimal development; and freedom from childhood and adult stress is required for an adaptation free of anxiety. Note, however, that many Asians honor a trio that values acceptance by peers, a posture of interdependence with others, and worry over task failure.

Consider the premise that all infants need physical expressions of maternal love. A majority of Americans believe that mothers who are not physically affectionate with their infants will create adolescents with a less effective adaptation to their society. This conviction, which is stronger today than it was in colonial America or is in many contemporary cultures, is neither a deduction from a formal argument, in close correspondence with proven facts, nor the product of a coherent, semantic narrative. Rather, faith in this idea is sustained by the ethical intuition that infants *should* receive frequent embraces and kisses in order to develop properly.

There are rare occasions when a society adopts an uncommon ethical idea. For a brief period Mao Zedong altered the primary target of loyalty from the family to the state. The seventh-century Mayans thought it morally acceptable to sacrifice young women to the gods for the welfare of the community. Societal conditions continually alter the ethical acceptability of particular actions, as ecological conditions alter the adaptive advantage of small or large beaks on the finches of the Galápagos Islands.

During the three decades that followed the end of the Second World War, a number of intellectuals worried that the rise in large bureaucratic institutions might foster a conformity to majority views and interfere with the traditional ethos which assumed that autonomy, freedom, and creativity were the reasons for America's greatness. This era spawned many research efforts designed to prove that the sacred quartet of autonomy, rationality, tolerance toward all lifestyles, and openness to ideas were ideal personality traits. When the student rebellions against the Vietnam war, prolonged by some advisers to the president who possessed those precious traits, were followed by bands of autonomous, academically talented youth retreating to communes hosting permissive sex and drugs, it became less obvious that the sacred quartet was the best profile to encourage.

Social scientists habitually select a trait that is adaptive in their society, usually more common among the privileged, and assume it can be attained with equal ease by any child regardless of the family's social class. The related concepts of self-control and self-regulation are examples. Children from better-educated families are more likely to persist with and maintain attention on a difficult cognitive task than those reared by families without a high school diploma. The class difference is mainly the product of variation in socialization. Parents from less advantaged class positions teach their children to be prepared to cope with the threats of attack, robbery, police harassment, and prejudice. These habits do not necessarily enhance perseverance on unfamiliar tests of intellectual skills.

Advantaged families teach their children self-control and reflection before acting because these traits are especially advantageous in school and in many of the professional positions in developed societies. The elites in most societies usually declare that the things they are good at are superior under all circumstances. It is more accurate to recognize that the disadvantaged have to handle different challenges. If a poor adolescent in an urban ghetto has the opportunity to earn a large amount of money for taking on an unpleasant task, or has to defend the self against a peer who threatens harm, it can be disadvantageous to vacillate too long and better to decide or act quickly. Biologists do not make this error. Large beaks on finches are better for cracking large seeds, small beaks better for small seeds. The ecology determines which type of seed is more prevalent, and neither large beaks nor small ones are inherently better all of the time.

Freud's writings contained at least three ethical premises that he believed were scientifically based insights gleaned from his observations of patients: humans naturally prefer sensory pleasure to maintaining a sense of virtue; freedom of choice is a natural, universal urge; and reason alone can free individuals from the distress caused by their repressed motives. Freud's emphasis on the centrality of personal freedom was a historical extension of events in Europe that began with the Magna Carta and were followed by philosophical treatises celebrating the seminal importance of freedom in human affairs.

The two traits celebrated by Americans since the Declaration of Independence, but not by medieval monks, were personal autonomy and the freedom to do as one chooses, as long as these properties did not infringe on the welfare of others. John Locke declared, "Children love liberty and, therefore, they should be brought to do the things that are fit for them, without feeling any restraint laid upon them."[31] The belief in the priority of the individual and his or her freedom, rather than the welfare of the family, clan, or community, separated Enlightenment Europe from most of the world's cultures.

Locke's premise lies behind the favorable evaluation of children's play. The founder of the Playground and Recreation Association of America wrote in 1920 that play is what we do when we are free and added that the freedom inherent in play is the freedom on which democracy rests.[32] One child psychologist wrote in 1922 that a parent's greatest sin was to obstruct a child's freedom. The behaviors that psychologists call play are actions that are neither coerced by others nor motivated by the desire to gain a pragmatically useful goal. Hawks soaring in the sky, butterflies flitting in the air, and ducks waddling in the water are also engaging in actions that are neither coerced by others nor obviously useful, but few biologists describe these animals as playing.

Young children building block towers, however, appear to me to be engaged in a useful activity that is motivated by the wish to perfect a talent because they usually display a serious facial expression and become upset if interrupted. I remember watching my five-year-old granddaughter repeatedly fill a bucket from an outdoor spigot, pour the water into a sprinkler, and then distribute the water on the nearby grass. After five careful repetitions of this arduous sequence, without getting her clothes wet, she replaced her serious facial expression and tense body posture with a smile as she exclaimed, "Isn't this fun!" This was not idle, carefree behavior without a purpose but a self-administered test of her competence.

I still feel a twinge of guilt over an event that occurred more than thirty years ago when I was a member of a faculty committee administering an oral examination to a doctoral candidate whose thesis was on children's play. When told to begin the questioning, I asked her, "What is play?" She remained silent for about two minutes, began to weep, and seconds later left the room and did not return to the university. I met her fifteen years later at Cambridge University and was relieved to learn that she eventually did receive a PhD from another university. I assume that her earlier silence reflected the realization that what she had believed was a clearly defined natural phenomenon was instead an ethical judgment she had imposed on children's behavior. The ethical premise hiding in the concept of play, and the related assumption that it is necessary for optimal development, is that children should be free to do as they wish. Affluent, educated parents in sixteenth-century Germany did not share that assumption. Many of these families sent their preadolescent sons to distant cities to apprentice with a craftsman in order to learn a skill rather than remain at home playing.

Less than a century after Locke, the Scottish social philosopher Adam Smith sensed earlier than others the shift in his society from a majority of lives spent with kin on the family farm to an increasing number of careers spent in manufacturing, trade, and commercial interactions with strangers. This prescient insight led him to endorse the morality of placing self's interests over the welfare of others. Smith suspected that this declaration in *The Wealth of Nations*, published in 1776, might bother the consciences of his fellow Christian citizens. Because he was certain that sympathy for the psychological states of others and the wish to be accepted and respected were human properties that could never be subdued, Smith made his claim palatable by stating that a posture of self-interest would lead, through invisible mechanisms, to benevolent changes in the society. This ethical ideal now dominates the theories of economists and evolutionary biologists, as well as the ideology of citizens in most of the world's societies.

Smith's declaration that a society in which each person was free to maximize his or her own welfare first would become the best society was not a profound discovery about the qualities of humans that were inherent in their genome. It was an ethical preference that the vicissitudes of history transformed over several centuries into an adaptive trait. Smith may have had a conflict of interest when he wrote *The Wealth of Nations*. He was a forty-year-old professor at the University of Glasgow in 1764 when the Duke of Buccleuch, a wealthy landowner with many business interests, hired him as a private tutor with a handsome annual stipend. Smith accepted the offer because he wanted to be free of burdensome academic responsibilities. But in doing so, Smith probably became psychologically indebted to the duke. It would have been difficult for Smith to betray his generous benefactor and argue that unrestrained capitalism was not the ideal form for an economy.[33]

Hunter-gatherer groups composed of twenty to forty individuals trying to survive in Africa a hundred thousand years ago would have regarded Smith's philosophical view as bizarre, as would Plato, Confucius, and Augustine. Jonathan Franzen's novel *Freedom*, acclaimed by many reviewers, questions the benevolent consequences of a personal freedom unconstrained by responsibilities to others.

A reasonable number of psychologists believe that at least two conditions contribute to the Tea Party's ideal of an autonomous adult able to cope with life's exigencies without help from others or the government. These conditions are a secure attachment to a parent during infancy and minimal stress during childhood. I consider first the presumed importance of an infant's attachment. The broadly held belief that a mother's sensitivity with and affection toward her infant are absolutely necessary for healthy development dominates a great deal of research by North Americans and Europeans whose eighteenth-century predecessors declared that the habits established during the first year or two were likely to be permanent. If adult autonomy were necessary for a satisfying life, and this trait was formed during the early years, careful attention to the parental practices that created this trait would guarantee a sunburst of joyous outcomes and mute parental worry over the child's future.

The British psychiatrist John Bowlby wrote a trilogy of books on attachment between 1969 and 1980 that asserted, with insufficient evidence, that an infant's emotionally gratifying emotional bond to the mother, called a secure attachment, had a profoundly lasting effect on the child's future. The assertion that the quality of the mother-infant relationship in the first year had a continuing effect on the child's future development, especially the trait of self-reliance, if we exclude the small proportion of infants who experienced unusually harsh abuse or neglect, is not yet affirmed by evidence. Marcel Zentner and I reviewed in 1996 the major studies that followed a large sample of children from infancy or early childhood to the adult years. The results did not support Bowlby's belief that the events of the opening years created moods or habits that resisted change and were preserved in a majority of children. Because material alterations in genes caused by early adversity can be reversed (due to epigenetic processes), it seems unreasonable to claim that the emotions, habits, and beliefs associated with that adversity resist change.[34]

Had Bowlby read more deeply in history, he would have realized that his exaggerated concern with the relation between the mother's behavior and the infant's future personality did not emerge in Europe until the early eighteenth century. This idea required a growing proportion of mothers who did not have to leave the home to work and the real possibility of status mobility for children from middle-class homes. Mothers were now given the responsibility of sculpting children who would advance the family's interests, or at least not harm them. Children who, a century earlier, had been plow horses had now become show horses.

Leon Battista Alberti, a fifteenth-century citizen of Florence, was certain that a mother's actions were irrelevant for the child's future. That responsibility rested with the father, whose task was to convince his children that they could control their destiny through the exercise of willpower. Thomas More devoted less than a page to the parental treatment of young children in his sixteenth-century classic treatise *Utopia*, and he never mentioned the importance of the emotional relationship between a parent and infant. Because More was describing an ideal community, his failure to dwell on the affection between mother and infant implies that this idea was not very salient in the consciousness of sixteenth-century citizens. The Old Testament forbids only one parental action: a father may not sell his daughter into harlotry. There are no sanctions against an aloof, unaffectionate mother. Bowlby's intuition finds no support in a comparison of adults who spent their infancy and childhood in the 1950s and 1960s on an Israeli kibbutz or in a family from another rural region in Israel. The kibbutz children were raised by several women in a group home with other children and saw their parents only in the evenings or on holidays. When the two groups were evaluated years later, the evidence revealed that the adults reared on the kibbutz were similar to the family-reared individuals in verbal descriptions of their personality traits, attitudes toward the mother, level of adaptation, and presence or absence of a mental illness.[35] The book reporting these results is rarely cited. I suspect this is because its conclusions are inconsistent with what many psychologists want to believe.

Flaubert's fictional character Emma Bovary behaved like many mothers of her social class when she took her infant to live with a wet nurse without worrying about the effects of this arrangement on her child's psychological development. Nor did Chinese experts during Mao Zedong's reign make dire predictions about the malevolent consequences of placing millions of infants in day-care centers because the parents were working either close to or, in some cases, far from the center housing the child. The several centers my colleagues and I visited in 1973 had few toys and an ambience marked by minimal activity and exploration. Because the centers were unheated, most infants were hampered by an excess of clothes and were not allowed to crawl on the cold floor. Some observers might regard this environment as "moderately depriving." There is no evidence, however, that this regimen produced large numbers of intellectually retarded adults, criminals, or mental patients. Many of the young Chinese who stood bravely against the government tanks in the 1989 protests in Tiananmen Square had spent their infant and early childhood years in one of these centers.

Young children born to Gusii mothers in southwest Kenya did not suffer psychological harm because their mothers were not especially affectionate, were unusually harsh disciplinarians, and had their preadolescent daughters care for them during most days. Most of the children growing up on the island of Kauai in a poor family with a working mother who placed her infant with a surrogate caretaker during the day developed adaptive traits. These facts led the authors to conclude, "As we watched these children grow from babyhood to adulthood, we could not help but respect the self-righting tendencies within them that produced normal development under all but the most persistently adverse circumstances." Thus, the belief that infants must have the continual nurture and physical affection of the mother is an ethical premise maintained by the inchoate feeling that that this form of rearing ought to be ideal for development.[36]

The authors of one of the first studies documenting the persistence of psychological problems from early childhood to adolescence came to the same conclusion thirty years earlier. There was no predictive relation between the number of psychological problems middle-class mothers observed in their twenty-one-month-olds in 1927 and the presence of problems during adolescence or adulthood. These psychologists confessed that they had given too much weight to the "troublesome and the pathogenic aspects and underweighted elements that were maturity inducing . . . many of our most mature

and competent adults had severely troubled and confus-
ing childhoods." It appears that most young children
with psychological burdens living in families that are not
seriously deprived grow toward health. This outcome is
even possible, although less likely, when the child's experiences are continually depriving, harsh, and abusive.
Some young European children who were orphaned
during the Second World War were adopted by caring
middle-class American families. Several years later, psychiatrists evaluating their adjustment were surprised to
learn how well they were doing and were forced to conclude that the possibility of adaptation for children who
had suffered extreme trauma was much greater than the
experts writing during the 1950s believed. The level of
recovery does not mean that the early stress had no malevolent influence. Rather, it means that later experiences
have the power to compensate to some degree for the un-
toward consequences of the adverse events. This is even
true if the stressful events altered the level of expression
of genes in the young child because, as I noted, some alterations in gene expression are reversible.[37]

Bowlby was influenced, perhaps unduly, by Freud's
statement that all forms of childhood anxiety were due to
the loss of a beloved person. Bowlby may have read Erik
Erikson's 1950 book *Childhood and Society*, which declared
that a mother's sensitive care creates a feeling of trust in

the infant. Thus, Bowlby was not the first scholar to argue that maternal behaviors have a profound and lasting effect on the young child. This idea had been in the air for about two centuries. Three later influences on Bowlby came from the observations of his colleague James Robertson, who noticed the extreme distress in two-year-olds who were alone in a crib on a pediatric ward, the writings of the animal ethologists Nikolaas Tinbergen and Konrad Lorenz, and Harry Harlow's discovery of the abnormal behaviors of infant rhesus monkeys separated from their mothers and reared on a wire object. Finally, a personal event may have played an influential role. Bowlby's nanny, with whom he had a close relationship, left the household when the future psychiatrist was four.

It is less well known that Robertson disagreed with Bowlby's interpretations of the child's crying on the ward. He tried, initially without success, to persuade Bowlby that the protests occurred only in children between one and two years of age and, furthermore, could be prevented by simply having any caring adult nearby. The crying did not imply that the child missed the mother, as Bowlby believed, but was caused by being alone in an unfamiliar place without any nurturing adult in the vicinity.[38] Bowlby was eventually responsive to evidence, for in the second volume of his trilogy, *Attachment and Loss: Separation*, published in 1973, he acknowledged that

Robertson was correct. Any nurturing person could calm most crying children who were frightened by being alone in an unfamiliar place.

It is not a coincidence that the probability that a child will cry when the mother unexpectedly leaves the child alone in an unfamiliar place is highest during the middle of the second year in children growing up in the different cultures of Botswana, Guatemala, Israel, and the United States. The reasons for this lawful developmental phenomenon lie with maturational growth of the brain. By eighteenth months, anatomical changes allow most children to compare their current condition with their memories of the past. This improvement in working memory permits children to recognize that they are in an unfamiliar setting and creates uncertainty. But because they are not mature enough to understand why they are alone and do not know what to do, they cry. Additional maturation during the third year permits older children to understand why they are alone and provides them with ways to reduce their uncertainty. Therefore, most three-year-olds no longer become distressed when a parent leaves them alone in a strange place.[39]

Although it is always dangerous to draw strong conclusions from a single case history, anecdotes can be illuminating. Anna Freud had accepted some young children into a residential home outside London during the period when German planes were bombing the British capital. One young girl from a middle-class family who was sent to this temporary home became extremely upset over being separated from her mother. She sat for hours either sucking her thumb or turned toward a wall. A psychologist on Freud's staff followed the girl's development and eventually established a warm, trusting relationship with her. As a grown woman she often visited the staff psychologist, who became convinced that the formerly distressed girl had become a well-adjusted woman with no signs of the earlier anxiety she expressed when separated from her parents.[40]

By contrast, the social class in which a child is reared has a profound and well-documented effect on future personality. These facts prompt the following hypothetical query. Suppose that one group of psychologists knew only the class of rearing of five thousand randomly selected thirty-year-olds and a second group of experts knew only their security of attachment and the affectionate sensitivity of their parents during the first two years of childhood. The evidence suggests that the experts who only knew the child's social class would be far more accurate in their predictions of which thirty-year-olds were depressed, socially anxious, obese, incarcerated for a crime, addicted to alcohol or an illicit drug, or seriously dissatisfied with their job or marriage. Yet, a sizeable number of talented psychologists continue to insist that the security or insecurity of an infant's attachment, based on the parents' behaviors, extends its influence indefinitely. Pretty ideas do not die easily. Mathematicians are allowed to use beauty as a criterion when deciding which equations best fit a natural phenomenon. Psychologists cannot rely on the attractiveness of their private ethical premises to decide which explanations are correct because nature does not favor any particular ethical preference.

The broad appeal of Bowlby's bold statements was facilitated by historical events in Europe and North America during and right after the Second World War. The rise in the proportion of women entering the workforce, which in the United States doubled from 40 to 80 percent between 1950 and 2000, led many to wonder whether this disruption of the usual arrangement during the past century, in which a biological mother continually tended her infant, was unhealthy for the child's future development. The enthusiasm for Bowlby's ideas was also aided by the public's abhorrent reaction to the cruelties of the Second World War, which created a deep yearning for a gentler conception of human nature in which trust and love, Erik Erikson's ideal prescription for the infant, replaced the dark images of emaciated adults gassed to death and thrown into mass burial pits or cremated in ovens in Nazi concentration camps.

The social scientists born after 1950 who were attracted to Bowlby's intuition that "gnawing uncertainty about the accessibility . . . of attachment figures is a principle condition for the development of unstable and anxious personality" may have projected their personal desire for more trusting relationships with friends, lovers, and colleagues on to young infants who were not mature enough to know whether their parents loved them. The ambiguous qualities of the infant, like tea leaves at the bottom of a cup, make it easy to imagine that infants deal with some of the same problems that adults confront. Some nineteenth-century American psychologists declared that the newborn's reflex grasping of a pencil placed in its palm was an early harbinger of adult greed, and most attributed to infants a narcissistic selfishness rather than a need for security. Japanese mothers living on the sparsely populated island of Hokkaido may have projected their feeling of isolation on their offspring, for they reported that their children were very lonely.[41] Poor, uneducated American mothers, frustrated by financial problems and boring work, are more likely than comfortable middle-class parents to describe their young infants as irritable and provide a persuasive example of adults attributing to children their own dominant mood.

At the moment, the quality of an infant's attachment to a parent is usually based on the behaviors of one-year-olds on two occasions in a laboratory when the parent leaves the infant in an unfamiliar room and returns a few minutes later (the procedure is called the Strange Situation). This strategy is marred by the fact that the infant's responses to the mother's departure and return are influenced, in part, by the child's temperamental biases, which are independent of the mother's sensitivity as a caretaker. Children are classified as securely attached if they cried a little when the mother left but were easily soothed by the mother when she returned. Insecurely attached children behave in two different ways. One group becomes so upset when the mother leaves that she is unable to soothe the infant when she returns. The other group does not cry when the mother leaves and ignores her when she returns. A third, very small group invented later, called *disorganized*, displays an unusual combination of stereotyped behaviors, sudden body immobility, an inconsistent combination of crying and avoidance of the mother, and signs of cognitive confusion.

These four groups of children display different behaviors even before the mother leaves the child, as well as at home. The insecurely attached children who could not be soothed were irritable, timid, and fearful in the familiar home setting and as newborns cried intensely when they lost the nipple they were sucking. They often sought contact with the mother and cried if they lost track of her. The insecurely attached children who ignored the mother in the laboratory were exploratory at home and unconcerned with the mother's location. These facts suggest that children's temperamental biases contributed to their reactions when the mother left them and returned in the Strange Situation and imply that the child's reactions to the mother's departure and return were not due exclusively to the quality of their interactions with their mother. That is why an insecure attachment at one year was not a good predictor of disobedience and aggression in preadolescent boys.[42]

The belief that the quality of the infant's attachment, inferred from behavior in the Strange Situation, exerts a continuing influence over many years remains an intuition rather than an established fact. The temptation to assume that good experiences in infancy must be followed by good traits in adulthood resembles the temptation that led Copernicus to assume that because God only made beautiful objects, it must be true that the orbit of the earth followed the beautiful trajectory of a circle. The human mind finds it hard to accept the possibility that something good can be followed by something bad or vice versa.

I suspect that one reason for the appeal of Bowlby's ideas is that most children in contemporary middle-class homes make no material contribution to their family.

They are pampered, well-fed guests at a small luxury hotel. This parasitic role renders them susceptible to needing reassuring signs of their worth. Parental caresses and
regular declarations of love assure children of their basic
value in the family. Sixteenth-century eight-year-olds in
rural farming villages who cared for younger siblings,
tended the family cow, helped with cooking or planting,
or gathered water and firewood, did not require this symbolic form of reassurance because they knew that they
made a substantial contribution to the family's welfare.
They had objective evidence of their intrinsic value. Preadolescent children in rural Zimbabwe, who became or-
phans when AIDS killed their parents, assumed the parental role and assigned their siblings appropriate work.
The youth born to parents who emigrated to California
from Mexico or Asia, who devoted many hours each week
to helping their family in some material way, reported
feeling more cheerful, happy, and satisfied than white
youth who made little or no sacrifices for their family.[43]

Nineteenth-century American children from poor
families may have had a stronger sense of their worth
than contemporary children from equally poor homes
because, during the years before mandatory public
schooling, many worked at unskilled jobs and shared
their earnings with their family. Today, all children are
required to be in school, and those who fail to master the

basic skills are doubly deprived. They feel intellectually inadequate and, in addition, are unable to use work to persuade themselves that they have some semblance of worth. Historical events have placed a psychological burden on many contemporary youth from disadvantaged homes that is heavier than the burden felt by those who lived in the same cities or towns 140 years ago.

If children or adults find it hard to believe in their intrinsic value, they become dependent on others, and especially the parents, to provide evidence for that reassuring thought. It is a uniquely Western premise, with an origin in the early eighteenth century, that a mother's love for her infant is a necessary foundation of the belief that the self is valued and possesses some measure of grace. Nineteenth-century middle-class Americans turned up the gain on this premise by assuming that women were responsible for the spiritual vitality of the family. The writer Hermann Hesse captured this perception of the sacred powers of women and the maternal role when he had Goldmund say to his friend Narcissus, who lay dying in his arms, "But how will you die when your time comes, Narcissus, since you have no mother? Without a mother one cannot love. Without a mother one cannot die."

The elimination of all stress, a derivative of Freud's conviction that anxiety was the primary villain in all neuroses, is a second ethically tinged idea that permeates research. The popular assumption that any form of anxiety is psychologically harmful is one reason why most experimental research on emotions centers on fear or anxiety rather than anger, sadness, shame, or guilt. If psychologists had been members of Plato's Academy they would have studied anger, because this emotion was the enemy of the harmonious civility Athenian citizens wished for their beloved city.

A second reason for the focus on anxiety or fear is that the scientists wanting to prove close relations between animal and human qualities were certain that they could create fear in a rat. They were less sure that they could create sadness, shame, or guilt. The assumption that a rat is in a state of fear is usually based on the display of body immobility (called freezing) or an exaggerated body startle to a tone (or light) that in the past had been followed by an electric shock. Rats who had undergone this conditioning regimen and became immobile to the presentation of a conditioned tone were assumed to be in a state of "fear."

It is worth noting, however, that Pavlov did not assume that the dogs he had conditioned to salivate to a tone that in the past had been followed by food powder were "hungry." Nor did Konrad Lorenz attribute an emotion to the goslings that followed him because he was the first moving object the newly hatched birds saw. It is not at all obvious that an emotional state is present when an animal, or person, displays a conditioned behavior. I automatically smile at a stranger who has smiled at me, but that brief, unconscious reaction does not mean I am in a "happy" state.

The popular premise that all forms of stress should be eliminated from a child's life is susceptible to a critique. A collection of papers on stress in a 2010 issue of the journal *Neuroscience and Biobehavioral Reviews* did not differentiate among the very different experiences that can be stressors and considered only the deleterious consequences of stress. The authors of these papers failed to consider the possible benevolent effects of mild or brief periods of stress, despite evidence indicating that such effects do occur. Infant squirrel monkeys that were stressed by being separated from their mother for an hour a day over a series of days developed more adaptive traits than the infant monkeys who were not stressed. The stressed animals were better at inhibiting an inappropriate behavior, were more likely to explore novel settings, and showed fewer signs of fear in these settings. The Mehinaku Indians of central Brazil are generally indulgent with their infants but treat disobedience in two- or three-year-olds harshly. The adult grabs the child's wrist and scarifies the calves and legs with a fish-tooth scraper as the child screams in pain. Because this form of punishment is predictable, and perceived by the child as just, these children became adults who are neither more nor less anxious than those from cultures that do not implement this stressful socialization.[44]

There is a serious inconsistency between the belief that all forms of stress interfere with healthy development and the memoirs or biographies of a small number of accomplished, satisfied adults who coped with unusually stressful childhoods. One reason is that some youths respond to the stress by generating a strong motive to eliminate the anxiety, shame, or guilt produced by the childhood experiences through unusual levels of achievement. Isaiah Berlin had to cope with harsh rejection by his classmates at an elite British boarding school because he was a recent Jewish immigrant from Russia. John Maynard Keynes was often whipped by a father he admitted hating. Johannes Brahms's family was so poor the future composer had to earn money during his adolescence by playing the piano at a brothel until the wee hours of each morning. Sherwin Nuland, a professor of medicine at Yale University and a respected writer, grew up in a poor family in New York, lost his mother when he was eleven years old, had an extremely harsh, uneducated father who regularly debased him in outbursts of rage, and, as a boy, felt deep shame when he appeared with the father in public. Yet, in a memoir written when he was seventy years old, Nuland forgave his father and declared his love for a parent that most Americans would regard as excessively cruel.[45]

Francis Wayland, an eighteenth-century Baptist minister and one of the presidents of Brown University, described with pride how he tamed the will of his disobedient, fifteen-month-old son by locking him in a closet for over twelve hours until the boy apologized for his sin of refusing food. If we assume that this level of harshness was a regular part of the boy's experience, modern readers might be surprised to learn that the boy did not become a criminal or develop a mental disorder but held the positions of minister, college teacher, magazine editor, and president of Franklin College. The Reverend Wayland's practices were not atypical for his historical era. Many eighteenth-century and early-nineteenth-century English parents locked their disobedient children in a dark room for hours or days in order to tame their will, and there is no evidence to indicate that most of these adults led unhappy lives. Many of the Jewish children who immigrated to America from Germany or Austria during the 1930s, some without their parents, became successful, productive adults, despite the stress of being removed from all that was familiar and having to adjust to an unfamiliar culture. Some told an interviewer that their stressful experiences had broadened their perspective and enriched their lives.[46]

A group of architects who had been nominated by their peers as unusually creative was compared with equally successful architects who were judged to be less original. The creative architects told an interviewer that they had experienced frequent rejection by and isolation from their adolescent peers. They added, however, that they believed the social rejection allowed them to develop effective defenses against the discomfort produced by a lack of friends. These defenses made it easier, when they became architects, to ignore the critical opinions of colleagues when they defied conventional norms in their original designs. Quakers, like Jews, were marginalized "outsiders" in seventeenth-century England and its American colony. Outsiders have the advantage of feeling free to entertain dissenting ideologies and less popular careers. When scientists began to make important discoveries that challenged dominant Christian premises, Quakers experienced less inhibition than devout Catholics or Anglicans over pursuing a scientific career. John Dalton, who was born in 1766 and achieved fame for his contributions to the atomic theory of matter, was a Quaker.

The assumption that the lack of close friendships during the adolescent or adult years is a serious stressor that frustrates a basic biological need and prevents sustained happiness has become popular over the past fifty years. A few psychologists amplified the gain on this bold declaration by suggesting that the physical pain of a broken leg shares important features with the "pain" of social rejection. They called the latter "social pain." A major reason for implying that physical pain shares important features with the feeling accompanying rejection is that a small number of brain sites are active in both states. This argument has flaws. The amygdala is activated by pictures of erotic couples as well as bloody surgical operations. That fact does not mean that scenes of sex and surgery evoke a common psychological state. Both my visual and motor cortex are active when I write, sip coffee, tie my shoes, pick up a soiled sock, and cut an apple, but these five acts do not belong to the same psychological category because my intentions and psychological states are different in each of these actions. It is misleading, therefore, to call the state produced by social exclusion "social pain."[47] Exclusion or rejection can evoke anxiety, anger, sadness, or self-hatred, but none of these states would be confused with the sensation of a toothache.

Poets, novelists, and lyricists are permitted to write about the "pain of love," but scientists should not treat casually constructed metaphors as deep insights into human nature. I hope that no psychologist decides that a hunger for food resembles a hunger for friendships. The positing of social pain is another example of the psychologists' fatal attraction to positing abstract categories based primarily on a common semantic term. Sixteenth-century botanists made the mistake of classifying wheat, which is a grass, with buckwheat, which is not a grass, because *wheat* was present in both terms.

The broad concern with the serious consequences of perceived social isolation or rejection rests on the unproven assumption that close relationships with others, especially members of the same age cohort, are biologically necessary for psychological health. I am excluding the relationships between child and parent, lovers, and marriage partners, for they have a different foundation. The popularity of the current view regarding the malevolent consequences of the absence of close friendships is due, in part, to the increased geographic mobility among Americans following the inventions of the automobile and airplane. These inventions made it possible for large numbers of adults to live far from their families and childhood friends in competitive social settings in which the ethic of self-reliance was a psychological burden to those who did not have challenging jobs or were marginalized.

A second reason is the increased awareness of and guilt over lingering racism in our society and the perception of exclusion by members of minority groups. These events motivated some experts to argue that optimal mental health required close friendships. These communications persuaded many citizens that they *ought* to have many close ties if they want to regard themselves as psychologically healthy. The seventeenth-century mathematician, physicist, and philosopher Blaise Pascal, who summarized his views on the human condition in his *Penséees*, did not believe that humans needed many close friendships to be happy. Rather, Pascal suggested, "All the unhappiness of men arises from one simple fact, that they cannot stay quietly in their own chamber. . . . To bid a man live quietly is to bid him live happily."

I suggested in the last chapter that many experiences are gratifying only if the individual believes that these states should be attained. An adolescent circumcision or a bar-mitzvah only enhances the person who believes in the sacredness of the ritual. If someone did not believe that close attachments to others were enhancing, which is true for those loyal to Buddhist philosophy, the knowledge that one enjoys many friendships would be less satisfying, and a lack of friends would not generate intense anxiety or depression. Jill Ker Conway, a former president of Smith College who spent her childhood on an isolated farm in Australia, did not regard her lack of childhood friends as a burden. Claude Lévi-Strauss chose to live a solitary life but did not seem to suffer because of the absence of friendships. We must distinguish between the feelings generated by the sensation of sweet foods, on the one hand, and the satisfaction that accompanies the attainment of a symbolically valued state, on the other. The latter prize requires a prior belief in the value of the state to be attained.

Contemporary youth and adults with access to cell phones, Facebook, Twitter, and e-mail are involved in a larger number of relationships than the members of my generation. But my adolescent friends and I did not feel particularly lonely. We must ask, then, what is it that the current cohort of young adults feels they are missing? I believe their subjective feeling of deprivation has two faces. First, as noted in chapter 2, many are not seriously committed to some ethical ideals that they believe must be honored. A fundamental requirement for feelings of serenity and satisfaction is, as Wallace Stevens recognized, commitment to a few unquestioned ethical beliefs. That is why neither Lévi-Strauss nor Pascal was unhappy, despite the absence of many friendships.

The muse of history, in a cruel mood, robbed large numbers of adults born after 1960 of an unquestioned faith in at least one sacred idea. The pictures of Nazi gas chambers and mass burial pits, American soldiers torching the huts of Vietnamese peasants, the taunting of naked Iraqi prisoners, and Hutu men slicing open the bellies of pregnant Tutsi women made it difficult to deny the ugly side of our two-faced species. A popular illustration in psychology textbooks is a figure that is perceived as a young, beautiful woman if one attends to one spot on the picture but as an old, ugly woman if the gaze shifts to another location. History has paralyzed the eye muscles of contemporary humans, making it difficult for them to shift their stare away from the human capacity for cruelty. This change in the dominant view of human nature is captured by the replacement of a naked, lactating woman as the symbol for nature in sixteenth-century Europe with the contemporary symbol of a lion killing a gazelle.

Earlier centuries witnessed equivalent horrors. The Inquisitors tortured and burned nonbelievers, but most populations outside Europe were unaware of these terrible actions. Today, information technology informs everyone—isolated villagers in New Guinea and residents of Chicago—of all horrendous crimes. The last two cohorts of Americans have found it more difficult than my generation to accept Wallace Stevens's advice to commit fully to some moral imperative in order to reassure themselves that they were OK. By OK, I mean the ability to whisper to the self at the end of most days that one possesses a goodness that originates within the person. A reasonable substitute that seemed attainable was to find at least one person who could be trusted to value his or her personhood under all circumstances.

A second factor contributing to the epidemic of loneliness is the increased distrust of others because of the omnipresent possibility of betrayal. This enhanced suspicion of the loyalty of others is due, in part, to changes in the socialization practices of American parents. After 1950 many parents became excessively concerned with perfecting their child's sense of self. Every child was a potential princess or prince. The removal of the earlier barriers to self-actualization in women meant that both sexes were to honor this imperative. The inevitable consequence of this preoccupation with creating the perfect self was that everyone became obsessed with aggrandizing their own egos. As might be expected, the celebration of self-actualization was accompanied by an increase in the frequency of betrayals by lovers, spouses, and friends. When the narcissistic concern with self was joined to the loss of faith in some ideal lying outside the self, millions found themselves searching for human ties through Facebook, Twitter, and cell phone conversations but, sadly, could not commit completely to another because of the need to remain vigilant to possible betrayal. Jack and Suzie, the lead characters in the film *The Baker Boys*, are excellent examples of a psychological condition missing from the Hollywood films of the 1940s. A *New Yorker* cartoon, illustrating a middle-aged couple, has the wife say to her husband, "I've decided to sell you on eBay."

I wish to be absolutely clear on this issue. It is true that, consciously, many contemporary North Americans and Europeans feel they are lonely. It is also true that this feeling can lead to sadness and compromises in the immune and cardiovascular systems. But the primary sources of the melancholic mood and compromised biology are the absence of an ethically praiseworthy goal worth working for with passion and a reluctance to commit to another because of the possibility of betrayal.

History, not biology, made loneliness a toxic condition. Although contemporary adults believe that their uncomfortable feelings are due to a lack of close friendships, their more fundamental deprivation is a reason for believing in something transcendent that would permit them the satisfaction of feeling worthy and vital. Those who have read John Stuart Mill's autobiography may remember that as a young man he decided to devote his life to improving the lot of humanity. Mill fell into a deep depression when he realized that if that wish were granted at that moment he would not feel happy. The loss of faith in a seminal ideal he had cherished for so long left him spiritually naked and, I suspect, lonely.

Buddhists would not regard the lack of close ties as a dangerous condition. There is a story of a Buddhist monk meditating under a tree when a former wife approaches, places his child before him, and says, "Here, monk, here is your son, nourish me and nourish him." The monk ignores them and sends the woman away. The Buddha, seeing this, says, "He feels no pleasure when she comes, no sorrow when she goes, I call him a true Brahman released from passion." American psychologists, especially those wedded to attachment theory and the notion that loneliness is a pathological condition, would regard the monk as suffering from a deep depression and in need of immediate therapy, perhaps because he had an insensitive mother when he was an infant.

Many years ago, perhaps in the 1980s, I saw a twenty-minute silent film whose author understood the nature of our present tragic condition. A man walking on an isolated country road trips, and one of his legs falls into a deep sinkhole from which he cannot escape. He waves for help whenever a car passes by, but no one stops. After awhile, both legs and his body have sunk into the hole and a passerby steals some of his clothes. In the final scenes, when only his head is visible, another passerby puts his foot on top of the victim's head, forcing him completely into the hole, and he disappears. Finis. The author of this chilling script did not intend to tell viewers that our victim lacked friendships. The message was that historical events have deprived many of the reassuring belief that most humans are usually loyal, honest, and kind, at least one person sincerely cares about them, and they need not fear betrayal by a stranger, friend, lover, or spouse. This uncomfortable state of mind has its origin in society rather than in deprivation of a biological need for friendships.

An article in the January 31, 2011, issue of the *New Yorker* first surprised me and then led to a deep sadness. A Japanese entrepreneur opened an agency that rents fathers, grandchildren, and temporary husbands. The English translation of the Japanese name for the business is "We want to cheer you up." A New Jersey businessman, who may have heard of the Tokyo success, started an agency that rents friends for $24.95 per hour. The message conveyed by these "start-ups" is that all deep feelings between friends or relatives are illusory. Perhaps we should drop the facade and admit that it makes no difference whether the person you hike with is a childhood friend or a rented companion. I confess to my terribly old-fashioned views by declaring that I hope this is not true. The Marquise du Châtelet would be proud of me for maintaining my illusion that Odysseus would not have persisted against storms, Scylla, and Circe in order to return home to Penelope, waiting patiently for him in Ithaka, if she were a rented wife.

To return to the central point, psychologists are ignoring the adaptive consequences of select stressors that give children an opportunity to learn how to cope with frustration, peer rejection, or harsh socialization. The child's immune system, too, requires the stress of infection to mature properly. The current parental habit of treating all sore throats with antibiotics and vaccinating children against common, nonfatal childhood diseases may not be in the best interests of the child. This conclusion should not be interpreted as implying that all childhood stressors are without serious consequences. What is likely to be true is considerably more nuanced. Some children are not seriously harmed by harsh socialization, peer rejection, or being the victim of bullies either because they had a resilient temperament or did not interpret the experience as reflecting on their personhood. And in some cases the stress allowed the child to acquire effective coping defenses that were of value later. I suspect that a childhood free of all stress can be as serious a risk factor as one filled with trauma. This more complex conclusion does not mean that I believe that physical or sexual abuse, neglect, and poverty are innocent experiences. These events can have palpable, undesirable influences on later development. But the exact forms of the later consequences are affected by the child's biology and idiosyncratic interpretations of the stressful events.

Some readers might ask whether any ethical beliefs have a privileged position in human biology, and if so how might they be discovered? Some social scientists assume that study of less modern cultures might reveal the ethics that are consonant with nature's plans. It is unlikely that ethnographies can accomplish that goal. Contemporary Americans allow their children to express anger and mild aggression because experts have told them that these are natural reactions and children may develop psychosomatic symptoms if their anger is always suppressed. However, Jean Briggs, who lived for several years with a group of Utku Eskimo in an area near Hudson Bay, challenged that assumption. She noted that every display of anger in children over two years of age was followed by parents and relatives becoming silent. The children were initially upset by this silent treatment, but tantrums stopped after a year or so, older children displayed little aggression, and the symptoms that were supposed to result from the suppression of anger were absent in these Eskimo children.[48] The consequences of suppressing the actions that accompany anger depend on the context in which children are growing. It is not adaptive for individuals living in an igloo nine months a year to express their anger easily. Hence, the correct answer to anyone asking whether it is more in accord with human nature to express anger or to suppress it is neither.

The belief that justified anger should not be suppressed has advantages in cultures in which a large number of strangers must compete for a small number of positions of dignity and status. In the film *El Norte* a young Guatemalan who fled his village for a job in Los Angeles learns from a coworker that in America everyone looks out for themselves first. Rather than acknowledge that the structure of American society forces this frame of mind, many find it more attractive to assume that expression of this mood is an inevitable remnant of our animal ancestry that we are powerless to subdue.

The results of scientific research can never be the sole basis for deciding what is psychologically optimal for all children in all cultures during all historical eras. Each person must make his or her own ethical evaluation of what is best, and this judgment is more often based on sentiments that rise from existing social conditions rather than logically consistent proofs, semantically coherent arguments, or correspondence with observations. The writer Louis Menand reminds us that each of us must figure out the ethical guides we wish to honor, "Go ahead, ask your genes what to do. You might as well be asking Zeus."[49]

If a society's ethics cannot be based only on scientific facts, readers may ask where a community can find the bases for its fundamental moral propositions? I suggest that the source lies with the feelings of the majority, which of course change with time. Most Americans regard unprovoked aggression, dishonesty, and coercion as morally indefensible and a referendum on each would reflect that belief. Indeed, increasing numbers of moral issues are placed on the local ballot each election day, suggesting that the larger community is ready to rely on majority opinion as a guide to ethical dilemmas.

The Supreme Court recognized the difficulty of defining pornography objectively when it declared that the attitudes of the local community should determine which books and movies violated sensibilities. The Court legitimized the private emotional reactions of the majority in a community as a participant in the establishment and maintenance of values. It is difficult to implement that strategy in American society all of the time because of the extraordinary diversity of opinion on critical issues and a resistance to having binding propositions rest on nonrational, sentimental grounds. That is why science was placed in the position of moral arbiter in the twentieth century.

Scientific facts have value because they can disconfirm the factual bases for a particular ethical premise and weaken its persuasive power. For example, research evidence was useful in refuting the belief of the majority during the early decades of the last century that black and

white children in segregated schools had equivalent educational opportunities. These facts allowed the Supreme
Court justices to appear rational when they decided that
segregated schools violated the Constitution. But it was
also necessary that, by the 1960s, a majority of Americans had come to believe that this practice was immoral.
Without that change in public opinion the Court might
have ruled differently. The nineteenth-century judges
sitting on the Massachusetts Supreme Judicial Court
failed to honor the article in the Bill of Rights guarantee-
ing every criminal a public defender and certainly would
not have ruled in favor of the legality of gay marriage.
Facts can prune the tree of morality, but they cannot be
the seedbed.

James Wilson, a colonial philosopher of law, defended
this position: "If I am asked—why do you obey the will
of God? I answer—because it is my duty to do so. If I am
asked again—how do you know this to be your duty? I
answer again—because I am told so by my moral sense
of conscience. If I am asked a third time—how do you
know that you ought to do that, of which your conscience
enjoins the performance? I can only say, 'I feel that such
is my duty.' Here investigation must stop; reasoning can
go no further."[50]

Psychologists should remain sensitive to the ethical
premises that occasionally penetrate their research and

affect the advice they give to clients. Scientists continue to search for the features of human brains that awarded our species its advantageous properties, especially language, reasoning, planning, morality, and the ability to control emotions. The neurons of the human frontal lobe have a little more space between them than the neurons in chimpanzee frontal lobes. Some scientists have suggested that this anatomical fact might explain our valued human competences. Scientists comment less often on the undesirable human traits that distinguish us from apes.

Imagine that chimpanzees, not humans, dominate the earth and have established university laboratories containing chimp scientists trying to understand why some members of the human species commit suicide, torture, hang, stone, or hack to death other members of their species, die while climbing or skiing on mountains in winter, are seriously injured in games observed by thousands gathered in large stadiums, abuse infants, develop addictions to alcohol or cocaine, cannot sleep at night, require children to sit for six hours a day in small rooms, become obese, incarcerate juveniles in prisons, enslave other humans, work until midnight even though they have sufficient food and shelter, wear clothes when it is hot, destroy forests, pollute streams, decide not to have children, and live in small apartments in high-rise buildings in densely crowded cities. Had the chimp scientists discovered that the neurons of the human frontal lobe had more space between them than the neurons of the chimpanzee brain, they might have argued that this feature probably explains why humans display these odd traits.

The suggestion that psychologists remain acutely aware of their ethical values does not mean that they should stop probing issues with ethical implications, only that they should not confuse those ideas with what is true in nature. The chance mutations that gave rise to humans and their unique brain allowed our species to anticipate the distant future, recall the deep past, and invent the concepts *bad*, *good*, and *best*. But the latter trio of abstract ideas does not specify their content. That is, they do not name the specific traits, acts, feelings, or beliefs that award a referential meaning to these terms. Hence, they resemble the open parameters in the equations of physicists and economists who insert the values that fit their preconceptions.

When Freeman Dyson was a young physicist, he showed some mathematical calculations to Enrico Fermi that he believed explained Fermi's empirical observations on the scatter of mesons. When Fermi asked how many open parameters Dyson had used, the younger man confessed that his equations had four open parameters, to which Fermi replied, "Johnny von Neumann used to say that with four parameters I can fit an elephant and with five I can make him wiggle his trunk."[51]

Three fundamental ideas penetrate most of the claims in this book. The suggestion to base more psychological concepts on patterns of evidence presumes that the context of observation, which includes the setting, the procedure, and the types of participants, is an important element in most patterns. Chapter 1 documented the profound influence of the context on behavior and biology in both animals and humans and urged advocates of a new concept to include a description of the context or to confirm that the new idea generalizes across settings. A large number of popular psychological concepts, including *fear, self-regulation, well-being,* and *agreeableness,* to name only a few, are contextually naked. They have an ambiguous meaning because the properties of the setting, the procedure with its unique evidence, and the qualities of the participants are unspecified. Analysis of the sex of the prominent character in prime-time television advertisements in seven different nations (Brazil, China, Thailand, Canada, Germany, South Korea, and the United States) revealed that South Korea was distinctive because its ads contained many more women than men as the primary character compared with the other six societies. This fact invites the guess that South Korea is probably the most gender-egalitarian society, as measured by the degree of gender equality in income, education, and life expectancy. But that inference is mistaken, for South Korea is less egalitarian than Germany, Canada, and the United States, countries that have fewer women as the primary character in television ads.[52] Once again, examining patterns of measures is more illuminating than restricting the evidence to one source of information.

Most classes of observations contain more than one pattern. Animals can be arranged into patterns based on their genomes and evolutionary history, latitude and longitude, size, longevity, and form of locomotion, or profile of symbolic meanings in various religions. The observer's purpose determines the pattern awarded privilege. But this fact does not negate the importance of searching for patterns. The advances in evolutionary theory over the past fifty years required biologists to acknowledge that the concept of *fitness* had to combine the genes that control the embryo's development, the genes that monitor adult traits, and the local ecology.

The second and third themes apply primarily to our species because only humans impose symbolic interpretations on experiences that, in many instances, engage a good to bad evaluation. That is why psychologists should develop procedures that can measure private understandings of an event, rather than assume that individuals are responding to the events that a camera records. Loss of a parent, a natural catastrophe, harsh socialization, abuse, social rejection, task failure, or an illicit sexual affair do not affect everyone similarly. A thirteenth-century woman from a small French village confessed that she felt no guilt when her sexual intimacies with a local priest were accompanied by intense carnal desire. But a feeling of sin did penetrate her mood when her sexual acts were not accompanied by libidinous ardor.

Children or adults who interpret an unpleasant experience as a sign of personal vulnerability or a lack of moral integrity are the most vulnerable to developing habits and moods that compromise adaptation. The smaller number who, for unknown reasons, construe the same event as the product of bad luck usually escape undesirable consequences. Some of these resilient souls were born with a special temperamental bias. Others exploited their life history or culture's premises to generate effective defenses against the stressful event. Recall that some of the American hostages held by Iranian terrorists for more than a year did not become unusually anxious. Patients who believe that the drug or form of psychotherapy they are receiving will be helpful are most likely to show serious improvement.

I noted that personal interpretations of experience are as basic in psychological theory as cells are in biology.

Interpretations of an event transcend the brain's response to the event, as mathematics transcends logic, thought transcends language, and faith transcends rationality. Variation in private interpretations is one reason for the extraordinary degree of variability found in most measurements. Adults lying in a scanner watching the same excerpt from a Hollywood film displayed different patterns of blood flow in the frontal lobes. Unfortunately, too few psychologists are trying to invent methods that might provide indices of these personal interpretations.

Suppose that a team of psychologists wished to know the variation among a hundred adolescents in the strength of their identification with their social class. The investigators might record changes in posture, talking, smiling, and heart rate while the youths watched a film portraying a competition between one adolescent from an advantaged family and one from a disadvantaged family. Disadvantaged youths who smiled and showed a large change in heart rate when the actor from the disadvantaged home gave a correct answer or when the advantaged actor failed can be regarded as more strongly identified with their class than those who expressed neither response. This strategy could be exploited to measure identifications with one's gender, religion, or ethnicity. This hypothetical example was meant only as an illustration of a procedure rarely used that could add important information to a person's conscious verbal descriptions of his or her profile of identifications.

The human moral sense is the third theme woven through the five chapters. Once children pass their second or third birthday, they cannot help imposing a good to bad evaluation on their experiences, actions, traits, feelings, and thoughts. Natural scientists who study inanimate matter or animals record what their procedures allow them to observe and typically suppress any temptation to wonder what nature should have revealed. Social scientists find it harder to suppress images of ideal states of affairs. These ethical intrusions seep into many investigations of human personality and pathology and have a profound effect on the advice therapists give their clients. I am not suggesting that psychologists stop studying ethically tinged questions, only that they recognize the biases that are bending their inquiries and inferences in a particular direction. These psychologists might profit from brooding on the advice the mathematician John von Neumann gave, in *The World of Mathematics*, to colleagues entangled in highly abstract mathematical systems that had strayed too far from natural events: "The only remedy seems to me to be the rejuvenating return to the source: the reinjection of more or less directly empirical ideas."

John von Neumann's request to pay close attention to what is observed will not, of course, yield explanations. A room full of DVDs and hard discs is an extremely quiet place. All scholars recognize that they also need rich ideas that bubble up from intuition to arrange their observations into a meaningful pattern. These theoretical ideas, however, will have to be more complex than those that dominate current explanations. An insecure attachment to a parent, attendance at a day-care center for several years, victimization by bullies, or a particular set of genes usually do not lead to a particular adult profile without being part of a pattern of conditions. Now the advice of the biologist J. B. S. Haldane deserves reflection: "The universe is not only queerer than we suppose but queerer than we can suppose." If more psychologists recited the von Neumann and Haldane quotes as mantras after their morning coffee they might achieve some of the deep insights that they, their mentors, and their mentors' mentors have sought for a very long time.

Some lines I wrote on yellow paper several years ago seem an appropriate way to end this book. Most people want to know why they're here when they should be asking what they are doing. In addition to the acts required for survival, they talk, listen, plan, plot, remember, anticipate, love, work, wonder, imagine, and try continually to prove they are worthwhile. These activities are occasionally interrupted by loss, hostility, catastrophe, rejection, failure, and regret, which permit anger, doubt, worry, shame, guilt, or sadness to disturb their mood. The fortunate who were born with genes that subdued the intruders or enjoyed a childhood that allowed them to learn coping defenses manage to tame the disturbances. A smaller group finds it harder to keep the interruptions at bay. Meanwhile, the muse of history, reclining on a cloud, is continually altering the scenery and rewriting the script so that new generations speak new lines, make new plans, remember new facts, wonder about new possibilities, and find new ways to feel worthwhile. The muse smiles as she watches each cohort rage wildly at ghosts, trying to make sense of a script with a permanently unfathomable meaning while insisting that their lines are better than those of their neighbors. Although the initial role assignments were determined by throws of the dice, the muse is willing to give a new role and a revised script to those who pay the proper fee. To a select few, she whispers her secret: "Play your role with passion, even if you suspect that it is expendable, and allow the compassion you had as a child to balance the urge to always maximize the self."

Notes

Missing Contexts

1. L. Rizzi and G. Dala-Zuanna, "The seasonality of conception," *Demography* 44 (2007): 705–728.
2. N. D. Eggum, N. Eisenberg, T. L. Spinrad, et al., "Predictors of withdrawal," *Development and Psychopathology* 21 (2009): 815–828; K. Dodge, "Context matters in child and family policy," *Child Development* 82 (2011): 433–442.
3. S. Milgram, *Obedience to Authority: An Experimental View* (New York: Harper and Row, 1974).
4. P. Galison, *Einstein's Clocks, Poincaré's Maps: Empires of Time* (New York: W. W. Norton, 2003).
5. D. Sabatinelli, P. J. Lang, A. Keil, and M. M. Bradley, "Emotional perception," *Cerebral Cortex* 17 (2007): 1085–1091; J. Vartiainen, M. Liljestrom, M. Koskinen, H. Renvall, and R. Salmelin, "Functional magnetic resonance imaging blood oxygenation level-dependent signal and magnetoencephalograpy evoked responses yield different neural functionality in reading," *Journal of Neuroscience* 31 (2011): 1048–1058.
6. A. Schafer, A. Schienle, and D. Vaitl, "Stimulus type and design influence hemodynamic responses towards visual disgust and fear elicitors," *International Journal of Psychophysiology* 57 (2005):

53–59; K. E. W. Laidlaw, T. Foulsham, G. Kuhn, and A. Kingstone, "Potential social interactions are important to social attention," *Proceedings of the National Academy of Science* 108 (2011): 5548–5553.

7. T. Sharon, M. Moscovitch, and A. Gilboa, "Rapid neocortical acquisition of long-term arbitrary associations independent of the hippocampus," *Proceedings of the National Academy of Sciences* 108 (2011): 1146–1151.

8. T. Striano and E. W. Bushnell, "Haptic perception of material properties by 3-month-old infants," *Infant Behavior and Development* 28 (2005): 266–289; A. E. Learmonth, N. S. Newcombe, and J. Huttenlocher, "Toddlers' use of metric information and landmarks to reorient," *Journal of Experimental Child Psychology* 80 (2001): 225–244; G. M. Alexander and M. Evardone, "Blocks and bodies: Sex differences in a novel version of the Mental Rotations Test," *Hormones and Behavior* 53 (2008): 177–184; D. A. Stapel and S. Lindenberg, "Coping with chaos: How disordered contexts promote stereotyping and discrimination," *Science* 332 (2011): 251–253.

9. R. M. Sapolsky, "The influence of social hierarchy on primate health," *Science* 308 (2005): 648–652; K. A. Sloman, D. Baker, G. S. Winberg, and R. W. Wilson, "Are there physiological correlates of dominance in natural trout populations?" *Animal Behavior* 76 (2008): 1279–1289; H. Vervaecke, H. De Vries, and L. van Elsacker, "An experimental evaluation of the consistency of competitive ability and agonistic dominance in different social contexts in captive bonobos," *Behavior Genetics* 136 (1999): 423–442; D. R. Robertson, "Social control of sex reversal in a coral-reef fish," *Science* 177 (1972): 1007–1009.

10. R. J. McMahon, K. Witkiewitz, and J. S. Kotler, "Predictive validity of callous-unemotional traits measured in early adolescence to multiple antisocial outcomes," *Journal of Abnormal Psychology* 119 (2010): 752–763; V. Reynolds, "How wild are the Gombe chimpanzees?" *Man* 10 (1975): 123–125; R. Slotow, G. van Dyk, J. Poule, B. Page, and A. Klacke, "Older bull elephants control young males," *Nature* 408 (2000): 425–426.

11. R. D. Williams, D. A. Marchuk, K. M. Gadde, et al., "Serotonin-related gene polymorphisms and central nervous system

serotonin function," *Neuropsychopharmacology* 28 (2003): 533–541; J. J. Arnett, "The neglected 95%: Why American psychology needs to be less American," *American Psychologist* 63 (2008): 602–614; A. Singh-Manoux, M. G. Marmot, and N. E. Adler, "Does subjective and social status predict health and change in health status better than objective status?" *Psychosomatic Medicine* 67 (2005): 855–861; C. E. Wright and A. Steptoe, "Subjective socio-economic position, gender and cortisol responses to waking in an elderly population," *Psychoneuroendocrinology* 30 (2005): 582–590; S. Ghane, A. M. Kolk, and P. M. Emmelkamp, "Assessment of explanatory models of mental illness: Effects of patient and interviewer characteristics," *Social Psychiatry and Psychiatric Epidemiology* 45 (2010): 175–182; U. M. Marigorta, O. Lao, F. Calafell, et al., "Recent human evolution has shaped geographical differences in susceptibility to disease," *BMC Genomics* 12 (2011): 55–69; J. O. S. Goh, E. D. Leshikar, B. D. Sutton, et al., "Cultural differences in neural processing of faces and houses in ventral visual cortex," *Social, Cognitive and Affective Neurosciences* 5 (2010): 227–235; R. M. Todd, J. W. Evans, D. Morris, M. D. Lewis, and M. J. Taylor, "The changing face of emotion," *Social, Cognitive, and Affective Neuroscience* 6 (2011): 12–23.

12. A. K. Beery and I. Zucker, "Sex bias in neurochemical and biomedical research," *Neuroscience and Biobehavioral Reviews* 35 (2011): 565–572; M. C. Keller, B. L. Fredrickson, O. Ybarra, et al., "A warm heart and a clear head," *Psychological Science* 16 (2005): 724–731.

13. J. Henrich, S. J. Heine, and A. Norenzayan, "The weirdest people in the world," *Behavioral and Brain Sciences* 33 (2010): 61–83; L. Boroditsky and A. Gaby, "Remembrances of times East: Absolute spatial representations of time in an Australian aboriginal community," *Psychological Science* 21 (2010): 1635–1639; K. R. Hill, R. S. Walker, M. Bozicevic, et al., "Co-residence patterns in hunter-gatherer societies show unique human social structure," *Science* 331 (2011): 1286–1289.

14. S. E. Asch, "Studies of independence and submission to group pressure," *Psychological Monographs* 70 (1956): 1–70; M. F. Lalancette and L. Standing, "Asch fails again," *Social Behavior and Personality* 18 (1990): 7–12.

15. V. R. Carney, A. J. C. Cuddy, and A. J. Yap, "Power posing," *Psychological Science* 21 (2010): 1363–1368.
16. M. Seaton, H. W. Marsh, F. Dumas, et al., "In search of the big fish: Investigating the coexistence of the big-fish-little-pond effect with the positive effects of upward comparisons," *British Journal of Social Psychology* 47 (2008): 73–103; A. Thornton and K. McAuliffe, "Teaching in wild meerkats," *Science* 313 (2006): 227–229; Y. Tong and M. R. Phillips, "Cohort-specific risk of suicide for different mental disorders in China," *British Journal of Personality* 196 (2010): 467–473; K. Y. Liu, M. King, and T. S. Bearman, "Social influence and the autism spectrum," *American Journal of Personality* 115 (2010): 1387–1424; S. Maggi, A. Ostry, K. Callaghan, et al., "Rural-urban migration patterns and mental health diagnoses of adolescents and young adults," *Child and Adolescent Psychiatry and Mental Health* 13 (2010): 4–13.
17. J. Diamond and J. A. Robinson, *Natural Experiments of History* (Cambridge, MA: Harvard University Press, 2010); V. Smil, "Genius loci," *Nature* (2001): 21.
18. W. J. Bossenbrook, *The German Mind* (Detroit, MI: Wayne State University Press, 1961); S. Ozment, *A Mighty Fortress: A New History of the German People* (New York: HarperCollins, 2004); P. A. Kuhn, "Chinese view of social classification," in *Language, History and Class*, ed. P. J. Corfield (Oxford: Basil Blackwell, 1991), 227–239.
19. J. Harwood, *Styles of Scientific Thought: The German Genetics Community, 1900–1933* (Chicago: University of Chicago Press, 1993).
20. F. Stern, *Einstein's German World* (Princeton, NJ: Princeton University Press, 1999); H. Kohn, *The Mind of Germany* (New York: Charles Scribner's Sons, 1960).
21. J. Block, *Lives through Time* (Berkeley, CA: Bancroft, 1971); S. W. Gregory and S. Webster, "A nonverbal signal in voices of interview partners effectively predicts communication, accommodation, and social status perceptions," *Journal of Personality and Social Psychology* 70 (1996): 1231–1240; S. B. Manuck, J. D. Flory, R. E. Ferrell, and M. F. Muldoon, "Social economic status covaries with central nervous system serotonergic responsivity as a function of allelic variation in the serotonin transporter gene-linked polymorphic region," *Psychoneuroendocrinology* 29

(2004): 651–668; E. Chen, S. Cohen, and G. E. Miller, "How low socioeconomic status affects 2-year hormonal trajectories in children," *Psychological Science* 21 (2010): 31–37; E. M. Tucker-Drob, M. Rhemtulla, K. Paige-Harden, E. Turkheimer, and D. Fask, "Emergence of a gene x socioeconomic status interaction on infant mental ability between 10 months and 2 years," *Psychological Science* 22 (2011): 125–133; J. Kagan and S. R. Tulkin, "Social class differences in child rearing during the first year," in H. R. Schaffer, ed. *The Origins of Human Social Relations*, ed. H. R. Schaffer (New York: Academic Press, 1971), 165–183.

22. N. M. Stephens, H. R. Markus, and S. M. Townsend, "Choice as an act of meaning," *Journal of Personality and Social Psychology* 93 (2007): 814–830; A. Firkowska, A. Ostrowska, M. Sokowska, Z. Stein, and M. Susser, "Cognitive development and social policy," *Science* 200 (1978): 1357–1362.

23. R. Rios and A. J. Zautra, "Socio-economic disparities in pain," *Health Psychology* 30 (2011): 58–66; N. E. Adler, T. Boyce, M. A. Chesney, et al., "Socioeconomic status and health," *American Psychologist* 49 (1994): 15–24; P. J. Gianaros, F. M. Van der Veen, and J. R. Jennings, "Regional cerebral blood flow correlates with heart period and high-frequency heart period variability during working-memory tasks: Implications for the cortical and subcortical regulation of cardiac autonomic activity," *Psychophysiology* 41 (2004): 521–539; N. A. Holtzman, "Genetics and social class," *Journal of Epidemiological and Community Health* 56 (2002): 529–535; M. Schiff, M. Duyme, A. Dumaret, J. Stewart, S. Tomkiewicz, and J. Feingold, "Intellectual status of working-class children adopted early into upper-middle-class families," *Science* 200 (1978): 1503–1504; R. W. Simm and L. E. Nath, "Gender and emotion," *American Journal of Sociology* 109 (2004): 1137–1176; M. Meltzer, P. Bebbiston, T. Brugha, R. Jenkins, S. McManus, and S. Stansfeld, "Job insecurity, socioeconomic circumstances, and depression," *Psychological Medicine* 40 (2010): 1401–1407; E. Turkheimer, A. Haley, M. Waldron, B. D'Onotrio, and I. I. Gottesman, "Socioeconomic status modifies heritability of IQ in young children," *Psychological Science* 14 (2003): 623–628.

24. L. Damrosch, *Tocqueville's Discovery of America* (New York: Farrar, Straus and Giroux, 2010).

25. P. J. Henry, "Low-status compensation," *Journal of Personality and Social Psychology* 97 (2009): 451–466; M. Akiba, G. K. Le Tendre, D. T. Baker, and B. Goesling, "School system effects on school violence in 37 nations," *American Educational Research Journal* 39 (2002): 829–853.

26. D. L. Vandell, J. Belsky, M. Burchinal, L. Steinberg, N. van der Grift, and NICHD Early Child Research Network, "Do effects of early child care extend to age 15 years?" *Child Development* 81 (2010): 737–756; E. Votruba-Drzal, R. L. Coley, C. Maldonado-Carreno, C. P. Li-Grining, and P. L. Chase-Lansdale, "Child care and the development of behavior problems among economically disadvantaged children in middle childhood," *Child Development* 81 (2010): 1460–1474.

27. J. J. Cutuli, K. L. Wiike, J. E. Herbers, M. R. Gunnar, and A. S. Masten, "Cortisol functions among early school-aged homeless children," *Psychoneuroendocrinology* 35 (2010): 833–845.

28. R. E. Zinbarg, S. Suzuki, A. A. Uliaszek, and A. R. Lewis, "Biased parameter estimates and inflated type 1 error rates in analysis of covariance (an analysis of partial variance) arising from variability," *Journal of Abnormal Psychology* 119 (2010): 307–319; R. M. May, "Uses and abuses of mathematics in biology," *Science* 303 (2004): 790–793; J. Collett and O. Lizardo, "Occupational status and the experience of anger," *Social Forces* 88 (2010): 2079–2084.

29. A. J. Oswald and S. Wu, "Objective confirmation of subjective measures of human well-being: Evidence from the U.S.A.," *Science* 327 (2010): 576–577.

30. R. P. McDonald, "Structural models and the act of approximation," *Perspectives on Psychological Science* 5 (2010): 675–686; F. Schmidt, "Detecting and correcting the lies that data tell," *Perspectives on Psychological Science* 5 (2010): 233–242, quotation on 237; J. W. Tukey, "Analyzing data: Sanctification or detective work?" *American Psychologist* 24 (1969): 83–91.

31. C. K. Peterson and E. Harmon-Jones, "Circadian and seasonal variability of resting frontal EEG asymmetry," *Biological Psychology* 80 (2009): 315–320; K. Allen, J. Blascovich, and W. V. Mendes, "Cardiovascular reactivity and the presence of pets, friends, and spouses," *Psychological Medicine* 64 (2002): 727–739.

32. R. Stark, A. Schienle, B. Walter, et al., "Hemodynamic responses to fear and disgust-inducing pictures: An fMRI study,"
International Journal of Psychophysiology 50 (2003): 225–234; C. M.
Stoppel, C. N. Boehler, H. Strumpf, et al., "Neural correlates
of exemplar novelty processing under different spatial attention
conditions," *Human Brain Mapping* 30 (2009): 3759–3771.

33. A. Alink, C. M. Schwiedrjik, A. Kohler, W. Singer, and L. Muckli,
"Stimulus predictability reduces responses in primary visual cortex," *Journal of Neuroscience* 30 (2010): 2960–2966; J. P. Johansen,
J. W. Tarpley, J. E. Ledoux, and H. T. Blair, "Neural substrates
for expectation-modulated fear learning in the amygdala and
periaqueductral gray," *Nature Neuroscience* 13 (2010): 979–986;
M. Zaretsky, A. Mendelsohn, M. Mintz, and T. Hendler, "In the
eye of the beholder: Internally driven uncertainty of danger recruits the amygdala and dorsomedial prefrontal cortex," *Journal
of Cognitive Neuroscience* 22 (2010): 2263–2275; C. O. Tan, "Anticipating changes in regional cerebral hemodynamics: A new role
for dopamine?" *Journal of Neurophysiology* 101 (2009): 2738–2740;
K. A. Zaghloul, J. A. Blanco, C. T. Weidemann, et al., "Human
substantia nigra neurons encode unexpected financial rewards,"
Science 323 (2009): 1496–1500; J. Machado, A. M. Kazama, and
J. Bachevalier, "Impact of amygdala, orbital frontal, or hippocampal lesions on threat avoidance and emotional reactivity in non-
human primates," *Emotion* (2009): 147–163; K. Sander, A. Brech-
mann, and H. Scheich, "Audition of laughing and crying leads
to right amygdala activation in a low-noise fMRI setting," *Brain
Research Protocols* 11 (2003): 81–90.

34. F. Ahs, T. Furmark, A. Michelgard, et al., "Hypothalamic blood
flow correlates positively with stress-induced cortisol levels in subjects with social anxiety disorder," *Psychosomatic Medicine* 68 (2006):
859–862; E. M. Eatough, E. A. Shirtcliff, J. L. Hanson, and S. D.
Pollak, "Hormonal reactivity to MRI scanning in adolescents,"
Psychoneuroendocrinology 34 (2009): 1242–1246; J. Pripfl, S. Robinson, U. Leodolter, E. Moser, and H. Bauer, "EEG reveals the effect
of fMRI scanner noise on noise-sensitive subjects," *Neuroimage*
(2006): 332–341; A. Raz, B. Lieber, F. Soliman, et al., "Ecological nuances in functional magnetic resonance imaging (fMRI):
Psychological stressors, posture, and hydrostatics," *Neuroimage*

25 (2005): 1–7; L. Schwabe, L. Haddad, and H. Schachinger, "HPA axis activation by a socially evaluated cold-pressor test," *Psychoneuroendocrinology* 33 (2008): 890–895; G. G. Brown, D. H. Mathalon, H. Stern, et al., "Multisite reliability of cognitive BOLD data," *Neuroimage* 54 (2011): 2163–2175; M. E. Raichle and M. A. Mintun, "Brain work and brain imaging," *Annual Review of Neuroscience* 29 (2006): 449–476; K. Fiedler, "Voodoo correlations are everywhere—not only in neuroscience," *Perspectives on Psychological Science* 6 (2011): 163–171.

35. S. J. Kim, H. S. Lee, and C. H. Kim, "Obsessive-compulsive disorder, factor-analyzed symptom dimensions and serotonin transporter polymorphism," *Neuropsychobiology* 52 (2005): 176–182; D. L. Liao, C. J. Hong, H. L. Shih, and S. J. Tsai, "Possible association between serotonin transporter promoter region polymorphism and extremely violent crime in Chinese males," *Neuropsychobiology* 50 (2004): 284–287; A. Serretti, L. Mandelli, C. Lorenzi, et al., "Temperament and character in mood disorders: Influence of DRD4, SERTPR, TPH, and MAO-A polymorphisms," *Neuropsychobiology* 53 (2006): 9–16; D. L. Liao, C. J. Hong, H. L. Shih, and S. J. Tsai, "Possible association between serotonin transporter promoter region polymorphism and extremely violent crime in Chinese males," *Neuropsychobiology* 50 (2004): 284–287.

36. C. E. Franz, T. P. York, L. J. Eaves, et al., "Genetic and environmental influences on cortisol regulation across days and contexts in middle-aged men," *Behavior Genetics* 40 (2010): 467–479; E. Maron, J. M. Hettema, and J. Shlik, "Advances in molecular genetics of panic disorder," *Molecular Psychiatry* 15 (2010): 681–701; A. Terracciano, S. Sanna, M. Uda, et al., "Genome-wide association scan for five major dimensions of personality," *Molecular Psychiatry* 15 (2010): 647–656.

37. S. Hohmann, K. Becker, J. Fellinger, et al., "Evidence for epistasis between the 5-HTTLPR and the dopamine D4 receptor polymorphisms in externalizing behavior among 15-year-olds," *Journal of Neural Transmission* 116 (2009): 1621–1629; W. Johnson, "Understanding the genetics of intelligence: Can height help? Can corn oil?" *Current Directions in Psychological Science* 19 (2010): 177–182; T. F. Mackay, "The genetic architecture of complex behaviors," *Genetica* 136 (2009): 295–302.

38. C. Ferdenzi, B. Schaal, and S. C. Roberts, "Human axillary odor: Are there side-related perceptual differences?" *Chemical Senses* 34 (2009): 565–571.

39. K. F. Condry, and E. S. Spelke, "The development of language and abstract concepts: The case of natural number," *Journal of Experimental Psychology: General* 137 (2008): 22–38; D. R. Bach, O. Hulme, W. D. Penny, and R. J. Dolan, "The known unknowns," *Journal of Neuroscience* 31 (2011): 4811–4820.

40. J. Albrecht, M. Demmel, V. Schopf, et al., "Smelling chemosensory signals of males in anxious versus nonanxious conditions increases state anxiety of female subjects," *Chemical Senses* 36 (2010): 19–27.

41. M. Bleich-Cohen, M. Mintz, P. Pianka, et al., "Differential stimuli and task effects in the amygdala and sensory areas," *NeuroReport* 17 (2006): 1391–1395.

42. A. de Tocqueville, *Democracy in America* (New York: Vintage, 1945); S. Haber, "Politics, banking, and economic development," *Natural Experiments of History*, ed. J. Diamond and J. A. Robinson (Cambridge, MA: Harvard University Press, 2010), 88–119; A. Macfarlane, *The Origins of English Individualism* (New York: Cambridge University Press, 1979).

43. W. Mischel, "Toward an integrative science of the person," *Annual Review of Psychology* 55 (2004): 1–22; S. Kato, *A History of Japanese Literature* (New York: Kodansha International, 1997); C. Ozawa-de Silva, "Too lonely to die alone: Internet suicide pacts and existential suffering in Japan," *Culture, Medicine, and Psychiatry* 32 (2008): 516–551; R. E. Nisbett, K. Peng, I. Choi, and A. Norenzayan, "Culture and systems of thought: Holistic versus analytic cognition," *Psychological Review* 108 (2001): 291–310; H. R. Markus, Y. Uchida, H. Omoregie, S. S. M. Townsend, and S. Kitayama, "Going for the gold," *Psychological Science* 17 (2006): 103–111; T. Masuda, P. C. Ellsworth, and B. Mesquita, "Placing the face in context: Cultural differences in the perception of facial emotion," *Journal of Personality and Social Psychology* 94 (2008): 365–381.

44. J. Goody, *The Theft of History* (New York: Cambridge University Press, 2009).

45. C. Hansen, *Language and Logic in Ancient China* (Ann Arbor: University of Michigan Press, 1983).

46. A. Tuohy and M. R. Phillips, "Cultural metaphors and reasoning," *Asian Folklore Studies* 50 (1991): 189–220; J. Spencer-Rogers, M. J. Williams, and K. Peng, "Cultural differences in expectations of change and tolerance for contradiction: A decade of empirical research," *Personality and Social Psychology Review* 14 (2010): 296–312.

47. A. Sen, "Internal consistency of choice," *Econometrica* 61 (1993): 495–521; Y. Hideki, "Modern trend of Western civilization and cultural peculiarities in Japan," in *The Japanese Mind*, ed. C. A. Moore (Honolulu, HI: East-West Press, 1967), 52–65, quotation on 63.

48. K. Miura, H. Inoue, and M. Tominaga, "Are there any differences of impression between real objects and their reproductions viewed through CRT displays and video projectors?" *Japanese Psychological Research* 24 (2002): 162–173; Y. Nihei, M. Terashima, I. Suzuki, and S. Morikawa, "Why are four eyes better than two? Effects of collaboration on the detection of errors in proofreading," *Japanese Psychological Research* 44 (2002): 174–180.

49. C. Chen, M. Burton, E. Greenberger, and J. Dmitrieva, "Population migration and the variation of the dopamine D4 receptor (DRD4) allele frequencies around the globe," *Evolution and Human Behavior* 20 (1999): 309–324; R. P. Ebstein, "The molecular genetic architecture of human personality: Beyond self-report questionnaires," *Molecular Psychiatry* 11 (2006): 427–445.

50. C. M. Kuhnen and J. Y. Chiao, "Genetic determinants of financial risk-taking," *PloS One* 4 (2009): e436; C. Chen, M. Burton, E. Greenberger, and J. Dmitrieva, "Population migration and the variation of the dopamine D4 receptor (DRD4) allele frequencies around the globe," *Evolution and Human Behavior* 20 (1999): 309–324.

51. A. Sen, *The Idea of Justice* (Cambridge, MA: Harvard University Press, 2009); R. Queinec, C. Beitz, B. Contrand, et al., "Copycat effect after celebrity suicides: Results from the French national death register," *Psychological Medicine* 41 (2011): 668–671.

TWO

Happiness Ascendant

1. J. M. Cooper, *Reason and Emotion: Essays on Ancient Moral Psychology and Ethical Theory* (Princeton, NJ: Princeton University

Press, 1999); E. Diener and R. Biswas-Diener, *Happiness: Unlocking the Mysteries of Psychological Wealth* (Malden, MA: Blackwell, 2008); M. E. P. Seligman, *Authentic Happiness: Using the New Positive Psychology to Realize Your Potential for Lasting Fulfillment* (New York: Free Press, 2002).

2. Y. Uchido and S. Kitayama, "Happiness and unhappiness in East and West: Themes and variations," *Emotion* 9 (2009): 441–456; F. F. Chen, "What happens if we compare chopsticks with forks? The impact of making inappropriate comparisons in cross-cultural research," *Journal of Personality and Social Psychology* 95 (2008): 1005–1018; J. L. Tsai, B. Knutson, and H. H. Fung, "Cultural variation in affect valuation," *Journal of Personality and Social Psychology* 90 (2006): 288–307.

3. C. J. Boyce, G. D. A. Brown, and S. C. Moore, "Money and happiness: Rank of income, not income, affects life satisfaction," *Psychological Science* 21 (2010): 471–475; C. A. Fulmer, M. J. Gelfand, A. W. Kruglanski, et al., "On 'feeling right' in cultural contexts: How person-culture match affects self-esteem and subjective well-being," *Psychological Science* 21 (2010): 1563–1569.

4. D. Kuhn, *The Age of Confucian Rule* (Cambridge, MA: Harvard University Press, 2009), 5.

5. D. G. Myers and E. Diener, "The pursuit of happiness," *Scientific American* 274 (1996): 56–57.

6. S. Bok, *Exploring Happiness: From Aristotle to Brain Science* (New Haven: Yale University Press, 2010); A. M. Abdel-Khalek, "Quality of life, subjective well-being, and religiosity in Muslim college students," *Quality of Life Research* 19 (2010): 1133–1143.

7. I. Kant, *Grounding for the Metaphysics of Morals* (Indianapolis, IN: Hackett, 1981), 27.

8. S. Banth and C. Talwar, "*Anasakti*, the Hindu ideal, and its relationship to well-being and orientations to happiness," *Journal of Religion and Health*, doi: 10.1007/s10943-010-9402-3.

9. C. D. Ryff, "Happiness is everything, or is it? Explorations of the meaning of psychological well-being," *Journal of Personality and Social Psychology* 57 (1989): 1069–1081.

10. W. Stevens, *Opus Posthumous* (New York: Knopf, 1957); D. M. McMahon, *The Pursuit of Happiness* (London: Penguin, 2006), 202.

11. L. Eiseley, *The Night Country* (New York: Charles Scribner's Sons, 1971), 224.
12. B. P. Dohrenwend, "Inventorying stressful life events as risk factors for psychopathology," *Psychological Bulletin* 132 (2006): 477–495; H. C. Heims, H. D. Critchley, R. Dolan, C. J. Mathias, and L. Cipolotti, "Social and motivational functioning is not critically dependent on feedback of autonomic responses: Neuropsychological evidence from patients with pure autonomic failure," *Neuropsychologia* 42 (2004): 1979–1988; W. Hirst, E. Phelps, R. I. Buckner, A. Cue, J. D. E. Gabrielli, and M. K. Johnson, "Long-term memory for the terrorist attack of September 11," *Journal of Experimental Psychology: General* 138 (2009): 161–176; R. Hoehn-Saric, J. S. Lee, D. R. McLeod, and D. F. Wong, "Effect of worry on regional cerebral blood flow in nonanxious subjects," *Psychiatry Research NeuroImaging* 140 (2005): 259–269.
13. A. K. Anderson and E. A. Phelps, "Is the human amygdala critical for the subjective experience of emotion? Evidence of intact dispositional affect in patients with amygdala lesions," *Journal of Cognitive Neuroscience* 14 (2002): 709–720.
14. L. Glanz, F. McCarty, E. J. Nehl, et al., "Validity of self-reported sunscreen use on parents, children, and lifeguards," *American Journal of Preventive Medicine* 36 (2009): 63–69; P. M. DiBartolo and A. E. Grills, "Who is best at predicting children's anxiety in response to a socially evaluative task?" *Journal of Anxiety Disorders* 20 (2006): 630–645; H. R. Riggio and R. E. Riggio, "Emotional expressiveness, extraversion, and neuroticism: A meta-analysis," *Journal of Nonverbal Behavior* 26 (2002): 195–218.
15. G. Murray, C. L. Nicholas, J. Kleiman, et al., "Nature's clocks and human mood: The circadian system modulates reward motivation," *Emotion* 9 (2009): 705–716; P. J. Rentfrow, S. D. Gosling, and J. Potter, "A theory of the emergence, persistence, and expression of geographic variation in psychological characteristics," *Perspectives on Psychological Science* 3 (2008): 339–341; T. J. Csordas, C. Dole, A. Tran, M. Strickland, and M. G. Storck, "Ways of asking, ways of telling," *Culture, Medicine, and Psychiatry* 34 (2010): 29–55; V. C. Plaut, H. R. Markus, and M. E. Lachman, "Place matters: Consensual features and regional variation in American well-being and self," *Journal of Personality and Social*

Psychology 83 (2002): 160–184; P. Raggatt, "Putting the 5-factor model into context: Evidence linking Big Five traits to narratives of individuals," *Journal of Personality* 74 (2006): 1321–1348; A. A. Stone, J. E. Schwartz, J. E. Broderick, and A. Deaton, "A snapshot of the age distribution of psychological well-being in the United States," *Proceedings of the National Academy of Sciences* 107 (2010): 9985–9990; R. Wuthnow, *America and the Challenges of Religious Diversity* (Princeton, NJ: Princeton University Press, 2006).

16. C. E. Osgood, "Objective indicators of subjective culture" in *Issues in Cross-Cultural Research*, ed. L. L. Adler (New York: New York Academy of Sciences, 1977), 435–458.

17. M. D. Back, A. C. Kufner, and B. Egloff, "The emotional time line, September 11, 2001," *Psychological Science* 21 (2010): 1417–1419.

18. A. Waugh, *The House of Wittgenstein* (New York: Doubleday, 2008).

19. W. O. Beeman, "Affectivity in Persian language use," *Culture, Medicine, and Psychiatry* 12 (1988): 9–30.

20. D. Bimler, "From color naming to a language space," *Journal of Cognition and Culture* 7 (2007): 173–199; C. Hookway, *Quine* (Stanford, CA: Stanford University Press, 1988).

21. D. S. Connelly and D. S. Ones, "Another perspective on personality," *Psychological Bulletin* 136 (2010): 1092–1122; S. J. Heine, E. E. Buchtel, and A. Norenzayan, "What do cross-national comparisons of personality traits tell us?" *Psychological Science* 19 (2008): 309–313; S. D. Gosling, O. P. John, K. H. Craik, and R. W. Robins, "Do people know how they behave? Self-reported act frequencies compared with on-line codings by observers," *Journal of Personality and Social Psychology* 74 (1998): 1337–1349; R. T. Edelman and S. R. Baker, "Self reported and actual physiological responses in social phobia," *British Journal of Clinical Psychology* 41 (2002): 1–14.

22. J. Kottler, *The Assassin and the Therapist: An Exploration of Truth in Psychotherapy and in Life* (New York: Routledge, 2010); R. T. Edelman and S. R. Baker, "Self-reported and actual physiological responses in social phobia," *British Journal of Clinical Psychology* 41 (2002): 1–14; F. Zhai, J. Brooks-Gunn, and J. Waldfogel, "Head start and urban children's school readiness: A birth cohort study in 18 cities," *Developmental Psychology* 47 (2011): 134–152.

23. D. G. Blanchflower and A. J. Oswald, "Hypertension and happiness across nations," *Journal of Health Economics* 27 (2007): 218–233.

24. J. Allik and R. R. McCrae, "Toward a geography of personality traits," *Journal of Cross-Cultural Psychology* 35 (2004): 13–28.

25. G. Firebaugh and M. B. Schroeder, "Does your neighbor's income affect your happiness?" *American Journal of Sociology* 115 (2009): 805–831; Boyce, Brown, and Moore, "Money and happiness"; E. Diener, W. Ng, J. Harter, and R. Arora, "Wealth and happiness across the world: Material prosperity predicts life evaluation, whereas psychosocial prosperity predicts positive feeling," *Journal of Personality and Social Psychology* 99 (2010): 52–61.

26. J. M. Twenge, "The age of anxiety," *Journal of Personality and Social Psychology* 79 (2006): 1007–1021.

27. D. Bok, *The Politics of Happiness: What Government Can Learn from the New Research on Well-Being* (Princeton, NJ: Princeton University Press, 2010); K. M. DeNeve and H. Cooper, "The happy personality: A meta-analysis of 137 personality traits and subjective well-being," *Psychological Bulletin* 124 (1998): 197–229; C. Graham, *Happiness around the World: The Paradox of Happy Peasants and Miserable Millionaires* (New York: Oxford University Press, 2009).

28. R. Veenhoven, "Life is getting better: Societal evaluation and fit with human nature," *Social Indicators Research* 97 (2010): 105–122.

29. G. Doblhammer and J. W. Vaupel, "Lifespan depends on month of birth," *Proceedings of the National Academy of Sciences* 98 (2001): 2934–2939.

30. L. Woolf, *The Journey Not the Arrival Matters: An Autobiography of the Years 1939 to 1965* (London: Hogarth, 1969), 158; M. A. Sprangers, M. Bartels, R. Veenhoven, et al., "Which patient will feel down, which would be happy? The need to study the genetic disposition of emotional states," *Quality Life Research* 19 (2010): 1429–1437; J. H. Stubbe, D. Posthuma, D. I. Boosma, and E. J. De Geus, "Heritability of life satisfaction in adults: A twin study," *Psychological Medicine* 35 (2005): 1581–1588; J. Kagan and N. Snidman, *The Long Shadow of Temperament* (Cambridge, MA: Harvard University Press, 2004).

31. V. Liberman, J. K. Boehm, S. Lyubomirsky, and L. D. Ross, "Happiness and memory: Affective significance of endowment

and contrast," *Emotion* 9 (2009): 666–680; J. Sugawara, T. Tarumi, and H. Tanaka, "Effect of mirthful laughter on vascular function," *American Journal of Cardiology* 15 (2010): 856–859; L. Harker and D. Keltner, "Expressions of positive emotion in women's college yearbook pictures and their relationship to personality and life outcomes across adulthood," *Journal of Personality and Social Psychology* 80 (2001): 112–124.

32. H. L. Urry, J. B. Nitschke, I. Dolski, et al., "Making a life worth living," *Psychological Science* 15 (2004): 367–372; C. S. Hayward, M. A. Stokes, D. Taylor, S. Young, and V. Anderson, "Changes in SWB following injury to different brain lobes," *Quality of Life Research* (in press).

33. D. Gilbert, *Stumbling on Happiness* (New York: Knopf, 2006).

34. D. Kahneman, A. B. Krueger, D. A. Schkade, N. Schwarz, and A. A. Stone, "A survey method for characterizing daily life experience," *Science* 306 (2004): 1776–1780.

35. A. B. Krueger, *Measuring the Subjective Well-Being of Nations: National Accounts of Time Use and Well-Being* (Chicago: University of Chicago Press, 2009).

36. Diener, Ng, Harter, and Arora, "Wealth and happiness across the world."

37. E. Kolbert, "Everybody has fun," *New Yorker*, March 22, 2010, 72–74, quotation on 74; A. Sen, "Well-being agency and freedom: The Dewey Lectures 1984," *Journal of Philosophy* 82 (1985): 169–221.

38. M. Morrison, L. Tay, and E. Diener, "Subjective well-being and national satisfaction: Findings from a worldwide survey," *Psychological Science* 22 (2011): 166–171; S. Oishi and U. Schimmack, "Culture and well-being: A new inquiry into the psychological wealth of nations," *Psychological Science* 5 (2010): 463–471.

39. C. J. Soto, O. P. John, and S. D. Gosling, "Age differences in personality traits from 10 to 65: Big Five domains and facets in a large cross-sectional sample," *Journal of Personality and Social Psychology* 100 (2011): 330–348.

40. M. E. P. Seligman, *Authentic Happiness: Using the New Positive Psychology to Realize Your Potential for Lasting Fulfillment* (New York: Free Press, 2002).

41. N. Gordimer, *Telling Times: Writing and Living, 1954–2008* (New York: W. W. Norton, 2010).

42. K. H. Trzesniewski and M. B. Donnellan, "Rethinking 'Generation Me': A Study of cohort effects from 1976–2006," *Psychological Science* 5 (2010): 58–75.

43. C. Crain, "Tea and antipathy," *New Yorker*, December 20, 27, 2010, 132–134; J. Gilder, *The Dance Most of All* (New York: Knopf, 2010).

44. Excerpted from O. Paz, "Petrifying Petrified," trans. E. Weinberger, *Hudson Review* 29 (1976): 341. In a story by Cervantes, Chanfalla is a con artist who deceives the leaders and residents of a village by pretending to evoke Samson demolishing the temple.

45. B. Bradlee, *New Yorker*, October 2, 2006, 52–57, quotation on 57; C. E. Osgood, W. H. May, and M. S. Miron, *Cross-Cultural Universals of Affective Meaning* (Urbana: University of Illinois Press, 1975); A. L. Berman, D. A. Jobes, and M. M. Silverman, *Adolescent Suicide*, 2nd ed. (Washington, DC: American Psychological Association, 2006); C. J. Graham, "Millennials and the myth of the post-racial society," *Daedalus* 140 (2011): 197–205.

46. A. Goodman, R. Joyce, and J. P. Smith, "The long shadow cast by childhood physical and mental problems on adult life," *Science* 108 (2011): 6032–6037; T. Judt, "Ill fares the land," *New York Review of Books* 42 (2010): 17–19, quotation on 17.

47. E. Diener, S. Oishi, and R. E. Lucas, "Personality, culture, and subjective well-being: Emotional and cognitive evaluations of life," in *Annual Review of Psychology*, ed. S. T. Fiske, D. L. Schacter, and C. Zahn-Waxler (Palo Alto, CA: Annual Reviews, 2003), 403–445.

48. S. Beckett, *Waiting for Godot* (London: Faber and Faber, 1956), 39.

THREE

Who Is Mentally Ill?

1. T. Friberg, "Burnout: From popular culture to psychiatric diagnosis in Sweden," *Culture, Medicine and Psychiatry* 33 (2009): 538–558; T. Grob and A. V. Horwitz, *Diagnosis, Therapy, and Evidence: Conundrums in Modern American Medicine* (Piscataway, NJ: Rutgers University Press, 2010).

2. R. C. Kessler, W. T. Chiu, O. Demler, and E. E. Walters, "Prevalence, severity, and comorbidity of 12-month DSM-IV disor-

ders in the National Comorbidity Survey Replication," *Archives of General Psychiatry* 62 (2005): 617–627; H. Kutchins and S. A. Kirk, *Making Us Crazy* (New York: Free Press, 1997).

3. Kessler, Chiu, Demler, and Walters, "Prevalence, severity, and comorbidity of 12-month DSM-IV disorders."

4. G. A. Miller, "The decades of the brain," *Perspectives on Psychological Science* 5 (2010): 716–743, quotation on 736; S. Beckett, *Endgame* (New York: Grove Press, 1958).

5. A. Frances, "Good grief," *New York Times*, August 14, 2010, 67.

6. D. J. Stein, K. A. Phillips, D. Bolton, K. W. M. Fulford, J. Z. Sadler, and K. S. Kendler, "What is a mental/psychiatric disorder?" *Psychological Medicine* 40 (2010): 1759–1765; R. J. McNally, *What Is Mental Illness?* (Cambridge, MA: Harvard University Press, 2011).

7. H. B. Woolston, "Rating the Nations," *American Journal of Sociology* 22 (1916): 381–390.

8. E. D. Klonsky, "Non-suicidal self-injury in the United States adults," *Psychological Medicine* 5 (2011): 1–6; M. Nock, "Self-injury," *Annual Review of Clinical Psychology* 6 (2010): 339–363; D. J. Kupfer and D. A. Regier, "Why all of medicine should care about DSM-5," *Journal of the American Medical Association* 303 (2010): 1974–1975.

9. V. Lux and K. S. Kendler, "Deconstructing major depression: A validation study of the DSM-IV symptomatic criteria," *Psychological Medicine* 40 (2010): 1679–1690.

10. M. J. Viron and T. A. Stern, "The impact of serious mental illness on health and health care," *Psychosomatics* 51 (2010): 458–465.

11. J. Radden, *The Nature of Melancholy: From Aristotle to Kristeva* (New York: Oxford University Press, 2000); J. Radden, *Moody Minds Distempered: Essays on Melancholy and Depression* (New York: Oxford University Press, 2009); L. C. Garro, "Cultural meaning of illness and the development of comparative frameworks," *Ethnology* 39 (2000): 305–334.

12. P. R. McHugh, *Try to Remember: Psychiatry's Clash over Meaning, Memory, and Mind* (Washington, DC: Dana Press, 2008).

13. W. Kim, I. Kim, and T. H. Nochajski, "Risk and protective factors of alcohol use disorders among Filipino Americans: Location of residence matters," *American Journal of Drug and Alcohol Abuse*

36 (2010): 214–219; S. R. Potochnick and K. M. Perreira, "Depression and anxiety among first generation immigrant Latino youth," *Journal of Nervous and Mental Disease* 198 (2010): 470–477.

14. T. I. Herrenkohl, R. Kosterman, W. A. Mason, J. D. Hawkins, C. A. McCarthy, and E. McCauley, "Effects of childhood conduct problems and family adversity on health, health behaviors, and service use in early adulthood," *Development and Psychopathology* 22 (2010): 655–665; M. T. Martin, R. D. Conger, T. J. Schofield, et al., "Evaluation of the interactionist model of socioeconomic status and problem behavior: A developmental cascade across generations," *Development and Psychopathology* 22 (2010): 695–713.

15. N. Lacey, "American imprisonment in comparative perspective," *Daedalus* (summer 2010): 102–114; B. Western and B. Pettit, "Incarceration and social inequality," *Daedalus* (summer 2010): 8–19.

16. A. S. Troy, F. H. Wilhelm, A. J. Shallacross, and I. B. Mauss, "Seeing the silver lining: Cognitive reappraisal ability moderates the relationship between stress and depressive symptoms," *Emotion* 10 (2010): 783–795.

17. R. A. Lanius, J. W. Hopper, and R. S. Menon, "Individual differences in a husband and wife who develop PTSD after a motor vehicle accident," *American Journal of Psychiatry* 160 (2003): 661–665.

18. T. Mann, *Diaries, 1918–1939* (New York: H. N. Abrams, 1982), 127.

19. K. Vickery, "Widening the psychiatric gaze: Reflection on PsychoDoctor depression, and recent transitions in Japanese mental health care," *Transcultural Psychiatry* 47 (2010): 363–391.

20. J. P. Johansen, J. W. Tarpley, J. E. Le Doux, and H. T. Blair, "Neural substrates for expectation-modulated fear learning in the amygdala and periacqueductal gray," *Nature Neuroscience* 13 (2010): 979–986.

21. A. Korszun, S. Stansfeld, and M. Frenneaux, "Depression postmyocardial infection," *British Journal of Psychiatry* 191 (2007): 455.

22. L. N. Yatham and M. Maj, *Bipolar Disorder: Clinical and Neurobiological Foundations* (Chichester, UK: Wiley-Blackwell, 2010); O. J. Bienvenu, E. S. Davydow, and K. S. Kendler, "Psychiatric disease versus behavioral disorders and degree of genetic influence," *Psychological Medicine* 41 (2011): 33–40; C. S. Gilmore, S. M. Malone, and W. G. Iacono, "Brain electrophysiological endophenotypes

for externalizing psychopathology: A multivariate approach," *Behavior Genetics* 40 (2010): 186–200.

23. D. K. Kinney, A. M. Miller, D. J. Crowley, E. Huang, and E. Gerber, "Autism prevalence following prenatal exposure to hurricanes and tropical storms in Louisiana," *Journal of Autism and Developmental Disorders* 38 (2008): 31–48; S. M. Sarasella, I. Marventano, F. R. Guerini, et al., "An autistic endophenotype results in complex immune dysfunction in healthy siblings of autistic children," *Biological Psychiatry* 66 (2009): 978–984.

24. E. Leibenluft, "Severe dysregulation, irritability, and the diagnostic boundaries of bipolar disorder in youths," *American Journal of Psychiatry* 168 (2011): 129–142; F. Hoeft, E. Walter, A. A. Lightbody, et al., "Neuroanatomical differences in toddler boys with fragile x syndrome and idiopathic autism," *Archives of General Psychiatry* 68 (2011): 295–305; S. E. Hyman, "The diagnosis of mental disorder: The problem of reification," *Annual Review of Clinical Psychology* 6 (2010): 155–179.

25. G. K. Murray, "The emerging biology of delusions," *Psychological Medicine* 41 (2011): 7–13.

26. C. Best, R. Tschan, A. Eckhardt-Henn, and M. Dietrich, "Who is at risk for ongoing dizziness and psychological strain after a vestibular disorder?" *Neuroscience* 164 (2009): 1579–1587; S. Nikolaus, C. Antke, M. Beu, and H. W. Müller, "Cortical GABA, striatal dopamine and midbrain serotonin as the key players in compulsive and anxiety disorders—results from in vivo imaging studies," *Reviews in the Neurosciences* 21 (2010): 119–139; M. A. Viar, E. N. Etzel, B. G. Ciesielski, and B. O. Olatunji, "Disgust, anxiety, and vasovagal syncope sensations: A comparison of injection-fearful and nonfearful blood donors," *Journal of Anxiety Disorders* 24 (2010): 941–945; U. Lueken, J. D. Kruschwitz, M. Muehlhan, J. Siegert, J. Hoyer, and H. U. Wittchen, "How specific is specific phobia? Different neural response patterns in two subtypes of specific phobia," *Neuroimage* 56 (2011): 363–372.

27. N. Nordquist and L. Oreland, "Serotonin, genetic variability, behaviour, and psychiatric disorders—a review," *Uppsala Journal of Medical Science* 115 (2010): 2–10; C. F. Zink, J. L. Stein, L. Kempf, S. Hakimi, and A. Meyer-Lindeberg, "Vasopressin

modulates medial prefrontal cortex—amygdala circuitry during emotion processing in humans," *Journal of Neuroscience* 30 (2010): 7017–7022; H. P. Jedema, P. J. Gianaros, P. J. Greer, et al., "Cognitive impact of genetic variation of the serotonin transporter in primates is associated with differences in brain morphology related to serotonin neurotransmission," *Molecular Psychiatry* 15 (2010): 512–546.

28. H. S. Lee, B. D. Korman, J. M. Le, et al., "Genetic risk factors for rheumatoid arthritis differ in Caucasian and Korean populations," *Arthritis and Rheumatism* 60 (2009): 364–371; T. Joiner, *Myths about Suicide* (Cambridge, MA: Harvard University Press, 2010).

29. L. K. G. Hsu, Y. M. Wan, H. Chang, P. Summergrad, B. Y. Tsang, and H. Chen, "Stigma of depression is more severe in Chinese Americans than Caucasian Americans," *Psychiatry* 71 (2008): 210–218.

30. A. H. Kemp, K. Griffiths, K. L. Felmingham, et al., "Disorder specificity despite comorbidity: Resting EEG alpha asymmetry in major depressive disorder and post-traumatic stress disorder," *Biological Psychology* 85 (2010): 350–354.

31. S. G. South and R. F. Kreuger, "Genetic and environmental influences on internalizing psychopathology varies as a function of economic status," *Psychological Medicine* 41 (2011): 107–117; J. Shi, J. B. Potash, J. A. Knowles, et al., "Genome-wide association study of recurrent early-onset major depressive disorder," *Molecular Psychiatry* 16 (2011): 193–201.

32. T. E. Moffitt, A. Taylor, J. Kokaua, B. J. Milne, G. Polanczyk, and R. Poulton, "How common are common mental disorders? Evidence that lifetime prevalence rates are doubled by prospective versus retrospective ascertainment," *Psychological Medicine* 40 (2010): 899–909; Radden, *Moody Minds Distempered.*

33. J. E. Le Doux, *The Emotional Brain: The Mysterious Underpinnings of Emotional Life* (New York: Simon and Schuster, 1996); S. L. Rauch, L. M. Shin, and E. A. Phelps, "Neurocircuitry models of post-traumatic stress disorder and extinction: Human neuroimaging research—past, present, and future," *Biological Psychiatry* 60 (2006): 376–382.

34. P. K. Keel and P. K. Klump, "Are eating disorders culture-bound syndromes?" *Psychological Bulletin* 129 (2003): 747–769; P. S. Mehler and A. E. Andersen, *Eating Disorders: A Guide to Medical Care and Complications*, 2nd ed. (Baltimore: Johns Hopkins University Press, 2010).

35. S. B. Stryer, *Anorexia* (Santa Barbara, CA: Greenwood, 2009); D. Forbes, R. Parslow, M. Creamer, et al., "A longitudinal analysis of posttraumatic stress disorder symptoms and their relationship with Fear and Anxious-Misery disorders: Implications for DSM-V," *Journal of Affective Disorders* 127 (2010): 147–152; A. Hussain, L. Weisaeth, and T. Heir, "Psychiatric disorders and functional impairment among disaster victims after exposure to a natural disaster: A population based study," *Journal of Affective Disorders* 128 (2011): 135–141; H. M. Zinzow, H. S. Resnick, J. L. McCauley, A. B. Amstader, K. J. Ruggiero, and D. G. Kilpatrick, "The role of rape tactics in risk for posttraumatic stress disorder and major depression results from a national sample of college women," *Depression and Anxiety* 27 (2010): 708–715.

36. S. McConville, "Word pictures of depression: Anhedonia," *British Journal of Psychiatry* 192 (2008): 105; D. W. Middlebrook, *Anne Sexton* (Boston: Houghton Mifflin, 1991).

37. J. R. Escobedo and R. Adolphs, "Becoming a better person: Temporal remoteness biases autobiographical memories for moral events," *Emotion* 10 (2010): 511–518.

38. K. S. Kendler, S. H. Aggen, G. Knudsen, E. Roysamb, M. C. Neale, and T. Reichborn-Kjennerud, "The structure of genetic and environmental risk factors for syndromes and subsyndromal common DSM-IV Axis I and all Axis II disorders," *American Journal of Psychiatry* 168 (2011): 29–39; J. Hannestad, J. D. Gallezot, B. Planeta-Wilson, et al., "Clinically relevant doses of methylphenidate significantly occupy norepinephrine transporters in humans in vitro," *Biological Psychiatry* 68 (2010): 854–860; K. P. Lesch, S. Selch, T. J. Renner, et al., "Genome-wide copy number variation analysis in attention-deficit/hyperactivity disorder: Association with neuropeptide Y gene dosage in an extended pedigree," *Molecular Psychiatry* 16 (2011): 491–503.

39. K. Langley, J. Heron, M. C. O'Donovan, M. J. Owen, and A. Thapor, "Genotype link with extreme antisocial behavior," *Archives of General Psychiatry* 67 (2010): 1317–1323; J. Dmitrieva, C. Chen, E. Greenberger, O. Ogunseitan, and Y. C. Ding, "Gender-specific expression of the DRD4 gene on adolescent delinquency, anger, and thrill seeking," *Social, Cognitive, and Affective Neuroscience* 6 (2011): 82–89.

40. H. Tavares, E. Carneiro, M. Sanches, et al., "Gambling in Brazil: Lifetime prevalences and socio-demographic correlates," *Psychiatry Research* 180 (2010): 35–41.

41. M. Rivers-Moore, "But the kids are okay: Motherhood, consumption and sex work in neo-liberal Latin America," *British Journal of Sociology* 61 (2010): 716–736.

42. E. Elliott, G. Ezra-Nevo, L. Regev, A. Neufeld-Cohen, and A. Chen, "Resilience to social stress coincides with functional DNA methylation of the Crf gene in adult mice," *Nature Neuroscience* 13 (2010): 1351–1353.

43. D. B. Goldston, S. D. Molock, L. B. Whitbeck, J. L. Murakami, L. H. Zayas, and G. C. N. Hall, "Cultural considerations in adolescent suicide prevention and treatment," *American Psychologist* 63 (2008): 14–31; I. A. Lang, D. J. Llewellyn, R. E. Hubbard, et al., "Income and the midlife peak in common mental disorder prevalence," *Psychological Medicine* 10 (2010): 1–8; J. Sareen, T. O. Afifi, K. A. McMillan, and G. J. G. Asmundson, "Relationship between household income and mental disorders," *Archives of General Psychiatry* 68 (2011): 419–427; N. Carragher and L. A. McWilliams, "A latent class analysis of DSM-IV criteria for pathological gambling," *Psychiatry Research* 187 (2011): 185–192.

44. E. Werner and R. S. Smith, *Vulnerable but Invincible: A Longitudinal Study of Resilient Children and Youth* (New York: McGraw-Hill, 1982); K. E. Pickett and R. G. Wilkinson, "Inequality: An underacknowledged source of mental illness and disorder," *British Journal of Psychiatry* 197 (2010): 426–428; S. Priebe, M. Bogic, D. Ajduikovic, et al., "Mental disorders following war in the Balkans," *Archives of General Psychiatry* 67 (2010): 518–528.

45. J. Das-Munshi, L. Becares, M. E. Dewey, S. A. Stansfeld, and M. J. Prince, "Understanding the effect of ethnic density on men-

tal health: Multi-level investigation of survey data from England," *British Medical Journal* 341 (2010): 5367–5371; Centers for Disease Control and Prevention, "Current depression among adults— United States, 2006 and 2008," *Morbidity Mortality Weekly Report* 59 (2010): 1229–1235; J. Zhang, N. Li, X. M. Tu, S. Xiao, and C. Jia, "Risk factors for rural young suicide in China: A case-control study," *Journal of Affective Disorders* 129 (2011): 244–251.

46. F. J. Sulloway, *Born to Rebel: Birth Order, Family Dynamics, and Creative Lives* (New York: Pantheon, 1996); F. J. Sulloway and R. L. Zweigenhaft, "Birth order and risk taking in athletics: A meta-analysis and study of major league baseball," *Personality and Social Psychology Review* 14 (2010): 402–416.

47. T. Frisell, P. Lichtenstein, and N. Langstrom, "Violent crime runs in families," *Psychological Medicine* 41 (2011): 97–105.

48. M. T. Martin, R. D. Conger, T. J. Schofield, et al., "Evolution of the interactionist model of socioeconomic status and problem behavior," *Development and Psychopathology* 22 (2010): 695–713; H. Meltzer, P. Bebbington, P. Brugha, et al., "Job insecurity, socio-economic circumstances and depression," *Psychological Medicine* 40 (2010): 1401–1407; J. G. Green, K. A. McLaughlin, and P. A. Berglund, "Childhood adversities and adult psychiatric disorders in the National Comorbidity Survey Replication 1," *Archives of General Psychiatry* 67 (2010): 113–123; S. Wicks, A. Hjern, and C. Dalman, "Social risk or genetic liability for psychosis? A study of children born in Sweden and reared by adoptive parents," *American Journal of Psychiatry* 167 (2010): 1240–1246; B. Sicherman, *The Quest for Mental Health in America, 1880–1917* (New York: Arno, 1980).

49. V. A. Mathur, T. Harada, T. Lipke, and J. Y. Chiao, "Neural basis of extraordinary empathy and altruistic motivation," *Neuroimage* 51 (2010): 1468–1475.

50. J. Updike, *Self-Consciousness* (New York: Fawcett Crest, 1989), 32; W. Gombrowicz, *A Kind of Testament* (London: Dalkey Archive Press, 2007).

51. J.-P. Sartre, *The Words*, trans. B. Frechtman (New York: George Braziller, 1964), 43.

52. I. Svensson, S. Nilsson, J. Wahlstrom, M. M. Jemas, L. Carlsson, and E. Hjelmquist, "Familial dyslexia in a large Swedish family:

A whole genome linkage scan," *Behavior Genetics* 41 (2011): 443–449; K. Dean, H. Stevens, P. B. Mortensen, et al., "Full spectrum of psychiatric outcomes among offspring with parental history of mental disorder," *Archives of General Psychiatry* 67 (2010): 822–829.

53. T. Insel, B. Cuthbert, M. Garvey, et al., "The research domain criteria (RdoC): Toward a new classification framework in research on mental disorders," *American Journal of Psychiatry* 167 (2010): 748–751.

54. D. Grabli, K. McCairn, E. C. Hirsch, et al., "Behavioural disorders induced by external globus pallidus dysfunction in primates," *Brain* 127 (2004): 2039–2054; K. S. Kendler and M. C. Neale, "Endophenotype: A conceptual analysis," *Molecular Psychiatry* 15 (2010): 789–797.

55. J. Kagan and N. Snidman, *The Long Shadow of Temperament* (Cambridge, MA: Harvard University Press, 2004); E. Whitley, F. Rasmussen, P. Tynelius, and G. D. Batty, "Physical stature and method-specific attempted suicide: Cohort study of one million men," *Psychiatry Research* 179 (2010): 116–118.

56. T. B. Lonsdorf, A. Golkar, K. Lindstom, et al., "5-HTTLPR and COMT Val 158 Met genotype gates amygdala reactivity and habituation," *Biological Psychology* 87 (2011): 106–112; J. Kagan, N. Snidman, V. Kahn, and S. Towsley, "The preservation of two infant temperaments into adolescence," *Monographs of the Society for Research in Child Development* 72 (2007): 1–75; J. A. Oler, A. S. Fox, S. E. Shelton, et al., "Amygdala and hippocampal substrates of anxious temperament differ in their heritability," *Nature* 466 (2010): 864–868; E. A. H. van den Hagen, L. Passamonti, S. Nutland, J. Sambronky, and A. J. Calder, "The serotonin transporter gene polymorphism and the effect of baseline on amygdalar response to emotional faces," *Neuropsychoendocrinology* 49 (2011): 674–680.

57. M. van der Werf, "Adolescent development of psychosis as an outcome of hearing impairment," *Psychological Medicine* 41 (2011): 477–485; L. Petersen, P. B. Mortensen, and C. B. Pedersen, "Paternal age at birth of first child and risk of schizophrenia," *American Journal of Psychiatry* 168 (2011): 82–88; A. D. Nguyen, M. E. Shenton, and J. J. Levitt, "Olfactory dysfunction in schizo-

phrenia: A review of neuroanatomy and psychophysiological measurements," *Harvard Review of Psychiatry* 18 (2010): 279–292; M. E. Calkins, W. G. Iacono, and D. S. Ones, "Eye movement dysfunction in first-degree relatives of patients with schizophrenia: A meta-analytic evaluation of candidate endophenotypes," *Brain and Cognition* 68 (2008): 436–461.

58. K. Pierce, D. Conant, T. R. Hazin, R. Stoner, and J. Desmond, "Preference for geometric patterns early in life as a risk factor for autism," *Archives of General Psychiatry* 68 (2011): 101–109.

59. Kagan and Snidman, *Long Shadow of Temperament.*

60. P. Huezo-Diaz, R. Uher, R. Smith, et al., "Moderation of antidepressant response by the serotonin transporter gene," *British Journal of Psychiatry* 195 (2009): 30–38; D. Foti, D. M. Olvet, D. N. Klein, and G. Hajcak, "Reduced electrocortical response to threatening faces in major depressive disorder," *Depression and Anxiety* 27 (2010): 813–820; F. Gressier, E. Bouaziz, C. Verstuyft, P. Hardy, L. Becquemont, and E. Corruble, "5-HTTLPR modulates antidepressant efficacy in depressed women," *Psychiatric Genetics* 19 (2009): 195–200; J. L. Stewart, A. W. Bismark, D. N. Towers, J. A. Coan, and J. J. Allen, "Resting frontal EEG asymmetry as an endophenotype for depression risk," *Journal of Abnormal Psychology* 119 (2010): 502–512.

61. F. Lamers, P. De Jonge, W. A. Nolan, et al., "Identifying depressive subtypes in a large cohort study: Results from the Netherlands Study of Depression and Anxiety," *Journal of Clinical Psychiatry* 71 (2010): 1582–1589; C. M. Lewis, M. Y. Ng, A. W. Butler, et al., "Genome-wide association study of major recurrent depression in the U.K. population," *American Journal of Psychiatry* 167 (2010): 949–957; M. Rietschel, M. Mattheisen, J. Frank, et al., "Genome-wide association—replication—and neuroimaging study implicates HOMER 1 in the etiology of major depression," *Biological Psychiatry* 15 (2010): 578–585.

62. A. L. Glenn, "The other allele," *Neuroscience and Biobehavioral Reviews* 35 (2011): 612–620; A. D. Boes, A. Bechara, D. Tranel, S. W. Anderson, L. Richman, and P. Nopoulos, "Right ventromedial prefrontal cortex: A neuroanatomical correlate of impulse control in boys," *Social Cognitive and Affective Neuroscience* 4 (2009):

1–9; F. E. Dupuy, A. R. Clarke, R. J. Barry, R. McCarthy, and M. Seilikowitz, "EEG coherence in children with attention-deficit/hyperactivity disorder: Differences between good and poor responders to methylphenidate," *Psychiatry Research* 180 (2009): 114–119; F. V. Rijsdijsk, E. Viding, S. De Brito, et al., "Heritable variations in gray matter concentration as a potential endophenotype for psychopathic traits," *Archives of General Psychiatry* 67 (2010): 406–413; R. G. Vaurio, D. J. Simmonds, and S. H. Mostofsky, "Increased intra-individual reaction time variability in attention-deficit/hyperactivity disorder across response inhibition tasks with different cognitive demands," *Neuropsychologia* 47 (2009): 2389–2396; J. T. Manning, S. Reimers, S. Baron-Cohen, S. Wheelwright, and B. Fink, "Sexually dimorphic traits (digit ratio, body height, systematizing-empathizing scores) and gender segregation between occupations," *Personality and Individual Differences* 49 (2010): 511–515.

63. S. A. Berenbaum, K. K. Bryk, N. Nowak, C. A. Quigley, and S. Moffat, "Fingers as a marker of prenatal androgen exposure," *Endocrinology* 150 (2009): 5119–5124; S. E. Medland, T. Zayats, D. Glaser, et al., "A variant in LIN28B is associated with 2D:4D finger length ratio, a putative retrospective biomarker of prenatal testosterone exposure," *American Journal of Human Genetics* 86 (2010): 519–525; M. S. Wallen, K. J. Zucker, T. D. Steensma, and P. T. Cohen-Kettenis, "2D:4D finger-length ratios in children and adults with gender identity disorder," *Hormones and Behavior* 54 (2008): 450–454.

64. J. Auger and F. Eustache, "Second to fourth digit ratios, male genital development and reproductive health: A clinical study among fertile men and testis cancer patients," *International Journal of Andrology* 34 (2011), doi: 10.1111/j.1365-2605.2010.01124.x; E. Nelson, C. Rolian, L. Cashmore, and S. Shultz, "Digital ratios predict polygyny in early apes, *Ardipithecus*, Neanderthals and early modern humans but not in *Australopithecus*," *Proceedings of the Royal Society B* 278 (2011): 1556–1563; A. Schwerdtfer, R. Heims, and J. Heer, "Digit ratio (2D:4D) is associated with traffic violations for male frequent car drivers," *Accident Analysis and Prevention* 42 (2010): 269–274; A. R. Smith, S. E. Hawkes-

wood, and T. E. Joiner, "The measure of a man: Associations between digit ratio and disordered eating in males," *International Journal of Eating Disorders* 43 (2010): 543–548; E. Nelson and S. Shultz, "Finger length ratios (2D:4D) in anthropoids implicate reduced prenatal androgens in social bonding," *American Journal of Physical Anthropology* 141 (2010): 395–405; E. I. De Bruin, P. F. De Nijs, D. H. Verhagen, and R. F. Ferdinand, "Autistic features in girls from a psychiatric sample are strongly associated with a low 2D:4D ratio," *Autism* 13 (2009): 511–521; T. Grimbos, K. Dawood, R. P. Burriss, K. J. Zucker, and D. A. Puts, "Sexual orientation and the second to fourth finger length ratio: A meta-analysis in men and women," *Behavioral Neuroscience* 124 (2010): 278–287; C. E. Schwartz, P. S. Kunwar, D. N. Greve, et al., "Structural differences in adult orbital and ventromedial prefrontal cortex predicted by infant temperament at 4 months of age," *Archives of General Psychiatry* 67 (2010): 1–7; J. M. Valla and S. J. Ceci, "Can sex differences in science be tied to the long reach of prenatal hormones?" *Perspectives on Psychological Science* 8 (2011): 134–146.

65. J. M. Coates and J. Herbert, "Endogenous steroids and financial risk taking on a London trading floor," *Proceedings of the National Academy of Sciences* 105 (2008): 6167–6172.

66. J. A. Quas, K. W. Alexander, G. S. Goodman, S. Ghatti, R. S. Edelstein, and A. Redlich, "Long-term autobiographical memory for legal involvement: Individual and sociocontextual predictors," *Cognitive Development* 25 (2010): 394–405.

67. G. Mazzoni, A. Scobaria, and L. Harvey, "Nonbelieved memories," *Psychological Science* 21 (2010): 1334–1340; E. Geraerts, D. S. Lindsay, H. Merckelbach, et al., "Cognitive mechanisms underlying recovered-memory experiences of childhood sexual abuse," *Psychological Science* 20 (2009): 92–98; E. F. Loftus, "Memories of things unseen," *Psychological Science* 13 (2004): 145–147; D. C. Rubin and A. Boals, "People who expect to enter psychotherapy are prone to believing that they have forgotten memories of childhood trauma and abuse," *Memory* 18 (2010): 556–562; S. J. Frenda, R. M. Nichols, and E. F. Loftus, "Current issues and advances in misinformation research," *Current Directions in Psychological Science* 20 (2011): 20–23; R. Meiser-Stedman,

T. Dalgleish, E. Glucksman, W. Yule, and P. Smith, "Maladaptive cognitive appraisals mediate the evolution of posttraumatic stress reaction," *Journal of Abnormal Psychology* 118 (2009): 778–787.

68. V. Miskovic, A. R. Ashbaugh, D. L. Santesso, R. E. McCabe, M. M. Antony, and L. A. Schmidt, "Frontal brain oscillations and social anxiety: A cross-frequency spectral analysis during baseline and speech anticipation," *Biological Psychology* 83 (2010): 125–132; V. Miskovic and L. A. Schmidt, "Frontal brain oscillatory coupling among men who vary in salivary testosterone levels," *Neuroscience Letters* 464 (2009): 239–242; D. H. Zald, D. L. Mattson, and J. V. Pardo, "Brain activity in ventromedial prefrontal cortex correlates with individual differences in negative affect," *Proceedings of the National Academy of Sciences* 99 (2002): 245–254; K. Domschke, A. Reif, H. Weber, et al., "Neuropeptide S receptor gene—converging evidence for a role in panic disorder," *Molecular Psychiatry* (2010): doi: 10.1038/mp.2010.81; S. B. Patten, "Correspondence," *Psychological Medicine* 40 (2010): 1757–1758; K. A. Raczka, N. Gartmann, M. Mechias, et al., "A neuropeptide S receptor variant associated with over-interpretation of fear reactions," *Molecular Psychiatry* 15 (2010): 1067–1074; D. H. Zald, N. D. Woodward, R. L. Cowan, et al., "The interrelationship of dopamine D2-like receptor availability in striatal and extrastriatal brain regions in healthy humans," *Neuroimage* 15 (2010): 53–62; C. A. Stifter, J. M. Dollar, and E. A. Cipriano, "Temperament and emotion regulation: The role of autonomic nervous system reactivity," *Developmental Psychobiology* 53 (2010): 266–279.

69. T. L. Yeh, I. H. Lee, K. C. Chen, et al., "The relationships between daily life events and the availability of serotonin transporters and dopamine transporters in healthy volunteers," *Neuroimage* 45 (2009): 275–279; K. Schwegler, B. D. Buser, R. Klaghofer, et al., "Cortisol reduces recall of explicit contextual pain memory in healthy young men," *Psychoneuroendocrinology* 35 (2010): 1270–1273; S. Diekelmann, I. Wilhelm, U. Wagner, and J. Born, "Elevated cortisol at retrieval suppresses false memories in parallel with correct memories," *Journal of Cognitive Neuroscience* 23 (2011): 772–781; E. Geraerts, D. S. Lindsay, H. Merckelbach, et al., "Cognitive mechanisms underlying recovered memory

experiences of childhood sexual abuse," *Psychological Science* 20 (2009): 92–98.

70. W. E. Copeland, G. Keeler, A. Angold, and E. J. Costello, "Post-traumatic stress without trauma in children," *American Journal of Psychiatry* 167 (2010): 1059–1065.

71. K. A. McLaughlin, J. G. Green, M. J. Gruber, N. A. Sampson, A. M. Zaslavsky, and R. C. Kessler, "Childhood adversities and adult psychiatric disorders in the National Comorbidity Survey Replication II," *Archives of General Psychiatry* 67 (2010): 124–132.

72. I. D. Waldman, "Statistical approaches to complex phenotypes," *Biological Psychology* 57 (2005): 1347–1356.

73. E. P. Hayden, D. N. Klein, H. I. Sheikh, et al., "The serotonin transporter promoter polymorphism and childhood positive and negative emotionality," *Emotion* 10 (2010): 696–702.

74. J. A. L. Donatelli, L. J. Seidman, J. M. Goldstein, M. T. Tsuang, and S. L. Buka, "Children of parents with affective and non-affective psychoses: A longitudinal study of behavior problems," *American Journal of Psychiatry* 167 (2010): 1331–1338; C. Gregg, J. Zhang, B. Weissbourd, et al., "High-resolution analysis of parent-of-origin allelic expression in the mouse brain," *Science* 329 (2010): 643–648; D. Planchard, Y. Loriot, A. Goubar, F. Commo, and J. C. Soria, "Differential expression of biomarkers in men and women," *Seminars in Oncology* 36 (2009): 553–565; B. H. Brummett, S. H. Boyle, I. C. Siegler, et al., "Effects of environmental stress and gender on associations among symptoms of depression and the serotonin transporter gene linked polymorphic region (5-HTTLPR)," *Behavior Genetics* 38 (2008): 34–43.

75. H. M. van Berge-Landry, D. H. Bovbjerg, and G. D. James, "Relationship between waking-sleep blood pressure and catecholamine changes in African-American and European-American women," *Blood Pressure Monitor* 13 (2008): 257–262; S. J. Garlow, D. Purselle, and M. Heninger, "Ethnic differences in patterns of suicide across the life cycle," *American Journal of Psychiatry* 162 (2005): 319–323; K. M. Grewen, K. C. Light, B. Mechlin, and S. S. Girdler, "Ethnicity is associated with alterations in oxytocin relationships to pain sensitivity in women," *Ethnicity and Health* 13 (2008): 219–241.

76. A. A. Fushan, C. T. Simons, J. P. Slack, and D. Drayna, "Association between common variants in genes coding sweet tastes signaling components and human sucrose conception," *Chemical Senses* 35 (2010): 579–592; C. E. Beardon and N. B. Freimer, "Endophenotypes for psychiatric disorders: Ready for primetime?" *Trends in Genetics* 22 (2006): 306–313.

FOUR

Helping the Mentally Ill

1. P. R. McHugh and P. R. Slavney, *The Perspectives of Psychiatry*, 2nd ed. (Baltimore: Johns Hopkins University Press, 1998).

2. M. Olfson and S. C. Marcus, "National trends in outpatient psychotherapy," *American Journal of Psychiatry* 167 (2010): 1456–1463.

3. S. Priebe, M. Bogic, D. Ajdekovic, et al., "Mental disorders following war in the Balkans," *Archives of General Psychiatry* 67 (2010): 518–528.

4. E. S. Valenstein, *Great and Desperate Cures: The Rise and Decline of Psychosurgery and Other Radical Treatments for Mental Illness* (New York: Basic Books, 1986); J. Moncrieff, *The Myth of a Chemical Cure: A Critique of Psychiatric Drug Treatment* (New York: Palgrave MacMillan, 2008); E. M. Tsapakis, "Efficacy and antidepressants in juvenile depression," *British Journal of Psychiatry* 193 (2008): 10–17.

5. R. Mendel, J. Hamann, E. Traut-Matausch, M. Buhner, and W. Kissling, "What would you do if you were me, doctor?" *British Journal of Psychiatry* 197 (2010): 441–447; E. C. van Geffen, R. van Hulten A. C. Egberts, and E. R. Heerdink, "Characteristics and reasons associated with nonacceptance of selective serotonin-reuptake inhibitor treatment," *Annals of Pharmacotherapy* 42 (2008): 218–225.

6. I. Veith, *Hysteria: The History of a Disease* (Chicago: University of Chicago Press, 1965).

7. C. Beard, R. B. E. Moitra, R. B. Weisberg, and M. B. Keller, "Characteristics and predictors of social phobia in a longitudinal study of primary care patients," *Depression and Anxiety* 27 (2010): 839–845; F. G. Graeff and H. Zangrossi, "The dual role of serotonin in defense in the modal action of antidepressants

on generalized anxiety and panic disorders," *Central Nervous System Agents in Medical Chemistry* 10 (2010): 207–217; C. McCabe, C. Mishor, T. J. Kowen, and C. J. Harmer, "The neural processing of aversive and rewarding stimuli during selective serotonin reuptake inhibited treatment," *Biological Psychiatry* 67 (2010): 439–445; J. Price, V. Cole, and G. M. Goodwin, "Emotional side effects of selective serotonin reuptake inhibitors," *British Journal of Psychiatry* 195 (2009): 211–217.

8. L. Almeida, T. B. Kashdan, R. Coelho, and A. Albino-Teixeira, "Healthy subjects volunteering for Phase 1 studies: Influence of curiosity, exploratory tendencies and perceived self-efficacy," *International Journal of Clinical and Pharmacological Therapy* 46 (2008): 109–118; N. Iovieno, A. van Nieuwenhuizen, A. Clain, L. Baer, and A. A. Nierenberg, "Residual symptoms after remission of major depressive disorder with fluoxetine and risk of relapse," *Depression and Anxiety* 28 (2011): 137–144; J. Hirshowitz, A. Kolevzon, and A. Garakani, "The pharmacological treatment of bipolar disorder," *Harvard Review of Psychiatry* 18 (2010): 266–278; S. B. Harvey and M. Hotopf, "Physical activity and common mental disorders," *British Journal of Psychiatry* 97 (2010): 357–364; B. M. Hoffman, M. A. Babyak, W. E. Craighead, M. Doraiswamy, M. J. Coons, and J. A. Blumenthal, "Exercise and pharmacotherapy on patients with major depression," *Psychosomatic Medicine* 73 (2011): 127–133; M. S. George and R. M. Post, "Daily left prefrontal repetitive transcranial magnetic stimulation for acute treatment of medication-resistant depression," *American Journal of Psychiatry* 168 (2011): 356–364.

9. J. Paris, *The Use and Misuse of Psychiatric Drugs: An Evidence-Based Critique* (Oxford: Wiley-Blackwell, 2010); R. Whitaker, *Anatomy of an Epidemic: Magic Bullets, Psychiatric Drugs, and the Astonishing Rise of Mental Illness in America* (New York: Crown, 2010).

10. E. F. Valenstein, *Blaming the Brain: The Truth about Drugs and Mental Health* (New York: Free Press, 1998), 165, 241.

11. I. Kirsch, *The Emperor's New Drugs: Exploding the Antidepressant Myth* (New York: Basic Books, 2010).

12. M. Incayawar, "Efficacy of Quechua healers as psychiatric diagnosticians," *British Journal of Psychiatry* 192 (2008): 390–391; B. O. Li, L. J. Kirmayer, and D. Groleau, "Therapeutic processes

in perceived helpfulness of bang ki from the symbolic feeling perspective," *Culture, Medicine, and Psychiatry* 34 (2010): 56–105.

13. T. J. Kaptchuk, E. Friedlander, J. M. Kelley, et al., "Placebos without deception," *PloS One* 5 (2010): e15591; A. Harrington, *The Cure Within: A History of Mind-Body Medicine* (New York: W. W. Norton, 2008).

14. F. Benedetti, E. Carlino, and A. Pollo, "How placebos change the patient's brain," *Neuropsychopharmacology* 36 (2011): 339–354; D. L. Morton, C. A. Brown, A. Watson, W. El-Deredy, and A. K. Jones, "Cognitive changes as a result of a single exposure to placebo," *Neuropsychologia* 48 (2010): 1958–1964; T. D. Wager, L. Y. Atlas, L. A. Leotti, and J. K. Rilling, "Predicting individual differences in placebo analgesia," *Journal of Neuroscience* 31 (2011): 439–452; S. C. Lindstome, M. Schulzer, K. Dinelle, et al., "Effects of expectation on placebo-induced dopamine releasing Parkinson disease," *Archives of General Psychiatry* 67 (2010): 857–865; Y. H. Qiu, X. Y. Wu, H. Xu, and D. Sackett, "Neural imaging study of placebo and analgesia in humans," *Neuroscience Bulletin* 25 (2009): 277–282; J. K. Zubieta and C. S. Stohler, "Neurobiological mechanisms of placebo responses," *Annals of the New York Academy of Sciences* 1156 (2009): 198–210.

15. J. M. Bostwick and K. A. Martin, "A man's brain in an ambiguous body," *American Journal of Psychiatry* 164 (2007): 1499–1505.

16. W. T. Roth, "Diversity of effective treatments of panic attacks: What do they have in common?" *Depression and Anxiety* 27 (2010): 5–11.

17. N. P. Freeman, N. Fava, J. Lake, M. A. Trivedi, K. L. Weisner, and D. Mischoulon, "Complementary and alternative medicine in major depressive disorder," *Journal of Clinical Psychiatry* 71 (2010): 669–681.

18. G. L. Staines, "The relative efficacy of psychotherapy," *Review of General Psychology* 12 (2008): 330–343; D. K. Fromme, *Systems of Psychotherapy* (New York: Springer, 2011); J. Curry, S. Silves, T. Rohde, T. Ginsburg, and C. Kratochuil, "Recovery and recurrence following treatment for adolescent major depression," *Archives of General Psychiatry* 68 (2011): 258–265; D. H. Barlow, "Negative effects from psychological treatments," *American Psy-*

chologist 65 (2010): 13–20; E. E. Logan and D. A. Marlett, "Home reduction therapy," *Journal of Clinical Psychology* 66 (2010): 201–214; D. Lynch, J. R. Laws, and T. J. McKenna, "Cognitive behavioral therapy to major psychiatric disorder: Does it really work?" *Psychological Medicine* 40 (2010): 9–21.

19. M. Prince, "The psychopathology of a case of phobia—a clinical study," *Journal of Abnormal Psychology* 8 (1913): 228–242.

20. F. McManus, B. Teerbhoy, M. Larkin, and B. M. Clark, "Learning to change the way of being," *Journal of Anxiety Disorder* 24 (2010): 581–589; D. R. Strunk, M. A. Bratman, R. J. Rubeis, and S. B. Hallon, "Therapists confidence in cognitive therapy for depression," *Journal of Consulting and Clinical Psychology* 78 (2010): 427–429; S. Hollon, "Cognitive and behavior therapy in the treatment and prevention of depression," *Depression and Anxiety* 28 (2011): 263–266.

21. J. D. Frank, *Persuasion and Healing: A Comparative Study of Psychotherapy*, 3rd ed. (Baltimore: Johns Hopkins University Press, 1991).

22. E. Hedman, G. Andersson, E. Andersson, et al., "Internet-based cognitive-behavioural therapy for severe health anxiety: Randomized controlled trial," *British Journal of Psychiatry* 198 (2011): 230–236; P. Carlbring, L. Maorin, C. Torngren, et al., "Individually tailored Internet-based treatments for anxiety disorders," *Behaviour Research and Therapy* 49 (2011): 18–24.

23. Curry, Silves, Rohde, Ginsburg, and Kratochuil, "Recovery and recurrence following treatment for adolescent major depression"; Lynch, Laws, and McKenna, "Cognitive behavioral therapy for major psychiatric disorder: Does it really work?"

24. A. Miyake, L. E. Kost-Smith, N. D. Finkelstein, S. J. Pollock, G. L. Cohen, and T. A. Ito, "Reducing the gender achievement gap in college science: A classroom study of values affirmation," *Science* 330 (2010): 1234–1237. A similar intervention designed to reduce the feelings of isolation among African-American college students did facilitate the students' grade record. See G. M. Walton and G. L. Cohen, "A brief social-belonging intervention improves academic and health outcomes of minority students," *Science* 331 (2011): 1447–1451.

25. A. Kleinman, *Rethinking Psychiatry* (New York: Free Press, 1991).

26. P. Elsass, J. Carlsson, K. Jespersen, and K. Phuntsok, "Questioning Western assessment of trauma among Tibetan torture survivors," *Torture* 19 (2009): 194–203.

27. J. Kagan, *What Is Emotion?* (New Haven: Yale University Press, 2007).

28. P. A. Rozario and N. Menon, "An examination of the measurement adequacy of the CES-B among African-American and women family caretakers," *Psychiatry Research* 179 (2010): 107–112.

29. S. Zammit, G. Lewis, J. Ossbash, C. Dalman, J. E. Guftafsson, and T. Allebeck, "Individual schools in neighborhoods," *Archives of General Psychiatry* 67 (2010): 914–922.

30. C. E. Osgood, W. H. May, and M. S. Miron, *Cross-Cultural Universals of Affective Meanings* (Urbana: University of Illinois Press, 1978); Y. Esmer and T. Pettersson, *Measurement and Mapping Cultures: Twenty Years of Comparative Values Surveys* (Boston: Brill, 2007).

31. J. Li, L. Wang, and R. W. Fischer, "The organization of Chinese shame concepts," *Cognition and Emotion* 18 (2004): 767–797; S. Simone-Schreier, N. Heinrichs, L. Alden, R. M. Rapee, et al., "Social anxiety and social norms in individualistic and collectivistic countries," *Depression and Anxiety* 27 (2010): 1128–1134.

32. E. A. Throop, *Psychotherapy, American Culture, and Social Policy* (New York: Palgrave Macmillan, 2009), 29.

33. P. Fischer, A. L. Ai, N. Aydin, D. Frey, and S. A. Haslam, "The relationship between religious identity and preferred coping strategies," *Review of General Psychology* 14 (2010): 365–381; H. Mirsalimi, "Perspectives of an Iranian psychologist practicing in America," *Psychotherapy Series Research Practice* 47 (2010): 151–161.

34. E. A. Sahdra, P. R. Shaver, and K. W. Brown, "The scale to measure non-attachment," *Journal of Personality Assessment* 92 (2010): 116–127.

35. A. Nehemas, "Friendships," in *Philosophy Bites*, ed. D. Edmonds and N. Warburton (New York: Oxford University Press, 2010), 38–46.

36. A. R. Teo and A. C. Gaw, "Hikikomori, a Japanese culture-bound syndrome of social withdrawal?" *Journal of Nervous and Mental Disease* 198 (2010): 444–449.

37. W. H. Auden, *The Age of Anxiety* (London: Faber and Faber, 1948).

38. C. Lane, *Shyness: How Normal Behavior Became a Sickness* (New Haven: Yale University Press, 2007); P. D. Kramer, *Against Depression* (New York: Viking, 2005); E. Watters, *Crazy Like Us: The Globalization of the American Psyche* (New York: Free Press, 2010).

39. K. S. Kendler, S. H. Aggen, G. P. Knudsen, E. Roysamb, M. C. Neale, and T. Reichborn-Kjennerud, "The structure of genetic and environmental risk factors for syndromal and subsyndromal common DSM-IV Axis I and all Axis II disorders," *American Journal of Psychiatry* 168 (2011): 29–39.

40. W. McGuire, *The Freud/Jung Letters*, trans. R. Manheim and R. F. C. Hull (Princeton, NJ: Princeton University Press, 1974).

41. M. Sabshin, *Changing American Psychiatry: A Personal Perspective* (Washington, DC: American Psychiatric, 2008), 254.

42. R. J. McMally, *What Is Mental Illness?* (Cambridge, MA: Harvard University Press, 2011).

FIVE

Promising Reforms

1. D. Magnusson, "The logic and implications of a person-oriented approach," in *Methods and Models for Studying the Individual*, ed. R. B. Cairns, L. R. Bergman, and J. Kagan (Thousand Oaks, CA: Sage, 1998), 35–64.

2. P. Knoeferle, T. B. Urbach, and M. Kutas, "Comprehending how visual context influences incremental sentence processing," *Psychophysiology* 48 (2011): 495–506; K. Das, B. Giesbrecht, and M. P. Eckstein, "Predicting variations of perceptual performance across individuals from neural activity using pattern classifiers," *Neuroimage* 51 (2010): 1425–1437.

3. T. Wilcox, J. A. Haslup, and D. A. Boas, "Dissociation of processing of featural and spatiotemporal information in the infant cortex," *Neuroimage* 53 (2010): 1256–1263; K. Kuraoka and K. Nakamura, "Impacts of facial identity and type of emotion on responses of amygdala neurons," *NeuroReport* 17 (2006): 9–12; L. W. Hyde, A. Gorka, S. B. Manuck, and A. R. Hariri, "Perceived social support moderates the link between threat-related

amygdala reactivity and trait anxiety," *Neuropsychologia* 49 (2011): 651–656; S. A. McCaughey, "The taste of sugars," *Neuroscience and Biobehavioral Reviews* 32 (2008): 1024–1043; L. A. Schmidt, N. A. Fox, K. Perez-Edgar, and D. H. Hamer, "Linking gene, brain, and behavior," *Psychological Science* 20 (2009): 831–837; N. A. Harrison, M. A. Gray, P. J. Gianaros, and H. D. Critchley, "The embodiment of emotional feelings in the brain," *Journal of Neuroscience* 30 (2010): 12878–12884.

4. T. Wilcox, J. A. Haslup, and D. A. Boas, "Dissociation of processing of futural and spatiotemporal inflammation in the infant cortex," *Neuroimage* 53 (2010): 1256–1263; V. M. Cassia, E. Valenza, F. Simion, and I. Leo, "Congruency as a non-specific perceptual principle contributing to newborns' face preferences," *Child Development* 79 (2008): 807–820.

5. R. B. Kearsley, "The newborn's response to auditory stimulation," *Child Development* 44 (1973): 582–590.

6. M. Zentner and J. Kagan, "Perception of music by infants," *Nature* 29 (1996): 383.

7. R. A. Hinde, "Through categories toward individuals," in Cairns, Bergman, and Kagan, *Methods and Models for Studying the Individual*, 11–31; M. L. Schwand, S. G. Lindell, R. L. Sjoberg, et al., "Gene-environment interactions and response to social intrusion in male and female rhesus monkeys," *Biological Psychiatry* 67 (2010): 323–330; B. B. Lahey, P. J. Rathouz, C. Van Hulle, et al., "Testing structural models of DSM-IV symptoms of common forms of child and adolescent psychopathology," *Journal of Abnormal Child Psychology* 36 (2008): 187–206.

8. C. S. Widom and L. M. Brzustowicz, "MAOA and the cycle of violence," *Biological Psychiatry* 60 (2006): 684–689; A. E. Kudwa, C. Bodo, J. A. Gustafsson, and E. F. Rissman, "A previously uncharacterized role for estrogen receptor beta," *Proceedings of the National Academy of Sciences* 102 (2005): 4608–4612.

9. J. Demos, *The Enemy Within: 2000 Years of Witch-Hunting in the Western World* (New York: Viking, 2008); A. S. Berman, D. A. Jobes, and M. M. Silverman, *Adolescent Suicide: Assessment and Intervention* (Washington, DC: American Psychological Association, 2006); S. M. Sylven, F. C. Papadopoulous, M. Olovsson, L. Ekselius, I. S. Poromaa, and A. Skalkidou, "Seasonality pat-

terns in postpartum depression," *American Journal of Obstetrics and Gynecology* 204 (2011): 413.e1–413.e6.

10. P. Rozin, A. Rozin, B. Appel, and C. Wachtel, "Documenting and exploring the common AAB pattern in music and humor," *Emotion* 6 (2006): 349–355; R. Naatanen, T. Kujala, and I. Winckler, "Auditory processing that leads to conscious perception," *Psychophysiology* 48 (2011): 4–22.

11. E. E. Werner and R. S. Smith, *Vulnerable but Invincible: A Longitudinal Study of Resilient Children and Youth* (New York: McGraw-Hill, 1982).

12. M. V. Rockman, S. S. Skrovanek, and L. Kruglyak, "Selection at linked sites shapes heritable phenotypic variation in *C. elegans*," *Science* 330 (2010): 372–375.

13. G. Conti and J. J. Heckman, "Understanding the early origins of the education-health gradient," *Perspectives on Psychological Science* 5 (2010): 585–605.

14. R. A. Poldrack, "Neuroimaging," *Cerebrum* (2010): 114–122.

15. A. H. Fischer, A. S. R. Manstead, P. M. Rodriguez Mosquera, and A. E. M. Van Vianen, "Gender and culture differences in emotion," *Emotion* 4 (2004): 87–94; M. I. Norton and D. Ariely, "Building a better America—one wealth quintile at a time," *Perspectives on Psychological Science* 6 (2011): 9–12.

16. J. Kagan, J. S. Reznick, J. Davies, H. Sigal, and K. Miyake, "Selective memory and belief," *International Journal of Behavioral Development* 9 (1986): 205–218.

17. J. M. Horn, R. Plomin, and R. Rosenman, "Heritability of personality traits in adult male twins," *Behavioral Genetics* 6 (1976): 17–30.

18. M. L. Slepian, M. Weisbuch, N. O. Rule, and N. Ambady, "Tough and tender: Embodied categorization of gender," *Psychological Science* 22 (2011): 26–28; G. D. Sherman and G. L. Clore, "The color of sin," *Psychological Science* 20 (2009): 1019–1025; L. Campbell-Sills, A. N. Simmons, K. L. Lovero, A. A. Rochlin, M. P. Paulus, and M. B. Stein, "Functioning of neural systems supporting emotion regulation in anxiety-prone individuals," *Neuroimage* 54 (2011): 689–696.

19. J. R. Gagne and K. J. Saudino, "Wait for it! A twin study of inhibitory control in early childhood," *Behavior Genetics* 40 (2010): 327–

337; R. R. McRae, A. Terracciano, F. De Fruyt, N. De Bolle, M. J. Gelfand, and P. C. Costa, "The validity and structure of culture level personality scores," *Journal of Personality* 78 (2010): 815–838; R. S. Laptook, D. N. Klein, T. M. Olino, M. W. Dyson, and G. Carlson, "Low positive affectivity and behavioral inhibition in preschool-age children," *Personality and Individual Differences* 48 (2010): 547–551; B. Reynolds, A. Ortengren, J. B. Richards, and H. de Wit, "Dimensions of impulsive behavior: Personality and behavioral measures," *Personality and Individual Differences* 40 (2006): 305–315; K. S. Kendler, S. H. Aggen, G. P. Knudsen, E. Røysamb, M. C. Neale, and T. Reichborn-Kjennerud, "The structure of genetic and environmental risk factors for syndromal and subsyndromal common DSM-IV axis I and all axis II disorders," *American Journal of Psychiatry* 118 (2011): 29–39.

20. B. B. Lahey, C. A. Van Holle, A. L. Singh, I. D. Waldman, and B. J. Rathooz, "Higher order genetics and environmental structure of prevalent forms of child and adolescent psychopathology," *Archives of General Psychiatry* 68 (2011): 181–189.

21. T. M. Achenbach, R. A. Krukowski, L. Dumenci, and M. Y. Ivanova, "Assessment of adult psychopathology," *Psychological Bulletin* 131 (2005): 361–382, quotation on 373; J. Derringer, R. F. Krueger, D. M. Dick, et al., "Predicting sensation seeking from dopamine genes," *Psychological Science* 21 (2010): 1282–1290.

22. Q. Wang, Y. Shao, and Y. J. Li, "My way or mom's way? The bilingual and bicultural self in Hong Kong Chinese children and adolescents," *Child Development* 81 (2010): 555–567; S. N. Doan and Q. Wang, "Maternal discussions of mental states and behaviors," *Child Development* 81 (2010): 1490–1503.

23. S. Braund and G. W. Most, *Ancient Anger*, vol. 32 of Yale Classical Studies (New York: Cambridge University Press, 2003).

24. E. S. Bromerg-Martin, M. Matsumoto, and O. Hikosaka, "Dopamine in motivational control," *Neuron* 68 (2010): 815–834.

25. L. M. Sankis, E. M. Corbitt, and T. A. Widiger, "Gender bias in the English language?" *Journal of Personality and Social Psychology* 77 (1999): 1289–1295.

26. R. E. Nisbett and T. D. Wilson, "Telling more than we can know," *Psychological Review* 84 (1977): 231–259; L. Sechrest, "Per-

sonality," in *Annual Review of Psychology*, ed. M. R. Rozenswieg and L. W. Porter (Palo Alto, CA: Annual Reviews, 1976), 1–27, quotation on 22; J. D. Mayer, S. C. Lin, and M. Korogodsky, "Exploring the universality of personality judgments," *Review of General Psychology* 15 (2011): 65–76.

27. J. Gilbert, "The Forgotten Dialect of the Heart," *The Great Fires: Poems, 1982–1992* (New York: Knopf, 1994), 5.

28. M. Kutas and K. D. Federmeier, "Thirty years and counting," in *Annual Review of Psychology*, ed. S. T. Fiske, D. L. Schacter, and S. E. Taylor (Palo Alto, CA: Annual Reviews, 2011), 621–648; J. Garcia and R. Koelling, "Relation of cue to consequence in avoidance learning," *Psychonomic Science* 4 (1966): 123–124.

29. M. du Sautoy, *Finding Moonshine: A Mathematician's Journey through Symmetry* (London: Fourth Estate, 2008), 353; F. Jacob, *The Statue Within: An Autobiography* (New York: Basic Books, 1988), 274.

30. J. M. Ogembo, "Cultural narratives, violence, and mother-son loyalty," *Ethos* 29 (2001): 3–29.

31. J. Locke, "Some thoughts concerning education," in *The Works of John Locke*, vol. 8 (London, 1794), 83.

32. L. Gulick, *A Philosophy of Play* (New York: Scribners, 1920).

33. N. Phillipson, *Adam Smith: An Enlightened Life* (New Haven: Yale University Press, 2010).

34. J. Bowlby, *Attachment and Loss*, vol. 1: *Attachment* (New York: Basic Books, 1969); T. Gregor, *Mehinaku: The Drama of Daily Life in a Brazilian Indian Village* (Chicago: University of Chicago Press, 1977); J. Kagan and M. Zentner, "Early childhood predictors of adult psychopathology," *Harvard Review of Psychiatry* 3 (1996): 341–350.

35. G. A. Guarino, *The Albertis of Florence* (Lewisberg, PA: Bucknell University Press, 1971); A. I. Rabin and B. Beit-Hallahmi, *Twenty Years Later: Kibbutz Children Grown Up* (New York: Springer, 1982).

36. Werner and Smith, *Vulnerable but Invincible*, 159.

37. C. Rathbun, L. Di Virgilio, and S. Waldfogel, "A restitutive process in children following radical separation from family and culture," *American Journal of Orthopsychiatry* 28 (1958): 408–415;

J. W. Macfarlane, "From infancy to adulthood," *Childhood Education* 39 (1963): 341–344; J. W. Macfarlane, L. Allen, and M. P. Honzik, *A Developmental Study of the Behavior Problems of Normal Children between 21 Months and 14 Years* (Berkeley: University of California Press, 1954); T. L. Roth and J. D. Sweatt, "Epigenetic remodeling of the BDNF gene by early-life adverse experience," *Hormones and Behavior* 59 (2011): 315–320.

38. F. C. P. van der Horst and R. van der Veer, "The ontogeny of an idea: John Bowlby and contemporaries on mother-child separation," *History of Psychology* 13 (2010): 25–45.

39. J. Kagan, R. B. Kearsley, and T. R. Zelazo, *Infancy* (Cambridge, MA: Harvard University Press, 1978).

40. I. Hellman, "Hamstead nursery follow-up studies," *Psychoanalytic Study of the Child* 17 (1967): 159–174.

41. D. W. Shwalb, B. J. Shwalb, J. H. Hyun, et al., "Maternal beliefs, images, and metaphors of child development in the United States, Korea, Indonesia, and Japan," *Annual Report of Research and Clinical Center for Child Development at Hokkaido University* 30 (2008–2009): 1–22.

42. M. D. S. Ainsworth, M. C. Blehar, E. Waters, and S. Wall, *Patterns of Attachment: A Psychological Study of the Strange Situation* (Hillsdale, NJ: L. Erlbaum, 1978); G. Shamir-Essakow, J. A. Ungerer, and R. M. Rapee, "Attachment, behavioral inhibition, and anxiety in preschool children," *Journal of Abnormal Child Psychology* 33 (2005): 131–143; M. W. Swingler, M. A. Sweet, and L. J. Carver, "Brain-behavior correlations: Relationships between mother-stranger face processing and infants' behavioral responses to a separation from mother," *Developmental Psychology* 46 (2010): 669–680; J. Kagan, *Unstable Ideas: Temperament, Cognition, and Self* (Cambridge, MA: Harvard University Press, 1989); R. M. P. Fearon and J. Belsky, "Infant-mother attachment and the growth of externalizing problems across the primary-school years," *Journal of Child Psychology and Psychiatry* (2011), doi: 10.1111/j.1469-7610.2010.02350.x.

43. J. Fuligni, "Social identity, motivation and well-being among adolescents from Asian and Latin American backgrounds," in *Health Disparities in Youth and Families,* ed. G. Carlo (Lincoln: Nebraska Symposium on Motivation, 2011), 97–120.

44. D. M. Lyons, K. J. Parker, and A. F. Schatzberg, "Animal models of early life stress," *Developmental Psychobiology* 52 (2010): 616–634; Gregor, *Mehinaku.*
45. S. B. Nuland, *Lost in America: A Journey with My Father* (New York: Vintage, 2003).
46. G. Sonnert and G. Holton, *What Happened to the Children Who Fled Nazi Persecution?* (New York: Palgrave Macmillan, 2006).
47. G. MacDonald and L. A. Jensen-Campbell, eds., *Social Pain* (Washington, DC: American Psychological Association, 2011).
48. J. L. Briggs, *Never in Anger: Portrait of an Eskimo Family* (Cambridge, MA; Harvard University Press, 1976).
49. L. Menand, "The gods are anxious," *New Yorker,* December 16, 1996, 5–6.
50. R. G. McCloskey, *Introduction to the Works of James Wilson* (Cambridge, MA: Harvard University Press, 1967), 132–133.
51. F. Dyson, "A meeting with Enrico Fermi," *Nature* 427 (2004): 297.
52. H. J. Paek, M. R. Nelson, and A. M. Vilela, "Examination of gender-role portrayals in television advertising across seven countries," *Sex Roles* 64 (2011): 192–207.

Index

Index

Cheever, John, 221–22
child guidance clinics, 147
Childhood and Society (Erikson), 303–4, 307
children: abuse and neglect, 179, 195–97, 258; aggression, 170, 179, 256–57, 310, 328; autism and bipolar diagnoses, 156–57; "big fish in the little pond effect," 27; brain development, 71–72, 305; bullying, 40–41; childhood and later mental health, 146–47, 195–97, 199–200, 224, 236, 238, 302–3, 314–17, 327; construal of context, 22; guilt, 217; historical childrearing practices, 295–96, 299–300, 311, 316; home size, 108; home vs. school behavior, 10; homeless, 40; intervention programs, 10, 230; in kibbutz, 300–301; Locke on, 293–94; masturbation, 208; measuring cognitive abilities, 19; moral sense, 338; over- and underachievers, 43–44; parents' mood projected onto, 308; play, 294–95; resiliency, 260, 303; self-control and self-regulation, 292–93; sense of self, 323; sense of worth, 311–12; social class's effects, 33–35, 38–39, 40–41, 179, 306–7, 311–12; understanding partial, 55, 56. *See also* high- and low-reactive infants (study); infants; young people
chimpanzees, 20–21, 263–64, 332–33. *See also* primates
China: Chinese/Western cultural differences, 61–69, 238; genes affecting personality in, 52, 66; Mandarin language, 62–63, 97, 271, 275–76; under Mao, 128, 291, 301; psychoanalysis in, 230; semantic networks, 271; suicide in, 177; well-being in, 105, 128. *See also* Asians
Chinese Americans, 162
class. *See* social class
climate, 68–69
cognitive abilities, 18–20, 33–35, 39–40, 73, 253–55
cognitive behavioral therapy, 206, 225, 227, 229. *See also* therapy
cognitive dissonance, reducing, 220
college, 38, 130–31, 176–77
color names, 99–100
commitment, lack of, 323–24
community size, 27–28

concentration, 169. *See also* ADHD
concepts, psychological: abstract broad-compass concepts, 90–91, 319; context important, 3–6, 73–74, 334 (*see also* context); generalization problematic, 24–27; meaning affected by evidence type/measurement, 15–18; naming, 279, 281–82. *See also specific concepts, such as* fear
concepts, types of, 75–76
conditioned behaviors, 314–15
conformation, 25
Confucius, 64, 104, 281
conscientiousness, 116
consciousness, 100, 104, 278
consistency, 60, 269
context: about, 14–22; answers dependent on, 95–96; behavior patterns activated by, 10–12; careers influenced by, 12–14; genetic context, 22–23; importance to psychological concepts, 3–5, 73–74, 334; local setting, 4–5, 9–10, 21, 250; observations/inferences influenced, 1–2, 7–8; and probable outcome, 70; Western vs. Asian philosophies re, 59–69. *See also* historical/cultural context; social class
Conway, Jill Ker, 320
Copernicus, Nicolaus, 76, 310
cortisol, 40, 51, 52, 189, 198–99
Costa Rica, 171–72
covariance analysis, 39–46, 48, 266–67
Crick, Francis, 75, 246
crime, 115, 116, 118, 148–49, 178–79. *See also* violence
crowding, 20–21
cruelty, capacity for, 321–23, 325–26
cultural differences. *See* historical/cultural context
cutting, 144, 217
cynicism, 121, 125, 130–31, 241–42

Dalton, John, 317
Darwin, Charles, 26, 76, 185, 288
day-care, 39–40, 301
Denmark, 82, 115, 182–83, 185
depression: assigning meaning to, 216–17; causes, 73–74, 145, 153–54, 163, 173–75, 191–92 (*see also* serotonin transporter molecule); dysthymia vs., 243; endophenotypes, 190–92; gender and cultural differences, 161–62, 202; historical/cultural con-

psychology and psychiatry (field)
(*continued*)
    observational bias, 8–9; patience
    needed, 284–88; physics' influence,
    72–73; single cause for each illness
    sought, 157–59; single measure-
    ments preferred, 261–62, 264–66;
    sources of evidence, 9, 101–4 (*see
    also* brain activity; verbal evidence);
    word choice important, 205–7. *See
    also* concepts, psychological; *and
    specific individuals and aspects, such as*
    therapy
psychotic depression, 156
Ptolemy, 232
PTSD. *See* post-traumatic stress
    disorder
punishment of self, 216–17

Quakers, 317
questionnaires, 116, 272–73, 275–76,
    282–83

rats, 24, 50, 187, 192, 313
reflex motor response, 192–93
religion and well-being, 96–97, 106
rent-a-relation agencies, 326
research studies: covariance analysis,
    39–46, 48, 266–67; flaws and biases,
    22–25. *See also specific studies*
resiliency, 197–98, 260, 303, 336
restlessness, 66–67
reward (concept), 6–7
risk-taking, 66–67, 194–95
Risperadal, 211
Ritalin, 169, 213–14
Robertson, James, 304
Rous, Peyton, 1, 9
Rousseau, Jean-Jacques, 237
Russell, Bertrand, 70, 94
Russian boys, 170
Ryff, Carol, 88–89

sadness, 113, 137, 143, 223–24, 243. *See
    also* depression
Salem witchcraft trials, 122
Sartre, Jean-Paul, 181, 278
satisfaction. *See* happiness; well-being
schizophrenia: cardiovascular prob-
    lems, 145; endophenotypes, 189; as
    family 1 disorder, 156, 157; margin-
    alization and, 235–36; single cause
    theory, 158–59; treatment, 209, 211
    (*see also* medication)

Schwartz, Carl, 187–88
the sciences, 25–26, 30, 246–47,
    284–87. *See also* biology; physics;
    psychology and psychiatry; *and
    specific individuals*
seasons, 22–23, 108, 258
Sechrest, Lee, 280–81
selective serotonin reuptake inhibitors
    (SSRIs), 211–12
self (concept), 17–18, 123–24, 129,
    323–24
self-control and self-regulation,
    292–93
self-esteem, 104, 279, 311–12
self-interest, 296–97
self-mutilation, 144, 217
self-punishment, 216–17
semantic networks, 67, 79, 97–98,
    99–100, 270–71, 277–78
Sen, Amartya, 64–65, 114
sensation seeking, 274–75
September 11, 2001, terror attacks, 98
serotonin: degradation gene, 258;
    transporter molecule gene, 51–52,
    66, 111–12, 191, 198, 201, 202
sex, biological, 20, 24, 193–94, 201–2,
    272, 334–35. *See also* boys; girls;
    men; women
sex workers, 171–72
Sexton, Anne, 166
sexual abuse, 183, 195–97
shame, 137, 167–68, 238, 248. *See also*
    guilt
Shao Yong, 82–83
Shweder, Richard, 31–32
shyness, 147–48, 186, 243, 273
sick societies, 136–37
skin conductance reactions, 6
smiling, 189
Smith, Adam, 296–97
social anxiety disorder (social phobia):
    career and, 147–48; diagnosis, 142;
    historical factors, 235–36; infant
    reactivity and, 188; shyness trans-
    formed into, 243; symptoms, 160;
    treatment, 212, 227. *See also* anxiety;
    family 2 disorders; shyness
social class: ambiguities, 106; anxiety/
    depression disorders and, 175–78;
    behavior influenced by, 32; bul-
    lying and, 40–41; and childhood
    memories, 196–97; children and,
    33–35, 38–39, 40–41, 179, 306–7,
    311–12; education levels and, 42–43;